T0313159

Engineering Patient Safety in Radiation Oncology

University of North Carolina's Pursuit
for High Reliability and Value Creation

Lawrence Marks • **Lukasz Mazur**
with contributions from
Bhishamjit Chera • **Robert Adams**

CRC Press
Taylor & Francis Group
Boca Raton London New York

CRC Press is an imprint of the
Taylor & Francis Group, an **informa** business

A PRODUCTIVITY PRESS BOOK

CRC Press
Taylor & Francis Group
6000 Broken Sound Parkway NW, Suite 300
Boca Raton, FL 33487-2742

© 2015 by Taylor & Francis Group, LLC
CRC Press is an imprint of Taylor & Francis Group, an Informa business

No claim to original U.S. Government works

Printed on acid-free paper
Version Date: 20150611

International Standard Book Number-13: 978-1-4822-3364-3 (Hardback)

Library of Congress Cataloging-in-Publication Data

Marks, Lawrence (Lawrence B.), author.
   Engineering patient safety in radiation oncology : University of North Carolina's pursuit for high reliability and value creation / Lawrence Marks, Lukasz Mazur, Bhishamjit S. Chera, and Robert D. Adams.
   p. ; cm.
   Includes bibliographical references and index.
   ISBN 978-1-4822-3364-3
   I. Mazur, Lukasz, author. II. Chera, Bhishamjit S., author. III. Adams, Robert D. (Registered radiologic technologist), author. IV. Title.
   [DNLM: 1. University of North Carolina at Chapel Hill. School of Medicine. 2. Radiation Oncology--organization & administration. 3. Radiotherapy--standards. 4. Patient Safety. 5. Quality Improvement. QZ 269]

   RC270.3.R33
   616.99'40757--dc23   2014037910

Visit the Taylor & Francis Web site at
http://www.taylorandfrancis.com

and the CRC Press Web site at
http://www.crcpress.com

We dedicate this book to the concept of interprofessional collaborations.
The practice of radiation oncology relies on the fusion of multiple fields
(e.g., clinical medicine, physics, dosimetry, radiation therapy, engineering).
The improvement work described in this book resulted from the infusion
of industrial engineers into the clinical arena. Advances in the sciences
often result from the concerted and interactive efforts of people from
diverse professions/disciplines, and the same is true for our clinical and
research activities. The world would be a better place if we were better able
to leverage each other's expertise in a synergistic and productive manner.
This book is also dedicated to the many patients who suffer
with cancer, whose outcomes we hope to improve through
our efforts. We especially dedicate this book to patients and
families harmed by the healthcare delivery system.

Contents

SECTION I

SECTION II

Preface

Radiation is a central curative and palliative therapy for many patients. It is therefore important for us to have safe and efficient systems to plan and deliver radiation therapy. However, several factors (e.g., rapid technological advances, financial reorganization, aging population, and evolving societal expectations) may be compromising our ability to deliver care in a highly reliable and efficient manner.

In this book, we portray our initial efforts at the University of North Carolina to address these challenges, that is, keeping our patients safe while continuously improving our care delivery processes. We presume little theoretical knowledge on high reliability and value creation, although some familiarity with these topics is clearly an advantage. Thus, the book is written with a mixed readership in mind: medical and administrative radiation oncology employees, industrial and management engineers, human factors professionals, safety managers, and reliability engineers— and, of course, their current and future students.

The book is divided into two sections and eight chapters. **Section I** consists of Chapters 1 to 3. It provides an introduction to basic concepts, methods, and tools that underlie our approach to high reliability and value creation and an overview of key safety challenges within radiation oncology.

Chapter 1 provides a broad overview of how the safety challenges within radiation oncology are currently perceived (i.e., with the focus on advanced technologies). We think that a focus on technology is important but somewhat misguided. We then contrast this with (what we believe is) the necessary and desired future state, with safety being the natural by-product of increased reliability and value creation at the organizational, workplace, and people levels.

Chapter 2 gives a broad overview of "past" and "current" challenges of patient safety issues within radiation oncology. An overview of incident rates and reported events is included. Although we recognize and applaud the multiple technology-based initiatives aimed at improving patient safety, we believe that technical solutions alone (at least for now) are not going to bring our field to the desired level of reliability.

Chapter 3 introduces a broad overview of the best practices from high-reliability organizations. We focus on the following key areas:

- leadership style and behaviors;
- culture of safety with an emphasis on error-reporting infrastructure,
- a need for robust improvement cycles;
- the use of Human Factors Engineering principles to design work and environments; and
- ways to help individuals engage, transform, and feel respected during continuous quality and safety improvement efforts.

Chapter 3 also reviews constructs that are commonly used in the study of organizational structures and their relationship with safety events. We compare and contrast these constructs and offer a preliminary assessment of how these constructs can be applied to radiation oncology. The lesson is that the nature of our practice (both on a broad macroscale and on a smaller microscale) determines the optimal methods to ensure high reliability and value creation.

In **Section II**, based on the beliefs outlined in the previous chapters, we describe our journey to high reliability and value creation at the University of North Carolina.

Chapter 4 provides an in-depth account of changes and initiatives taken at the organizational level. This includes personal reflections on why this work was initiated, along with specific examples of how the organizational leadership supports high reliability and value creation.

Chapter 5 describes our efforts to optimize workplaces and work processes for people so that human error can be minimized. We rely heavily on the hierarchy of effectiveness for error prevention and the principles of Human Factors Engineering.

Chapter 6 focuses on people and their decision-making processes and behaviors. We offer ways to engage, transform, and respect people during transition to high reliability and value creation.

Chapter 7 summarizes our research program on mental workload that is synergetic with our clinical activities. We also provide ideas for future research at the organizational, workplace, and people levels.

Chapter 8 provides a summary of key points and concluding remarks. We emphasize that high-reliability and value creation organizations, despite all improvement efforts, are not immune to errors. Continuous diligence is needed, with continuous support from leadership to nurture a culture of safety and empower people to improve processes.

Acknowledgments

Portions of this book (e.g., text, illustrations, tables) were adapted from some of our previous publications and are cited as such. We thank Mark Kostich for many of the photographs. We thank the faculty and staff in the Department of Radiation Oncology at the University of North Carolina (UNC) for their participation and assistance with the improvement activities. We recognize that everyone does not necessarily share our enthusiasm for this work, and that people have many competing priorities; thus, we appreciate everyone's willingness to be involved in these improvement activities. We especially thank our department managers and members of our Quality and Safety Committee, including (in no particular order) Kathy Burkhardt, John Rockwell, Patricia Saponaro, Kenneth Neuvirth, Dana Lunsford, Lori Stravers, Lauren Terzo, Kinley Taylor, Nancy Coffey, Prithima Mosaly, and Gregg Tracton, who courageously help us lead our improvement work. We are indebted to Dr. Marianne Jackson, a board-certified gynecologist, retrained as an industrial engineer and Lean expert, who was instrumental in helping us spearhead our improvement agenda at UNC.

We also want to thank our students—resident physicians, physicists, dosimetrists, and radiation therapists—for their active and inspiring participation in our improvement activities. Special thanks go to Dr. Aaron Falchook and Dr. Michael Eblan for engaging with us on our research activities to quantify mental workload and performance during provider–computer interactions.

We are grateful to the UNC healthcare system, the Medical Center Improvement Council, the School of Medicine, the Institute for Healthcare Quality Improvement, and the Cancer Center for their ongoing support of this work. Some of the research presented was funded by grants from Accuracy, Elekta, the Agency for Healthcare Research and Quality (AHRQ), and the UNC Innovation Center. We have also received support via a grant from the Centers for Disease Control and Prevention (CDC) to pursue some of these improvement initiatives in our breast cancer clinic. We are especially indebted to Dr. Prithima Mosaly, who assisted with much of the research work, and to Kinley Taylor, who helped coordinate the improvement aspects of the CDC-funded project as well as our global departmental quality initiatives. Thanks also to Adrian Gerstel,

Jayne Camporale, Drs. Deborah Mayer, Donald Rosenstein, and Thomas Shea, and Jean Sellers, for their efforts on the CDC grant, and to Dr. Tina Willis, Celeste Mayer, and Glen Spivak for their continual encouragement and guidance in our improvement work. L. M. also thanks his many colleagues at Duke who helped him get started in this area for their support, encouragement, and participation.

Thanks to Michael Sinocchi, Jill Jurgensen, Jay Margolis, and Sophie Kirkwood at Taylor & Francis Group for their skillful assistance and patience in the bringing this book to fruition.

We are thankful for our families, who have supported and encouraged our professional careers and who patiently try to share our enthusiasm.

We are especially thankful to Ivette Duran-Mazur who assisted with the design of the cover.

ABOUT THE COVER

The artistic rendition by Ivette Duran-Mazur illustrates several of the concepts presented in this book. The three white swirls represent the three layers of the Swiss Cheese Model that we used to structure our book (e.g. organizational, workplace, and people). The thicker light blue line passing through the three swirls represents the complex interactions among these three layers that can lead to unforeseen events. The swirls and straight lines are meant to be reminiscent of cloud chamber tracings depicting the path taken by some "radiation beams." The back-projection of the lines to different points emphasizes the need for multiple perspectives when considering complex systems.

About the Authors

Lawrence Marks was born and raised in Brooklyn, New York. He studied chemical engineering at Cooper Union and earned his MD from the University of Rochester. He did his residency training in radiation oncology at Massachusetts General Hospital and then served on the faculty of Duke University for 19 years. There, he studied radiation-induced normal tissue injury and became interested in Human Factors Engineering and patient safety. In 2008, he moved to the University of North Carolina to become the Dr. Sidney K. Simon Distinguished Professor of Oncology Research and the chairman of the Department of Radiation Oncology. Over the last six years, he and Dr. Mazur and others have been systematically applying engineering principles from high-reliability and value creation organizations to improve safety. In his clinical work, he has particular interest in the care of patients with cancers of the lung or breast. He has been active in ASTRO (American Society for Radiation Oncology) and currently serves on its Board of Directors as the chairman of the Clinical Affairs and Quality Council. He lives with his wife of 29 years, Caryn Hertz, in Chapel Hill. They have three sons, none of whom is planning a career in medicine.

Lukasz Mazur earned his BS, MS, and PhD in industrial and management engineering from Montana State University. As a student athlete at Montana State University, he earned a spot in the Bobcats Hall of Fame for his efforts on a tennis team. While working at North Carolina State University, he was awarded the Alumni Outstanding Extension Service Award for his outreach work, highlighting his passion for quality and safety work in the healthcare industry. Currently, he is an assistant professor in the Radiation Oncology Department at the UNC School of Medicine. His research interests focus on engineering management as it pertains to continuous quality and safety improvements and human factor engineering with a focus on workload and performance during human–computer interactions.

Robert Adams earned his BS in biology/radiology from Averett University, a MS in healthcare administration from the University of North Carolina, and a doctorate in higher education administration from North Carolina State University. He is an assistant professor in the Radiation Oncology Department at the UNC School of Medicine, and directs both the UNC healthcare radiation therapy and the medical dosimetry educational programs. He is certified in radiation therapy and medical dosimetry. His research interests focus on clinical work practices, patient safety, and educational issues for radiation therapists and medical dosimetrists. He has served on several national and international boards of directors and editorial review boards. He is both a Fellow and an Award of Excellence recipient from the American Association of Medical Dosimetrists. He has published over 50 peer-reviewed articles, 10 book chapters, and recently completed an R25 National Cancer Institute recent grant developing "Computer-Based Medical Dosimetry Clinical Learning Modules."

Bishamjit S. Chera is an assistant professor and director of patient safety and quality in the Department of Radiation Oncology at the University of North Carolina. He earned his BS in biology from Winthrop University in 2000 and an MD from the Medical University of South Carolina in 2004. He completed his residency training in radiation oncology at the University of Florida. His clinical expertise is in head and neck and skin cancers. His major areas of research pertain to head and neck cancer and translating quality assurance/control/improvement principles and methodologies from high-reliability organizations to radiation oncology. He has written on the incorporation of practical quality assurance approaches (e.g., process/Human Factors Engineering and Lean methodologies) in the daily activities of radiation oncology departments/clinics.

Section I

This section provides an introduction to basic concepts, methods, and tools that underlie our approach to high reliability and value creation and an overview of key safety challenges within radiation oncology.

1

An Introduction and Guide to This Book

LEARNING OBJECTIVES

After completing this chapter, the reader should be able to:

1. Broadly understand some of the current challenges to safety in radiation oncology;
2. Understand the Swiss Cheese Model (e.g., the interdependence of the organizational, workplace, and people levels); and
3. Broadly understand how changes at the organizational, workplace, and people levels affect reliability and value creation within radiation oncology.

1.1 A BRIEF OVERVIEW OF THE SAFETY CHALLENGES WITHIN RADIATION ONCOLOGY

Radiation oncology is a modest-size field with about 4,000 practicing radiation oncologists in the United States. Nevertheless, the clinical impact of radiation therapy (RT) is significant. Approximately 50% of patients with cancer receive RT, with about 600,000 patients treated annually in the United States alone. RT plays an important role in the curative and palliative management of most malignancies and is also used to treat some benign conditions.

The clinical practice of RT enjoys a long-standing reputation for being generally safe. This is a tribute to the founding members of our field, who, recognizing the risks of RT, instilled within the very fabric of our field the need for careful oversight and clinical observation. Furthermore, the involvement of physicists, engineers, and other technical and quantitative-minded individuals, integral to our practice, brings an objective and systematic approach to quality assurance (QA).[1] For decades, radiation treatment centers have used numerous techniques to ensure high reliability and patient safety and have generally been successful.

The rate of "potential quality/safety events" within radiation oncology is difficult to estimate, as there are marked interstudy and interdatabase differences in the methods used to define an event. Further, there are certainly inaccuracies and biases in the reporting of events. Nevertheless, based on the available data, a reasonable estimate is that there is an event during the course of treatment in approximately 1%–3% of patients, but the vast majority of these events are not clinically relevant.[2-18] Importantly, however, about 1 in 1,000–10,000 treated patients is affected by a reportable event with potentially serious consequences (the supporting data are detailed in Chapter 2). This rate may compare unfavorably with highly reliable industries such as commercial aviation ($\approx$1 death in 4.7 million passenger flights)[19] or other areas of medicine, such as anesthesiology ($\approx$1 death in 200,000 procedures).[20] However, these comparisons might not be totally fair because the reporting thresholds are different. If in aviation we were to count faulty take-offs, landings, or unplanned returns to the airport, and if in anesthesiology we reported intubation failures or ventilator equipment/tube malfunctions, aviation and anesthesiology might not appear as favorable. Nevertheless, the relatively high rate of any type of event within radiation oncology is cause for concern as it suggests inherent shortcomings of our current systems.

Further, the event rates noted may not be reflective of modern practice. Recent technological advances (e.g., medical imaging, computer-based planning systems, and radiation delivery/control systems) have driven a rapid evolution in clinical practice and have had a mixed effect on event rates. Some technologies clearly have dramatically *reduced* the rate of some errors. For example, computer-based systems obviate the need for manual data transfer (e.g., by dosimetrists from the planning system to the patient's chart and by therapists from the patient's chart to the treatment machine), thereby essentially eliminating that type of data transfer error. However, other changes in practice appear to have strained our existing QA procedures (e.g., tracking of the technical review of the RT chart has become more difficult). These and other evolving safety challenges within RT are discussed in detail in Chapter 2.

There is reason to suspect that the *risks associated with incidents* (defined as events reaching the patients) might be *increasing*. Given the uncertainties in collected quantitative data related to the probability of an incident and their clinical severities, it is challenging to prove or disprove this suspicion. Conceptually,

$$Risk_{incident} = Probability_{incident} \times Severity_{incident}$$

Changes in radiation oncology practice may have influenced both the probability of incidents and their severity. It is unclear if the probability of incidents is increasing or decreasing, but there is a suggestion that the severity per incident might be increasing, leading to a net increasing risk (Figure 1.1).

A summary of some of the factors in modern radiation oncology practice that generally tend to decrease and increase the probability of events and their severities is given in Table 1.1.

Based on these forces, we submit that the slope in Figure 1.1A might be positive or negative, and that the slope of Figure 1.1B is almost certainly strongly positive. In concert, this leads us to believe that the slope of Figure 1.1C is most likely positive, although the degree of positivity is uncertain. We further explore many of these factors in more detail in Chapter 2.

Recent developments in our professional community also suggest a growing concern with safety. In 2008, the American Society for Radiation Oncology (ASTRO), American Association of Physicists in Medicine (AAPM), and the National Cancer Institute (NCI) held a conference

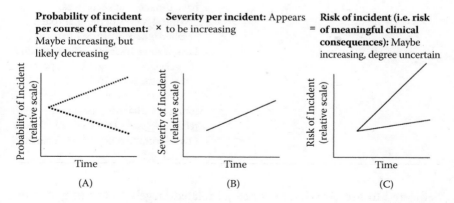

FIGURE 1.1
Left, probability of event; middle, severity of event; right, risk of event. All are presented in a relative and arbitrary scale.

TABLE 1.1

Example Factors Tending to Change the Probability or Severity of Events

Factors Tending to *Decrease* the Probability or Severity of Events	Factors Tending to *Increase* the Probability or Severity of Events
• Increased number of clinical guidelines. • Increased availability of "dose/volume/outcome" data/standards. • Readily available information via the Internet. • Enhanced communication technology better facilitating information transfer. • Electronic medical records systems (making information more readily available). • Record and verify systems. • Better-integrated computer systems. • Hardware/software interlocks to prevent incorrect treatment or alert users to potential issues. • Image-guided RT. • Collision detection software and hardware on machines reducing the risk for potentially catastrophic collisions. • End-to-end testing for many procedures.	• Older/sicker patients. • Increased use of combined modality therapy and complex multidisciplinary care. • Staff working in an increasing number of clinical sites, with more handoffs. • Higher doses per fraction, shorter fractionation schedules. • Trend toward using tighter margins. • Increased demands on staff, reduced reimbursement. • Increasing amount of data to consider. • Multiple electronic medical record systems to contend with (often where some critical information is not readily apparent or readily highlighted). • Data transfer is automatic and some errors may not be readily apparent. • A single software/hardware problem can affect a large number of patients. • Increased number of computer systems, often outpacing the ability to integrate systems. • Electronic systems may propagate errors such that a single error may have broader consequences. • Technical review of the chart often cumbersome and difficult to track. • Loss of some traditional downstream "QA checks" (e.g., light fields, portal films) in the era of IMRT. • Monitor unit calculations are less intuitive with fancier treatment techniques (e.g., IMRT vs. non-IMRT). • Overall complacency with information technology.

dedicated to growing safety concerns related largely to the introduction of new technologies. In 2010, a series of articles in the *New York Times* reported several disturbing clinical events that highlighted safety issues in our field.[21–24] The incidents and concerns brought to the fore in the lay and academic press were largely focused on technical factors; thus, many of the more recent quality initiatives within RT have understandably focused on the mechanical and computer aspects of new high-technology treatments (e.g., intensity-modulated radiation therapy, IMRT). RT safety was the focus of subsequent congressional hearings, a public meeting sponsored by the Food and Drug Administration (FDA), and the ASTRO/AAPM-sponsored "Call to Action" meeting (which was filled to capacity). In 2010, ASTRO also responded with a multifaceted Target Safely campaign with key elements that included[25]:

1. Create a national database for event reporting (the Radiation Oncology Incident Learning System [RO-ILS] was recently launched).
2. Accelerate an ongoing effort (Integrating the Healthcare Enterprise-Radiation Oncology [IHE-RO]) to ensure device manufacturers can transfer treatment information from one machine to another seamlessly to reduce the chance of medical incidents.
3. Enhance the radiation oncology practice accreditation programs (the Accreditation Program for Excellence [APEx] recently launched).
4. Advocate for new and expanded federal initiatives to help protect patients from radiation incidents; support the immediate passage of the Consistency, Accuracy, Responsibility, and Excellence in Medical Imaging and Radiation Therapy ("CARE") Act, which among other things requires national standards for RT treatment team members.
5. Work with cancer support organizations to help cancer patients and their families know what to ask their doctors when radiation is a possible treatment option.
6. Expand educational programs related to QA and safety.

1.2 THE FOCUS OF SAFETY INITIATIVES ON TECHNICAL/ EDUCATION VERSUS ORGANIZATIONAL/ WORKPLACE/BEHAVIORAL ISSUES

We applaud the multiple technology-based initiatives aimed at improving patient safety, such as the efforts to promote interconnectivity between different RT-related products. We understand the need for a strong focus on these technical factors. We also applaud the education and training

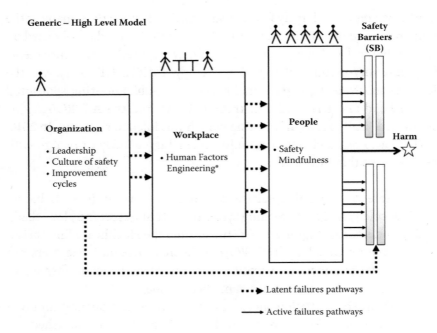

FIGURE 1.2

Conceptual representation of the Swiss Cheese Model. Left, organizational level with three key elements: leadership, culture of safety, and improvement cycles. Middle, workplace with Human Factors Engineering. Right, people with one key element: safety mindfulness. *In this book, for convenience, we place Human Factors Engineering at the workplace level to emphasize the interplay between a person and the person's physical environment that markedly influences the worker's human ability to perform his or her job well and directly influences reliability, safety, and quality. We recognize that the discipline of Human Factors Engineering is broader (see Section 1.3.2.1).

efforts to promote safety and quality. However, we believe that technical solutions alone are not going to bring our field to the desired level of reliability and value creation.

The successful practice of radiation oncology rests with people and in their ability to repeatedly perform diverse tasks in a reliable and predictable manner. However, people do not perform their tasks in a vacuum. We embrace a concept (often termed the Swiss Cheese Model) that people's actions (far right-hand side of Figure 1.2) are influenced by upstream *latent* failure pathways (contributory factors that may lie dormant for long periods of time) at the organizational, workplace, and people levels (e.g., policies, programs, schedules, work flows, training, perceptions).[26] The worker's action that is linked to the incident (e.g., forgetting to do something) is often referred to as the *active* failure.

Highly reliable organizations embrace this concept and are preoccupied with ways latent and active failure pathways can occur in the system. They work hard to detect and correct small emerging latent failure pathways and to see these as potential clues to additional latent failures pathways elsewhere in the system. They anticipate specific pathways that are at risk of occurring and build into their processes initiatives intended to prevent occurrence of these pathways. For example, the workplace and work flows should be "engineered" to minimize/prevent human errors (e.g., it is not physically possible for an anesthesiologist to attach a tube intended to carry oxygen to a gas tank containing nitrogen). For most activities involving human performance, the goal of the upstream initiatives is to facilitate worker behaviors and decisions that maximize the likelihood of the desired outcome.

Further, essentially all upstream initiatives are imperfect and may even generate additional latent failure pathways. Even if the upstream initiatives were optimal, this is still a probabilistic matter, and the involvement of humans creates some uncertainty. High-reliability and value creation organizations acknowledge this uncertainty. They acknowledge that their staff operates under variable abilities and training, conditions, equipment configurations, and work scenarios. It is recognized that the total composite of these elements and the human component determine the safety of the system. Thus, *multiple* methods are used to maximize worker behaviors, decisions, and task execution under any circumstances. A worker's broad awareness of, and appreciation for, these concepts (e.g., the potential presence of latent failures pathways, the risk of active failures pathways, and the critical role that they play in improving their [and the broader system's] overall performance) is often referred to as *safety mindfulness*. Safety mindfulness is particularly important in interactively complex systems, such as medicine, for which the overall performance of the system can be difficult to predict (this concept is developed more fully in Chapter 3).

In recognition that our systems are often imperfect, most processes have multiple built-in safety barriers, formally and informally defined QA and quality control (QC) steps to identify errors or question something that seems out of the ordinary. An interesting question is whether one considers these safety barriers as part of a reliable system or as a symptom/acknowledgment of upstream unreliability. High-reliability and value creation organizations are structured to detect unexpected active and latent failures and their pathways. Workers operate with safety mindfulness to more readily notice and act on *weak signals of potential failures* (i.e., associated with subtle deviations from the expected) before they evolve into *larger signals* (i.e., associated potentially with "large" system accidents). This is analogous to having the mindset to bring your car in for service when there is a subtle noise or dysfunction rather than waiting for the breakdown. Because medicine is a human endeavor, it is not possible to prevent all human errors; thus, safety barriers will always be considered. This can perhaps be better represented by the Venn diagram-like representation shown in Figure 1.3, which emphasizes this point; workers function within workplaces, and workplaces are defined by organizational decisions, in nested configuration. If one considers the three components of organization, workplace, and people to be in series as presented in Figure 1.2, it is instinctive to place the barriers only on the far right-hand side where people directly interact with patients. In the nested configuration, it becomes clear that those safety barriers can also be applied to the organization and workplace as shown in Figure 1.3.

Patient harm usually occurs as a result of one or several latent failure pathways interacting with active failure pathways, depicted as the arrow propagated throughout organizational, workplace, and people levels to the "patient harm" in Figure 1.3 (top). Typically, most human errors do not cause patient harm as sufficient safety barriers are present in work flows to prevent them (Figure 1.3, bottom). However, final outcomes alone are not the primary interest of high-reliability and value-creating organizations. Rather, they mainly focus on their practices to produce a robust and reliable system. They closely monitor metrics that assess the system's performance in the hopes of detecting signals of latent and active failures and their respective pathways. Further, they continuously promote staff safety mindfulness.

It is important to emphasize that the Swiss Cheese Model described is the classical form that is widely understood among safety experts. An alternative interpretation of the term Swiss Cheese Model has been offered by which the different pieces of cheese represent *sequential steps* in a multistep process, and that errors manifest at the end of the process may have had their nidus at an earlier step. A sequential process-oriented representation of the Swiss Cheese Model is shown in Figure 1.4. Although this is true, the message of the classical Swiss Cheese Model shown in Figures 1.2 and 1.3 is more powerful.

Our desire to write this book was based on our strong belief that our field of radiation oncology needs to embrace the concepts of the

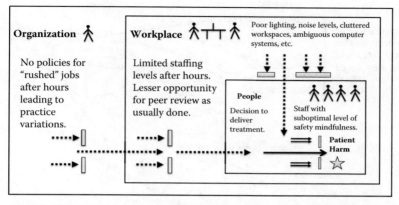

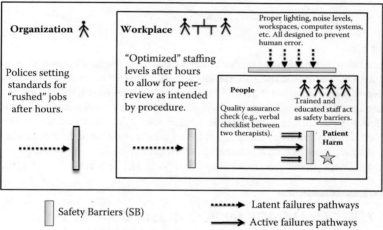

FIGURE 1.3

Conceptual representation of the Swiss Cheese Model using a Venn-like diagram. Top, example of the Swiss Cheese Model with safety barriers *not* present, with a series of events leading to patient harm. Bottom, example of the Swiss Cheese Model *with* safety barriers present at *all* three levels.

organizational Swiss Cheese Model, and promote safety mindfulness at all levels, to maximize patient safety.

We acknowledge that all the activity shown in Figures 1.2 and 1.3 is also contained within even larger organizational structures (e.g., societal, governmental, etc.). Challenges related to these larger structures (e.g., regulation, legislation, equitability, insurance, etc.) can also influence patient safety and are briefly discussed in Chapter 8.

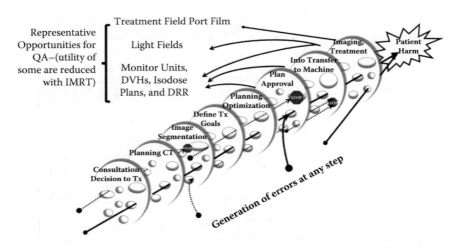

FIGURE 1.4

Espoused alternative temporal version of the Swiss Cheese Model illustrating the approximate steps between consultation and treatment with external beam radiation therapy. At any step in the process, latent (dotted line) and active (solid line) failure pathways exist, creating a probability to generate errors. Active failure pathways originating downstream have fewer opportunities for correction (angled solid line). Further, because errors in treatment delivery are always manifest at the treatment machine (even if their genesis is, at least in part, more upstream), therapists are frequently incorrectly "blamed" for delivery errors. (With permission from Marks LB, Jackson M, Xie L, et al., *PRO*, 2011;1:2–14.)

1.3 THE CHALLENGE IN PROMOTING SAFETY IN RADIATION ONCOLOGY: LESSONS FROM HIGH-RELIABILITY AND VALUE CREATION ORGANIZATIONS

The challenge for radiation oncology facilities is to develop highly reliable systems that deliver value to every patient. Value from the patient's viewpoint is the provision of service that provides maximum therapeutic benefit with the least amount of cost, harm, and effort. It has been simply described as the ratio of "benefit to bother." Value is tightly linked to reliability and efficiency of processes and thus the overall quality and cost of the care delivery system. Conceptually,

$$Value_{patient} \cong Reliability \ and \ Efficiency_{process} \cong Quality \ and \ Cost_{system}$$

The opposite of reliability and value is waste. In a world of limited time and resources, any waste within the system serves (at least) as a distraction and (more often) as a hindrance to reliability and value. We define waste broadly, and on all levels, such as waste related to:

- Organizational (e.g., unclear or conflicting goals, unnecessary meetings, redundant/ambiguous policies, insufficient training of personnel, etc.);
- Workplace (e.g., poor lighting, slow/cumbersome computer systems, cluttered clinic rooms, missing/broken equipment, interruptions, etc.);
- People (e.g., decisions leading to unnecessary tests or evaluations, rushing, unnecessary work-arounds, etc.).

Besides leading to lost time, rework, and excessive rechecking, waste creates anxiety, frustration, poor communication, and low employee satisfaction. The relentless elimination of waste in any form will enable the ready delivery of value to the patient at lowest cost. So, how do we get there? We believe that the following concepts borrowed from high-reliability and value creation organizations can help guide radiation oncology centers.

1.3.1 Organizational Level

The successful delivery of RT requires concerted efforts of multiple individuals at all levels in the organization. Their activities need to be harmonized to develop systems that can prevent serious incidents and eliminate waste (i.e., creating value for patients). At the organizational level, this requires at least the following three concepts: (1) leadership, (2) a culture of safety, and (3) improvement cycles (Figure 1.5).

1.3.1.1 Leadership

We emphasize leadership first because, without it, virtually no significant organizational change can succeed or can a well-functioning organization (once created) be maintained.[27] This is true in essentially all types of organizations (e.g., from industries to sports teams). The same is true in medical environments and might be especially important within radiation oncology treatment centers because of their complexity.

Leaders in radiation oncology treatment centers, both clinical and administrative, must set a clear vision and goals for a culture of safety. They need to continually reinforce the need for the staff to cooperate with each other and understand (and work to improve) their work flow.

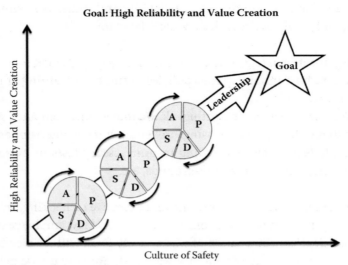

Improvement Cycle: **P** – Plan, **D** – Do, **S** – Study, **A** – Act

FIGURE 1.5

This conceptual figure illustrates the symbiotic relationship between the culture of safety (*x* axis), high reliability and value creation (*y* axis), and continuous improvement cycles (PDSA). Each of these components is mutually dependent on, and reinforcing of, the others. As such, the relative positions of the three components are somewhat arbitrary. At the organizational level, leaders must be the driving force behind improvement cycles, and these cycles promote the culture of safety (e.g., safety mindfulness among the staff and robust systems). Similarly, there must be some degree of a culture of safety to successfully perform the PDSA cycles. Building a culture of safety and systematically improving processes through the PDSA approach will increase reliability and value creation. The sizes of the pie charts on the leadership arrow pointing toward the goal (shown using a star symbol in the top right corner) are deliberate, with Plan (P) being the largest, indicating the need for thoughtful planning and readiness of all stakeholders before relatively rapid improvements (Doing, D), Studying (S), and Acting (A), as no major improvement can be typically achieved in one leap. (Figure conceptually adapted from the teaching of Mark Chassin, president and chief executive officer at Joint Commission, 2012 Institute for Healthcare Improvement [IHI] Annual Conference.)

For example, people do not always readily understand the upstream and downstream consequences of their wants and actions. Even when understood, these issues can be readily forgotten. Seemingly modest changes or shortcuts to "my own work" can have unanticipated implications. Strong leaders promote a deep understanding of the interconnectedness among all the members of the organization. Leaders send this message overtly, by verbalizing it, and implicitly through their actions (e.g., by inviting all staff to operational meetings, by inviting broad staff participation in policy-making meetings, etc.).

When leaders become fully committed to high reliability and value creation, improvement efforts can be implemented, coordinated, and sustained over time and permeate every level of the organization. Leaders need to encourage staff to be involved in improvement activities, to celebrate/reward the people involved in improvement initiatives, and to follow up on operational concerns and revelations of unsafe practices. Leaders need to be actively involved in these initiatives to send a clear message of their commitment. It is critical that the leader's commitment to high reliability and value creation be felt and seen by the staff on a continual basis.

Leaders inspire staff to follow and make their own commitment to a vision of high reliability and value creation. This might take a long time as these concepts have not always been given the highest priority. Seemingly competing considerations (e.g., meeting patient and referring physician expectations, maintaining clinical volumes, research productivity) are often given a greater priority (maybe because their "rewards" are more readily apparent). Nevertheless, the true potential of the culture of safety, and the improvement cycles, can only be realized if all staff buy in, both in theory and in practice (i.e., via active participation). Less-than-complete participation might still yield improvements, but they will not be optimal. Thus, leaders need to continually encourage all staff to participate. Further, even if high reliability and value creation are achieved, a widespread personal commitment to continuous improvement efforts is needed for sustainability. Entropy is a strong, ever-present concept. Systems decay and often become obsolete as practice evolves. Sustainability requires the continued concerted efforts from all staff. Leaders can help by setting clear expectations and continuing to recognize, celebrate, and reward behaviors that promote safety.

The activities of the leaders and staff are mutually reinforcing. Winning over the hearts and minds of the staff provides encouragement to the leaders to continue to promote their vision. However, they can be mutually damaging as well. If leaders fail to consistently, actively lead by example and to totally embrace these concepts, staff can easily become skeptical and frustrated. Similarly, continual staff skepticism can cause the leader to become frustrated.

Leadership practices from some high-reliability and value creation organizations are described in more detail in Chapter 3. In Chapter 4, we present how we apply these concepts and practices in our department at the University of North Carolina (UNC).

1.3.1.2 Culture of Safety

A culture of safety is one in which workers feel comfortable raising concerns about safety, efficiency, quality, reliability, value, and so on without concern for retaliation or reprimand. The culture supports the workers as active participants in the identification, implementation, and assessment of initiatives aimed at addressing these concerns. Workers not only are expected to engage in such improvement activities but also are encouraged and rewarded. Indeed, in a robust culture, workers should feel this as an obligation. It is obvious that supportive leadership is a critical underpinning of a successful culture of safety.

Creating a culture of safety can be a transformational experience for the staff. They begin to see their work differently, no longer accepting the existing way of performing their jobs with all of the problems, workarounds, and resulting frustrations. Instead, they begin to rethink why work is done in the current manner and how it might be restructured and even reconceptualized. Workers learn that they have two jobs: to do their job and to improve the manner in which they do their job.

This type of culture is not something that leadership can mandate. Rather, this culture evolves, almost on a person-by-person basis, driven by each individual's understanding, motivation, abilities, and desire to make constructive change in his or her work environment. An important catalyst for this evolution is empowerment of all staff to report and act on any safety-related issues.

To do that, staff must feel psychologically safe to report events and human errors without fear of potential negative consequences to self-image, status, or career. This builds trust and a broad sense of respect. This creates a positive-feedback loop in which workers become increasingly engaged in improvement cycles and greater empowerment and responsibility, which in turn further solidifies trust and respectfulness. Ideally, when events and human errors are discovered, leadership will naturally defer to the most informed and experienced individuals, regardless of their position in the organization, to resolve issues. We further explore a culture of safety in Chapter 3. In Chapters 4, 5, and 6, we present our efforts at UNC to maintain a positive and healthy attitude toward a culture of safety.

1.3.1.3 Improvement Cycles

Complex systems involving multiple people with diverse tasks can be difficult to change. Effective solutions are not always obvious, and sometimes the apparently obvious ideal solution can have unintended negative consequences. Well-intentioned people, motivated to make positive change, can inadvertently make matters worse by instituting nonvetted change. Therefore, it is most helpful for there to be a systematic and *not* random manner in which problems and potential solutions are considered. The Plan–Do–Study–Act (PDSA) cycle is a common approach taken to formalize this iterative process. This intentional, scientific approach to improvement recognizes the benefits of learning from experimentation, pilot studies, observing for the unintended consequences, and being prepared to modify the improvement approach as needed.

The PDSA concept might feel somewhat "out of line" as high-reliability industries such as commercial aviation or nuclear power cannot operate under trial-and-error conditions to address problems (as the first error can be catastrophic). This can be true to radiation oncology facilities as well. Thus, we must emphasize that the application of improvement cycles based on the PDSA is always to be safeguarded for patients as the first iteration is often not the optimal solution. Broad participation of staff from diverse functional subunits of the organization is needed to help ensure that all aspects of a particular problem are adequately considered. Broad participation also promotes acceptance for the changes by all constituents. Scholars studying high-reliability and value creation industries speculate that their long-term organizational effectiveness depends on robust PDSA improvement cycles that require close interrelationships among key personnel in various functions.[28] Some well-known approaches that provide structure to improvement initiatives include Lean, Six Sigma, and change management programs.

The power of each of these approaches lies in a systematic nature rather than a specific structure. Healthcare experts emphasize that use of a systematic approach is crucial to avoid failures common in many efforts to improve quality and safety.[29,30] In Chapter 2, we provide a detailed overview of PDSA cycle implementation. In Chapter 6, we present examples of our improvements based on the PDSA methodology.

1.3.2 Workplace Level

High-reliability and value creation organizations recognize that the workplace has a profound influence on worker performance. The workplace is broadly defined to be the physical space itself (e.g., desk, telephones, technology, etc.); the environment (e.g., temperature and noise level, etc.); as well as the demands placed on the worker. Many industries have performed extensive research to develop workplaces that optimize performance. One common conclusion from this research is that human performance can be improved by reducing distractions and making the information and tools needed to perform tasks readily available. Although this seems obvious, many healthcare workplaces are designed with suboptimal regard for these concepts. Often, physician's work areas are cluttered, noisy, and poorly organized for easy information flow. The broad study of optimizing the work environment to maximize the likelihood that tasks are performed as intended is often referred to as Human Factors Engineering.

1.3.2.1 Human Factors Engineering

According to the International Ergonomics Association, the discipline of Human Factors Engineering covers three major domains: (1) physical ergonomics, concerned with physical activity; (2) cognitive (or information-processing) ergonomics, concerned with mental processes; and (3) organizational ergonomics (also called macroergonomics), concerned with sociotechnical system design. Thus, the discipline of Human Factors Engineering recognizes all levels of the Swiss Cheese Model (organization, workplace, and people). In this book, for convenience, we place Human Factors Engineering at the workplace level to emphasize the interplay between a person and the person's physical environment that markedly influences the worker's human ability to perform their job well and directly influences reliability, safety and quality. A prerequisite that dovetails with this concept is the need for there to be clarity of expectations regarding tasks to be performed at each workplace.

It is particularly important for complex organizations, wherever possible, to clearly define task demands placed on operators and design the workspace to facilitate the anticipated tasks. As examples, providers need ready access to patient medical records, medical instruments and supplies used during patient visits, and so on. Clinical examination rooms should be stocked with all of the essential materials that providers need to perform the examination, preferably located in clearly labeled and consistent locations. Providers required to provide an *International Classification of Diseases, Tenth Revision (ICD-10)* code for a patient need ready access to easy-to-use lookup tables. Nurses asked to page or call a physician should have ready access to accurate, up-to-date phone directories. The same is true for clerical staff, transporters, therapists, dosimetrists, and everyone in a department. Similarly, if we expect workers to be able to concentrate, we need to provide them with a quiet environment with minimal interruptions and appropriate lighting. Time spent searching for materials, telephone numbers, or computer log-in instructions is all waste. Thus, optimally standardized processes and corresponding workplace design can maximize human and team performance. These seemingly obvious items are often considered trivial instead of opportunities to create a safer environment.

Broadly speaking, the work environment needs to be made predictable and reliable so that it supports standard processes. Workloads need to be optimal. Research shows that workloads that are too low can lead to boredom, daydreaming, and multitasking, which can reduce situational awareness. On the other hand, if workload is too high, performance can suffer from anxiety and rushing. Nevertheless, there needs to be some flexibility in workload to support unexpected events and planned innovations. Selected concepts of Human Factors Engineering are further discussed in detail in Chapter 3. In Chapter 5, we present examples of how we applied Human Factors Engineering thinking at UNC to improve our workplaces.

1.3.3 People Level

Superficially, most human errors can be directly linked to decisions and behaviors of individual people. Therefore, individuals are often blamed for errors. However, as noted in Figures 1.2 and 1.3, most human errors are caused largely by the existence of multiple latent failures at the organizational and workplace levels. To better understand this phenomenon, we must better understand how and why people behave and make decisions under various conditions and the impact of organizational and workplace factors on people's safety mindfulness. No one goes to work thinking, "I am going to make an error today." People are well meaning and want to perform well. Rather, we place people in environments and in situations that may increase the risk of human error.

1.3.3.1 Safety Mindfulness

Humans are imperfect. Their participation in any endeavor, including the delivery of healthcare, introduces the possibility of human error stemming from their behaviors or decision-making processes. On the other hand, our inability to turn all tasks over to robots attests to the unique cognitive abilities that humans possess. Indeed, for a huge number of societal tasks, particularly those in healthcare, human participation is required. Human decision making and oversight, and thus safety mindfulness, are required to address the needs of patients with complex clinical problems, such as patients with cancer involving multiple organs who have patient-specific concurrent medical conditions, family relationships, and emotional responses to illness. So, although human involvement in the system is essential, it also generates defects (e.g., the lack of information/material needed for task completion). When a system is compromised by defects, individuals tend to try to quickly fix the problems using work-arounds so they can move on to the next task.

For a simple example, if an examination room lacks needed equipment, the provider "borrows" it from the adjacent examination room (essentially creating the defect elsewhere). Work-arounds are often done without addressing the underlying root causes or without correcting the root causes of latent failures and their associated pathways. In this case, it is preferable to determine how the rooms are monitored for equipment needs and stocked with the necessary supplies to find out why the desired materials are not being replaced as needed is preferred. Another variation when the system is *not* compromised by defects occurs when individuals deviate from standard procedures and processes by taking shortcuts to get work done *faster*. For example, rather than specifying a desired treatment parameter in the record and verify system, the provider verbally tells the simulator therapist, who forgets to tell the dosimetrist, whose plan then does not meet the provider's expectation. Unfortunately, shortcuts can lead to serious incidents.

When defects are present, the management challenge is to transform *Quick-Fixing* behavior like work-arounds into *Initiating* behaviors by empowering people to engage in PDSA-based problem-solving behaviors.[31] Workers need to be encouraged to call attention to the defects and provide the organization with the opportunity to take preventive action and potentially eliminate the latent and active failures and their respected pathways. In the absence of defects, the most desirable approach

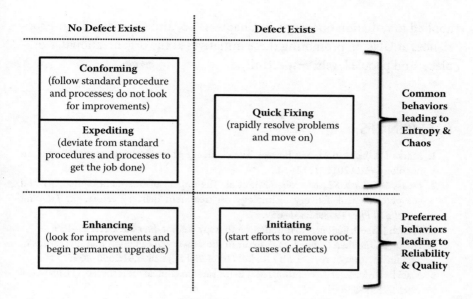

FIGURE 1.6

Categories of behaviors and decision making under conditions of defect and no defect. Preferred behaviors are *Enhancing* and *Initiating* as they promote individual and organizational learning toward high reliability and value creation. The remaining three behaviors—*Conforming, Expediting,* and *Quick Fixing*—lead to systems decay and potential chaos. (Adapted from Mazur L, McCreery J, Chen S-J. *J Healthcare Eng* 2012;4:621–648.)

is to encourage individuals to continue to use the agreed-on work flows while continually looking for opportunities for improvement, termed *Enhancing* behaviors.[31] Leadership should reinforce *Enhancing* behaviors via accolades to the staff and celebration of compliance and participation in quality improvement. In contrast, *Conforming* behaviors (e.g. not looking for the opportunities to improve) and *Expediting* behaviors (e.g. taking shortcuts, "doing favors," "helping out") should be limited, and not routinely done, as they promote uncertainty, false expectations, and unreliability (Figure 1.6).[31]

The importance of leadership is readily apparent at the people level. A worker who "gets the job done" via a series of work-arounds is frequently seen as a "can do person" and often receives accolades. The real accolades should be saved for the worker who analyzes and eliminates the underlying latent and active failure pathways that are generating the need for the work-arounds.

In Chapter 3, we further discuss how the concepts from high-reliability and value creation organizations, and normal accident theory, can be applied to radiation oncology. In Chapters 4, 5, and 6, we detail our experiences at UNC in promoting these initiatives at the organizational, workplace, and people levels, respectfully.

REFERENCES

1. Marks LB, Jackson M, Xie L, et al. The challenge of maximizing safety in radiation oncology. *PRO* 2011;1(1):1–14.
2. Fraass BA, Lash KL, Matrone GM, et al. The impact of treatment complexity and computer-control delivery technology on treatment delivery errors. *Int J Radiat Oncol Biol Phys* 1998;42:651–659.
3. French J. Treatment errors in radiation therapy. *Radiat Ther* 2002;11:149–159.
4. Huang G, Medlam G, Lee J, et al. Error in the delivery of radiation therapy: results of a quality assurance review. *Int J Radiat Oncol Biol Phys* 2005;61:1590–1595.
5. Macklis RM, Meier T, Weinhous MS. Error rates in clinical radiotherapy. *J Clin Oncol* 1998;16:551–556.
6. Marks LB, Light KL, Hubbs JL, et al. The impact of advanced technologies on treatment deviations in radiation treatment delivery. *Int J Radiat Oncol Biol Phys* 2007;69:1579–1586.
7. Patton GA, Gaffney DK, Moeller JH. Facilitation of radiotherapeutic error by computerized record and verify systems. *Int J Radiat Oncol Biol Phys* 2003;56:50–57.
8. Yeung TK, Bortolotto K, Cosby S, et al. Quality assurance in radiotherapy: evaluation of errors and incidents recorded over a 10 year period. *Radiother Oncol* 2005;74:283–291.
9. Barthelemy-Brichant N, Sabatier J, Dewe W, et al. Evaluation of frequency and type of errors detected by a computerized record and verify system during radiation treatment. *Radiother Oncol* 1999;53:149–154.
10. Ford EC, Terezakis S. How safe is safe? Risk in radiotherapy. *Int J Radiat Oncol Biol Phys* 2010;78:321–322.
11. Williamson JF, Thomadsen BR. Foreword. Symposium "Quality assurance of radiation therapy: The challenges of advanced technologies." *Int J Radiat Oncol Biol Phys* 2008;71:S1.
12. Williams TR. Target safely. http://www.huffingtonpost.com/tim-r-williams-md/target-safely_b_544270.html. Accessed August 4, 2010.
13. Dunscombe P. What can go wrong in radiation treatment? Presented at the AAPM/ASTRO Safety in Radiation Therapy meeting; Miami, FL; June 24–25, 2010.
14. Ibbott GS. What can go wrong in radiation treatment: data from the RPC. Presented at the AAPM/ASTRO Safety in Radiation Therapy meeting; Miami, FL; June 24–25, 2010.
15. Dansereau RE. *Misadministrations—Event Summaries and Prevention Strategies.* Troy, NY: State of New York Department of Health; 2010. BERP 2010-1.
16. Donaldson L. *Towards Safer Radiotherapy.* London, UK: British Institute of Radiology, Institute of Physics and Engineering in Medicine, National Patient Safety Agency, Society and College of Radiographers, the Royal College of Radiologists; 2007.
17. World Health Organization. *Radiotherapy Risk Profile: Technical Manual.* Geneva, Switzerland: WHO; 2008.

18. Ortiz Lopez P, Cosset J-M, Dunscombe P, et al. Preventing accidental exposures from new external beam radiation therapy technologies. International Commission of Radiological Protection Publication 112. *Ann ICRP* 2009;39(4).
19. Federal Aviation Administration http://www.faasafety.gov/. Home page.
20. Institute of Medicine. *To Err Is Human. Building a Safer System*. Washington, DC: National Academy Press; 1999.
21. Bogdanich W. Safety features planned for radiation machines. *New York Times* June 10, 2010:A19.
22. Bogdanich W. V.A. is fined over errors in radiation at hospital. *New York Times* March 18, 2010:A20.
23. Bogdanich W, Ruiz RR. Radiation errors reported in Missouri. *New York Times* February 25, 2010:A17.
24. Bogdanich W. Radiation offers new cures, and ways to do harm. *New York Times* January 24, 2010:A1.
25. ASTRO. Safety is no accident. A framework for quality radiation oncology and care. 2012.
26. Reason J. Human error: models and management. *BMJ* 2000;320:768–770.
27. Kotter J. *Leading Change*. Cambridge, MA: Harvard Business School Press; 1996.
28. Liker J. *The Toyota Way: Fourteen Management Principles from the World's Greatest Manufacturer*. New York, NY: McGraw-Hill; 2004.
29. Kenny C. *Transforming Health Care: Virginia Mason Medical Center's Pursuit of the Perfect Patient Experience*. New York, NY: CRC Press, Taylor & Francis Group; 2011.
30. Toussaint J, Gerard R. *On the Mend: Revolutionizing Healthcare to Save Lives and Transform the Industry*. Cambridge, MA: Lean Enterprise Institute; 2010.
31. Mazur L, McCreery J, Chen S-J. Quality improvement in hospitals: what triggers behavioral change? *J Healthcare Eng* 2012;4:621–648.

2

Broad Overview of "Past" and "Current" Challenges of Patient Safety Issues in Radiation Oncology

LEARNING OBJECTIVES

After completing this chapter, the reader should be able to:

1. Understand the care delivery process involved in radiation therapy;
2. Understand the range of event rates reported in radiation therapy; and
3. Understand many of the changes within radiation therapy, and more broadly within medicine and society, that may impact patient safety.

2.1 BRIEF INTRODUCTION TO RADIATION THERAPY PROCESSES

Readers familiar with RT processes should skip to Section 2.2. The broad goal of three-dimensionally (3D) planned external beam RT is to design and deliver high-energy photon beams to cancer targets while minimizing radiation risks to surrounding normal tissues. The potential for errors in RT is high because the planning and delivery processes include numerous handoffs between RT professionals, each interpreting and inputting information via multiple electronic systems (i.e., electronic health records [EHRs] and images). Thus, to ensure patient safety, a high level of accuracy is achieved via highly specified protocols and multiple QA steps conducted throughout the following generic stages (Figure 2.1):

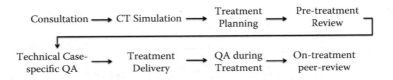

FIGURE 2.1
Radiation therapy process (generic flow for external beam). The use of pretreatment peer review is variable.

1. *Consultation:* The physician (radiation oncologist) evaluates the patient to determine if RT is an appropriate method of treatment. If yes, a tentative prescription is generated, also including tentative decisions regarding things such as positioning, immobilization, concurrent therapies (e.g., chemotherapy), and so on.

2. *Computed tomographic (CT) simulation:* The optimal position for treatment is determined and the patient is positioned accordingly on the CT simulation machine. For the patient to be positioned in a reproducible manner for treatment, patient-specific immobilization devices/positioning aids are often made. Markers might be placed on the skin to delineate things such as scars, palpable masses, or tentative field borders based on clinical landmarks. CT images of the patient in the treatment position are obtained for treatment planning. This may include a single CT data set, or multiple image sets (e.g., during multiple phases of the respiratory cycle for so-called four-dimensional [4D] planning). The physician typically reviews the images to ensure that they adequately visualize the target tissues and all areas that might be traversed by the treatment beams. A tentative isocenter for the treatment might be determined, and reference tattoos are often placed on the patient's skin (for later alignment with the lasers present in the CT simulator and treatment rooms). The desired images for planning are transferred to the treatment planning software.

3. *Treatment planning:* The radiation oncologist segments the images to define the target tissues (e.g., gross tumor and regional lymph nodes) and together with a medical dosimetrist defines the adjacent critical structures. The physician defines a series of dosimetric goals (e.g., treat the target with margin to a minimum of dose X and limit the normal tissue to dose Y, etc.). The medical dosimetrist or medical physicist uses the treatment planning software to design candidate radiation treatment plans (a series of radiation beams intended to

deliver the desired radiation dose distribution) that are then evaluated and redesigned (with the physician) in an iterative fashion until an acceptable/optimal plan is defined. Once approved, the radiation treatment plan is transferred to the record-and-verify system that is used to operate the treatment machine.

4. *Pretreatment peer review:* The segmented images and (where appropriate) the beam arrangement are reviewed by a panel of radiation oncology professionals (e.g., other radiation oncologists, medical physicists, medical dosimetrists) to ensure that the patient can be treated safely and efficiently. At the University of North Carolina (UNC), the peer review for intensity-modulated radiation therapy (IMRT) cases is done prior to treatment planning, and for three-dimensional (3D) cases is often done postplanning. Pretreatment review is integral to our procedures at UNC, and we have a daily meeting to facilitate this. Most centers perform some form of peer-review, but it is commonly performed after treatment has been initiated.

5. *Technical case-specific QA:* For some treatment plans (typically including all IMRT cases), the physicist will perform patient/plan-specific QA to verify that the information has been transferred appropriately to the treatment machine and that the plan delivers the intended dose distribution.

6. *Treatment delivery:* The radiation therapists position the patient as desired on the treatment table (emulating the position from the simulator) using the immobilization devices/positioning aids, tattoos, and alignment lasers. The accuracy of positioning is assessed using imaging (2- or 3D) and the patient is repositioned as needed. The treatment is delivered by the radiation therapists according to the approved radiation treatment plan in the record-and-verify system using a linear accelerator.

7. *QA during treatment:* The radiation oncologist reviews the images taken before and during the course of treatment to ensure appropriate localization. The radiation oncologist and nurse clinically evaluate the patient (typically weekly) during the course of therapy to manage acute toxicities. Changes to the treatment plan are made as necessary.

8. *On-treatment peer review*: At UNC, we have a weekly meeting where all of the cases that have initiated therapy during the prior week are reviewed. The goals are to review the localization images to the finalized treatment plans. Most radiation oncology facilities perform this type of on-treatment peer review.

All stages involve obtaining, interpreting, and transferring information from various electronic data storage systems. Even though RT professionals utilize sophisticated technologies to help control the process, many of the steps remain largely dependent on individual performances. Therefore, errors can occur at virtually any stage of the RT process.

2.2 RATES AND TYPES OF EVENTS REPORTED AND THE NEED FOR BETTER REPORTING

Estimating event rates is challenging. The definition of an event is ambiguous, and underreporting is the norm. Even if a consistent definition were applied, there have been only limited attempts to estimate the rates of particular types of events.

For example, incidents (defined as events reaching the patient) in treatment delivery are, by their nature, more readily identified and objective. They are essentially always manifested at the treatment machine, even if its cause was upstream, for example, by an ambiguous physician directive or, as is often the case, as the result of a series of latent failure pathways throughout the process. Thus, most of the data regarding the incidents are focused on treatment delivery, with some attribution bias. With these caveats stated, several data sources can be used to infer information about event rates (Table 2.1).

2.2.1 Population/Registry Data

New York State has maintained a central registry of reportable radiation events between 2001 and 2009. This database contains 230 events derived from an unknown number of patients/treatments. Using estimates based on radiation utilization and cancer incidence rates in New York State, one can estimate that the rate of events is 230/373,000. Of these, 37/230 were incidents that required medical intervention. From this, one can estimate

TABLE 2.1

Event Rates (%)

	Per Treatment	Per Course	Per Fraction	Per Field
Multiple-Center Series				
United Kingdom, 2006		0.04 (0.003)[a]		
Pennsylvania State, 2009	0.0025 (0.0006)[a]			
New York State,[b] 2009	0.06 (0.01)[a]			
Single-Institution Series				
Fraass, 1998	0.44	1.20		
Macklis, 1998		3.06		0.18 (0)[a]
Barthelemt-Brichant, 1999				3.22
Patton, 2003	0.17	3.3		
Huang, 2005		1.97	0.29	
Yeung, 2005		4.66	0.25	
French, 2006			0.32 (0.05)[a]	0.037 (0.005)[a]
Marks, 2007	0.10			

Source: Reproduced with permission from Marks LB, Jackson M, Xie L, et al., *PRO,* 2011;1:2–14.
[a] Estimated "serious" incident rate.
[b] NY state regions outside the metropolitan New York City area.

a serious incident rate of about 1/10,000 treated patients (i.e., 37/373,000). Therapist error was implicated in 84% of the events.[1] A review from the United Kingdom noted 181 events during 6.25 years, corresponding to an estimated rate of 40 incidents (3 clinically significant) per 100,000 courses of therapy.[2] This rate of 3/100,000 is a similar order of magnitude to the New York State registry report.

2.2.2 Institutional Data

Several institutional series noted event rates per patient, field, or treatment course (Table 2.1). Obviously, as one alters the denominator, the reported rate varies. The definition of an event between these reports was also inconsistent. Typically, all treatment deviations were included, whether or not they were clinically meaningful. In concert, these studies suggested that approximately 1% of patients have at least a minor incident during their course of treatment, with the majority of incidents causing no lasting harm. Nevertheless, their occurrence might reflect underlying problems. As expected, this 1% rate is far higher than that estimated from the NY or UK series because the threshold for reporting to an external agency is higher than that used in an institutional review.

2.2.3 Type of Events

Some reports provided data regarding the types/causes of events. The New York State data implicates therapist error in 84% of events, failure to follow policies and procedures in 63%, and physics-/dosimetry-related tasks in 27%, with some attributed to multiple causes. A World Health Organization (WHO) report reviewed significant events over three decades leading to death or injury in 3,125 patients.[3] These 3,125 incidents were associated with treatment planning in about 55%, the commissioning of new machines/systems in 25%, and data transfer and treatment delivery each in about 9%. Among the 4,616 WHO events not leading to patient harm, the identified sources of error were more diverse and included treatment planning in 9%, data transfer in 38%, treatment delivery in 18%, medical decision/assessment in 16%, simulation/imaging in 7%, and other causes in 28%. Reviews from Calgary and ROSIS (Radiation Oncology Safety Information System), a voluntary registry containing 1,200 events from 110 largely European centers, implicated standards, procedures, or practices in about 60%, communication in about 15%, materials/equipment in about 10%, and knowledge/skill in 10%.[4] Thus, serious incidents appear most associated with errors in machine commissioning, dose calculation, treatment planning, and data transfer. We recognize that the attribution of errors to a specific portion of a complex process is inexact and are reporting the data as presented in the report.

Multiple reports noted a shift in the type/frequency of errors with the introduction of new technologies (e.g., a decline in data entry errors with record-and-verify systems), but an increase in errors during equipment transitions when multiple machine types were used concurrently and tasks were thus less standardized.[5,6] High technology brings with it some automation, a sense of infallibility, and increased detachment between the operator and patient, which may lead to relatively more low-technology errors (e.g., forgetting to do something simple in a low-technology environment [such as placing a wedge or a block in the machine tray] that is no longer necessary in the high-technology setting with dynamic wedges and multileaf collimators [MLCs] as block replacements).[5,6] The inconsistencies in the data reported result from variable definitions, reporting requirements (e.g., voluntary vs. mandatory and anonymous vs. regulatory), and confusion between types and causes of error.

2.2.4 The Need for Better Reporting

Going forward, our field needs to embrace cultural changes to adopt a more systematic approach to reporting events and understanding the causes of errors. We need to develop clear criteria and definitions to categorize different types of events, errors, their causes, and so on to facilitate analyses that lead to methods of prevention. It is particularly critical that this issue be addressed by the organizers of central data repositories so their pooled data are most meaningful. For each event, if possible, there needs to be a clear distinction between what happened (or almost happened), when it occurred, who was involved, and what were the multiple steps (e.g., both latent errors and active errors) leading to the event. The American Society for Radiation Oncology (ASTRO) and American Association of Physicists in Medicine (AAPM) are working together with Clarity to form a radiation-oncology PSO (patient safety organization), with the hope that it will become a robust registry of events/errors within our field, capturing this sort of detailed data. The Radiation Oncology Incident Learning System (RO-ILS) was launched in June 2014 as our field's PSO.

Further, it is important that we not waste time/effort arguing about nomenclature and not force everyone to learn that nomenclature (as that would be a barrier to reporting). Experts in the field of quality and safety have ascribed a specific nomenclature (e.g., event vs. incident; error [slip vs. lapse vs. mistake]; and QA vs. quality control [QC] vs. quality management) to the study of systems and human performance. The majority of people do not need to take the time to learn these distinctions, and they do not want to learn them. If we want everyone to embrace reporting, we need to make sure that reporting is made as easy as humanly possible, and that reporting does not require understanding the jargon/nomenclature of the field of quality and safety. Therefore, in the ASTRO/AAPM PSO, it is intended that there will be two levels of reporting. At the first level, any worker within an organization can report an event. At that level, the worker is asked to describe his or her concern in broad terms, using the vernacular. Within each organization, there will be a specified person who will perform a second-level review of the described event that will be more detailed, such as addressing what happened (or almost happened), when it occurred, who was involved, and what were the multiple steps (e.g., both latent and active error pathways) leading to the event. Thus, the designated second-level reporting person within each organization will need to be more versed in the jargon and techniques of analysis used in the field of quality and safety.

The focus should not be on eliminating every cause of every event. Rather, we should focus our attention on latent and active failure pathways that can cause real patient harm or those that reflect systemic problems that might cause harm. Therefore, it is anticipated that not all things reported at level 1 will lead to a "full/official" submission to the PSO.

It should be emphasized that the ASTRO/AAPM-sponsored PSO will not be the only specialty-specific registry of events. Within the United States, federal legislation affords legal protections to reporting within the PSO structure. It was not practical for ASTRO/AAPM to piggyback onto one of the existing international registries to meet the need for reporting of events within the United States.

2.3 THE CHANGING PRACTICE OF RADIATION ONCOLOGY

There *appears* to be an increasing problem related to patient safety and quality within our field. The truth is hard to know. The metric one used to measure patient safety and quality will likely influence one's conclusion regarding whether things are getting better or worse. In either case, there is an increasing focus on high reliability and value creation. Many forces in our specialty are influencing the real and perceived changes in the practice of radiation oncology (discussed further in the following sections). A summary of some factors tending to change the probability or severity of events within RT and the apparently increasing risk of incidents (as the product of the incidence times the severity) is also presented in Table 1.1 and Figure 1.1. Several of the major factors are discussed next.

2.3.1 2D to 3D to IMRT

2.3.1.1 2D to 3D

The practice of radiation oncology has markedly changed since the beginning of the 2000s. Traditionally, planning and delivering radiation treatments was relatively easy both to conceptualize and to actualize. With our field's origins within diagnostic radiology, tumor targets were localized and defined based on fluoroscopy and planar imaging (2D planning). The orientations of treatment beams were largely limited to those that could be filmed and where the anatomy (from that perspective) was understood. The desired beam apertures were defined by (literally) drawing with crayon or wax pencil on the hard-copy films. On the treatment machine, the beams' apertures were created by physical blocks with shapes based on those crayon drawings. Dose distributions were easy to understand as they represented the weighted intersection of groups of (almost always) axial beams. Calculations of "beam-on" time (or monitor units) for each beam were relatively simple and indeed could be estimated mentally by experienced RT professionals. The accuracy of the beam localization and shape was easily assessed with a portal film. This is a radiograph generated by the treatment beam passing through the patient, essentially providing a 2D picture of what was being treated. Gross errors in dosing and delivery were relatively uncommon because the processes were relatively intuitive and relatively easy to check. This approach suffered from inaccuracies in target and normal tissue localization.

Three-dimensional treatment planning is a major advance in our field. It allows the planner to better understand the 3D relationship between the target and surrounding normal tissues as viewed from any arbitrary orientation. This planner can consider a wider array of possible beam orientations and more conformal beam shaping (compared to 2D planning). Studies to relate quantitative 3D dose/volume parameters to tumor and normal tissue outcomes were enabled, thus facilitating research leading to refined clinical practice for our field.

The changes in routine practice required in the transition from 2D to 3D planning are largely in the *planning* of treatment. Work flows are modified to incorporate the 3D imaging, image segmentation, beam design, calculation, and data transfer (Figures 2.2A and 2.2B).

Challenges in understanding/visualizing the 3D dose distribution (relative to the underlying anatomy) ushered in the use of dose-volume histograms (DVHs) as surrogate representations of the 3D data.

The adoption of 3D planning raises some quality and safety challenges, including:

- the need for physician competence in 3D image interpretation (i.e., target and normal tissue definition);

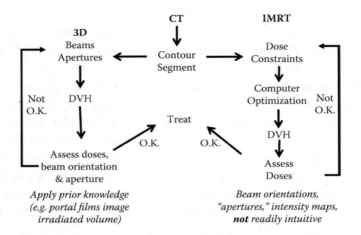

FIGURE 2.2(A)

The "work flow" for conventional three-dimensional (3D) planning versus intensity-modulated radiation therapy. Both are based on 3D anatomy. For conventional 3D, prior knowledge can be applied to assess the acceptability of a proposed treatment. (Reproduced with permission from Marks et al., *Int J Radiat Oncol Biol Phys* 2007;69(1):4–12.)

- interconnectivity of various electronic imaging/planning/treatment tools to be sure that information is transferred and interpreted correctly; and
- the need to appreciate the shortcomings of DVHs. DVHs are, at best, surrogates for the true 3D dose distribution. DVHs discard all spatial information, and the definition of a "safe" versus "unsafe" DVH is unclear in many settings.

Nevertheless, the widespread use and success of 3D treatment planning has been achieved without apparent major quality and safety concerns. Physicians largely obtained the needed skills to segment 3D images, and our physics/computer colleagues defined robust ways to transfer data (and monitor that data transfer).

One reason why the adoption of 3D planning may not have caused more problems with safety and quality is that it typically did *not* radically change *how* treatment was delivered. Certainly, there are some changes at the treatment machine; for example, therapists need to be comfortable delivering beams from unconventional orientations, and sometimes port-film verification of a treatment beam is not possible. Nevertheless, for the most part, the actual tasks performed by the therapists, and the machine itself, are similar to the 2D processes. Even with 3D planning, treatment

	Comparison of the Generic Steps for Three Types of Planning[a]		
	"2D" traditional	3D	IMRT
	MD consultation and decision to treat		
	Review of diagnostic images		
	Fluoroscopy to localize target, define treatment iso-center, and beam orientation	CT[b] imaging in the treatment position. Targets and normal tissue volumes defined on 3D images	
Planning	Beam shaping done "manually" (e.g. wax pencil on film)	Software used to assist with the "manual" definition of beam orientations and beam apertures. Typically each beam is conformally-shaped to include the 3D-defined target	Desired 3D dose constraints defined, and beam orientation is typically selected as well. Software used to compute the "optimal" beam-intensity maps (for each of the selected beams) to yield (as best as "possible") the desired 3D dose constraints. A "deliverable" beam intensity map is generated that approximates the computed "optimal" beam-intensity maps
	Doses calculated on one or several 2D planes	Doses calculated in 3D, and can be viewed in any arbitrary plane. DVHs used to help interpret the 3D doses	
	Physicians approve plan. Information transferred to treatment machine either manually or electronically	Physicians approve the plan. Information transferred to treatment machine; typically electronically	
	Therapists review plans, align patient's isocenter		
	Therapists review/check the field's borders		
Treatment	+/– IGRT and treat		
	Portal films aid in verifying iso-center localization and irradiated volumes		Portal films (and other imaging methods) aid in verifying iso-center localization only

FIGURE 2.2(B)
Comparison of the Generic Steps for 2D, 3D, and IMRT Planning. a. Steps shown are a gross oversimplification of workflow (e.g. IMRT has been suggested to require 54 tasks from patient evaluation to implementation[9]). This simplified version is intended to make the point discussed. b. Other 3D imaging tools can be used as well.

beams are still largely axial, plans are still largely weighted sums of the intersection of the beams, and thus treatment plans are still relatively easy to conceptualize and check. Calculations of beam-on times are still relatively intuitive, and portal films are still largely obtainable and useful to verify both the localization and the irradiated volume.

2.3.1.2 3D to IMRT

The move to IMRT is a much larger change with regard to *planning* and *delivery* processes. The delivered dose is no longer a "simple" weighted sum of the intersection of the beams; thus, treatment plans are not easy to conceptualize. Calculations of beam-on times are no longer intuitive. Portal films can be used to verify isocenter localization but are not typically adequate to verify the irradiated volume. Importantly, the therapist's role has been markedly altered (discussed further in the following material).

The MLC-based IMRT increases the monitor units (MUs) per delivered dose. Catastrophic failures of the system (e.g., MLCs mispositioned), although extremely rare, can have dramatic clinical consequences because the ratio between unintended/intended doses may be high. By comparison, failure to place a physical wedge (as routinely used with 2D and 3D) typically has lesser, rarely catastrophic, dosimetric effects. IMRT markedly increases the number of parameters that need to be correctly generated/transferred, thus increasing opportunities for error. Indeed, IMRT has been largely made possible (despite the large number of treatment parameters) by robust electronic interconnections and automated treatment delivery tools. Without these enhancements, the delivery of IMRT would be impractical and not very safe.

2.3.1.3 Reliance on Image Segmentation

Both 3D RT and IMRT rely on image segmentation. Institutions evolving from 2D to 3D to IMRT were able to refine their image segmentation skills. Segmentation errors with 3D can often be detected on digitally reconstructed radiographs (DRRs) or simulator/portal films. For example, the base of the tongue can be somewhat challenging to segment on axial CT, but its location is generally easy to identify on lateral planar images relative to soft tissue/bony landmarks. Thus, when reviewing the digitally reconstructed radiograph from a 3D plan (or from the corresponding portal film), one can appreciate if the image segmentation on the CT was done "approximately correctly." Gross errors are readily apparent. The user's prior knowledge from the 2D era can be used to help verify the accuracy of the 3D processes. Conversely, institutions rapidly moving from 2D to IMRT may have had less opportunity to refine image segmentation skills. And, segmentation errors are more challenging to detect with IMRT because they are not reflected in DVHs, and portal films (if taken at all) do not readily represent the irradiated volume (Figure 2.2A).

2.3.1.4 Collisions

With conventional planning, treatment beams were almost always static and oriented from "standard directions" and within the axial plane. With 3D planning, the ability to treat from nonstandard directions increased the possibility of a collision between the patient (or table) and the treatment machine (i.e., gantry). This was not too much of a risk as long as the therapists were within the treatment room to review the setup because the beams were largely static. However, new tools enable the therapist to move the table and gantry remotely, from outside the room. Historically, there was much reluctance to enable this function because collisions can be catastrophic. Nevertheless, as the number of beams being used has increased (from about 2–4 in the 2D era to about 2–6 with 3D and even more with IMRT), the time needed to go in and out of the treatment room increased accordingly. This, plus the lesser-perceived value in viewing the light fields on the patient's skin and the increasing use of arc-based therapies, has increased the desire to enable remote-controlled movement of the table and gantry. Collisions are thus a concern. The development of devices to remotely detect possible collisions has lessened the risks of enabling this remote movement feature.

2.3.2 Evolving Role of Radiation Therapists

Essentially all incidents are ultimately manifest at the treatment machine, where the therapists deliver the actual treatment. Often, these end-of-the-line staff are blamed for errors even if there are multiple contributing factors (e.g., latent failures and their respected pathways) or if the error occurred further upstream (e.g., a calculation error in dosimetry or an ambiguous directive from the physician). The critical role that end-of-the-line therapists play emphasizes the importance of discussing the impact of the technological evolution (from 2D to 3D to IMRT) on the therapist's role.

Radiation therapists who are more senior (e.g., trained > 10 years ago) were trained on older linear accelerators and were taught and required to think about the correct field size (that they manually set), gantry position for the treatment fields (also manually set), and field shapes (determined by "blocks" that they manually placed onto the machine). Historically, therapists routinely assessed the correctness of the patient setup by looking at the actual light field, field size, gantry angle, and block patterns on the skin and then comparing these parameters with the printed (or written) information from dosimetry and considering if it made sense from a clinical perspective (e.g., whether the light field was shining on the location of the target). Therapists instinctively knew the approximate number of monitor units typically used for various beams.

Changing technologies have altered this work flow and made some of these traditional QA/QC tools less useful. For example, review of the light field on the patient's skin and review of portal films, both long-standing QA procedures in traditional RT, are less applicable in the era of IMRT and image-guided radiation therapy (IGRT). Computer/remote control of the gantry and table and the use of MLCs to shape the fields (rather than cerrobend blocks) obviate the need for the therapists even to enter the treatment room between fields. This makes review of the light fields cumbersome and almost quaintly old fashioned. Currently, radiation therapists are trained to retrieve electronic information about a patient on a computer screen and review this for accuracy. The broad embrace of advanced technologies may promote an underappreciation of the physical limitations of our systems (a concept discussed in more detail in Chapter 3, Section 3.1.1.5). As with many things electronic, there is an underlying presumption that the information is correct (call it a societal/human nature bias). Thus, technology and automation often promote complacency and might inadvertently reduce safety mindfulness.

Further, the electronic environment displays much more information (compared to the paper chart), and it is often not practical to realistically verify all of the critical components. Diligence, checklists, reminders, and so on are often needed to assist with these tasks. The broad concept of a therapist reviewing the chart for correctness is not as fervently emphasized in today's training programs compared to therapists' training 10–20 years ago. Their review to make sure that things "make sense from a clinical perspective" is more challenging compared to the 2D/3D era (e.g., there is often no light field to check). On the other hand, therapists are taking on an increasing role in the review of pretreatment IGRT images and often make decisions regarding the adequacy of setup and the needed shifts to improve localization.

2.3.3 Image-Guided Therapy and Tighter Margins

Imaging tools (broadly defined to include conventional imaging [planar or 3D images] and other imaging-like tools, such as Calypso) allow us to "image" the patient on the treatment table. Essentially all technologies allow pretreatment imaging and some (e.g., planar radiographs and Calypso) also allow imaging *during* treatment. This approach can markedly reduce the degree of intra- and inter-fraction setup variation—clearly a potential advantage for our patients. We now have unprecedented verification of the accuracy of patient setup on the treatment machine. However, overreliance on imaging can result in an increase in marginal misses caused by an underestimation of the degree of microscopic extension.

Traditional margins around a target consider multiple sources of uncertainty in concert, including target delineation, microscopic spread, target motion, and patient setup (Figure 2.3A). Discrete target definitions (GTV, CTV, ITV, PTV, defined in figure) formally decouple these uncertainties; for example, CTV addresses microscopic spread beyond the GTV, ITV addresses CTV motion, and PTV broadly addresses setup inaccuracies. As technologies address these uncertainties (e.g., gating and IGRT shrink ITV and PTV margins, respectively), there is a widely embraced perceived ability to shrink overall margins (Figure 2.3A and 2.3B). However, tumor control may suffer with tighter margins. At least two published reports noted an increased rate of local failure, with the adoption of advanced technologies and tighter margins.[7,8] The authors of these reports should be commended for openly sharing their experiences. Their reports suggested that (at least) some of the margin ascribed to our uncertainties regarding gross target definition and intra-/interfraction motion also helped mitigate some uncertainty in tumor infiltration.

2.3.4 Time Demands/Expectations

2.3.4.1 Increased Time Demands of the Changing Work Flow

Newer technologies require increased efforts for many members of the radiation oncology team; for example, for image segmentation, iterative dose calculations, patient-specific QA, image acquisition/review, treatment delivery, or machine/MLC maintenance/repair. Individual's tasks are more interdependent, with more handoffs, thus increasing opportunities for delay and suboptimal information transfer, for example, dosimetrist image segmentation → MD image segmentation and specification of dose/volume constraint → dosimetrist planning → MD review → dosimetrist replanning → iteratation and so on. The time pressures on all involved are increased. The need for unambiguous communication and for easy-to-use tools is increased. A recent ASTRO-sponsored report noted that there are

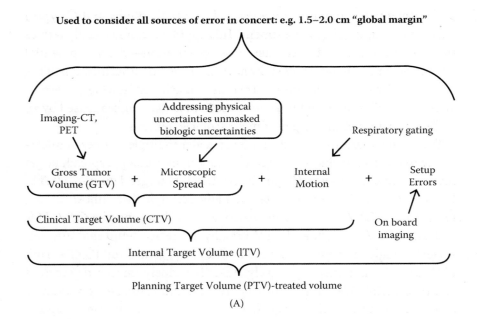

FIGURE 2.3(A)

(A) Margins are defined to compensate for microscopic spread, internal motion, and setup errors, as noted. Advances in imaging (e.g., CT) decrease uncertainty regarding GTV. Technology such as respiratory gating allows us to better control internal motion. Technologies such as image-guided therapy or cone beam CT allow us to mitigate/reduce patient setup errors. Adaptation of these technologies has led to a reduction in global margins and, in some instances, a decline in local control, perhaps because of the unmasking of uncertainties regarding microscopic spread (i.e., biologic uncertainty). (Reproduced with permission from Marks et al., *PRO*, 2011.)[9]

approximately 54 tasks performed by the physician, dosimetrist, physicist, and therapist (with about 15 handoffs) for a patient receiving IMRT.[10]

2.3.4.2 Addressing Expectations

Care providers, including referring physicians, patients, and administrators have been accustomed to our historic ability to proceed with consultation, simulation, and treatment initiation in rapid succession. With advanced technologies, this is less practical and might be dangerous. Rushing is a contributing factor in errors. The transition to 3D, and particularly IMRT, lengthens the planning process. Administrators and providers need to be educated about the increased complexity of modern techniques and possible hazards of work-arounds. Similarly, patients and others must recognize that

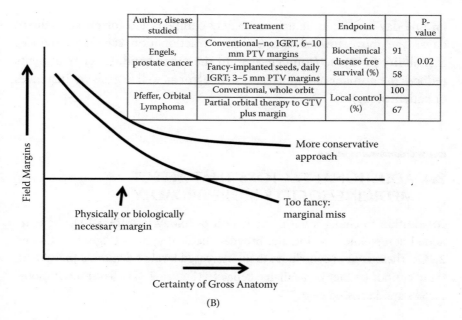

Author, disease studied	Treatment	Endpoint		P-value
Engels, prostate cancer	Conventional–no IGRT, 6–10 mm PTV margins	Biochemical disease free survival (%)	91	0.02
	Fancy-implanted seeds, daily IGRT; 3–5 mm PTV margins		58	
Pfeffer, Orbital Lymphoma	Conventional, whole orbit	Local control (%)	100	
	Partial orbital therapy to GTV plus margin		67	

FIGURE 2.3(B)

(B) As our certainty of our gross anatomy increases, there is a tendency and ability to reduce the field margin. However, there is probably a physical or biologically necessary margin related to our uncertainty of microscopic spread. If this uncertainty is not acknowledged, then reducing the margin may lead to a marginal miss. (Reproduced with permission from Marks et al., *PRO*, 2011.)[9]

the increased capabilities of modern machines might lead to more frequent downtimes. The instinct to move patients to different machines is, at best, logistically challenging, but often is tremendously burdensome because some complex IMRT plans are machine specific, and replanning, optimization, and QA must be repeated. Despite these concerns, clinical care often dictates that we do rush a treatment plan, create work-arounds, or replan for patients—all activities that stress the system and may lead to errors. Thus, the realistic goal is not to totally eliminate these activities but to create systems that minimize their frequency and to enable systems to evolve in response to changes in clinical practice.

2.3.5 Shorter Treatment Schedules

Traditional RT is delivered over many days or weeks. Thus, the dosimetric/clinical effects of a treatment deviation on a given day are diluted by the many other days of correct treatment delivery. Further, a deviation on one day can often be approximately compensated for on subsequent days. The move toward shorter/faster fractionation schedules reduces this ability to correct/compensate. On the other hand, fewer treatments reduces the number of opportunities for error as well (e.g., fewer instances of patient setup).

2.4 ADDITIONAL FACTORS THAT AFFECT MEDICINE/SOCIETY MORE BROADLY

In addition to changes within radiation oncology (Figure 2.4A), there are added complexities within the broader medical system (Figures 2.4B and 2.4C). These factors contribute to an increased level of demands that potentially cannot be met by available capacity (Figure 2.4D). Several additional factors are discussed next.

2.4.1 Electronic Health Records

Electronic health records have the potential to improve an individual's care (e.g., by improved access to information, data sharing between providers, data integration, etc.). Discrete data elements can be tracked over time to better personalize care. On a population level, the EHR can facilitate monitoring care trends across groups of patients and over time. Variations in treatments can be more readily and accurately associated with variations in outcomes, helping to better define optimal treatments. The possibilities are seemingly endless, and the opportunities for real improvements in the quality and efficiency of care are exciting. However, the transition from a paper chart to an EHR can be disruptive. Even when fully functional, it takes time to re-create work flows within EHRs. Some functions are diminished: Multiple notes cannot be easily viewed concurrently or in rapid sequence; thus, the *clinical context* can often be difficult to appreciate.[11] Notes typically cannot be annotated, and data entry/retrieval can be cumbersome. Some capabilities that are particularly helpful in our field cannot be readily replicated in the EHR, such as drawing/comparing serial pictures to document changes in tumor extent or normal tissue response. The lack of connectivity between many hospital EHRs and the (radiation) oncology-specific EHRs presents particular concerns (e.g., double data entry, unavailability of records to other departments, omissions, and

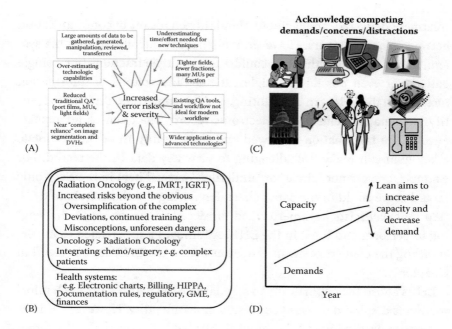

FIGURE 2.4

(A) Confluence of events shown may have increased the risks of errors in radiation oncology. The increased use of advanced technologies results, at least in part, from the physician's desire to provide state-of-the-art care, as well as from patient, competitive, and financial pressures. (B) Sources of increased complexity can be somewhat arbitrarily divided into categories as shown: within radiation oncology, general oncology (e.g., including issues related to chemotherapy and surgery), and broader issues affecting the whole health system. (C) Interventions aimed to reduce errors should consider the competing demands, concerns, and distractions that people face (e.g., government regulations, educational missions, legal concerns, monetary/billing issues). (D) In concert, these many factors have increased demands to the point that they might exceed capacity. When there was excess capacity, minor inefficiencies in the workplace were more tolerable; work-arounds and redos were relatively easy to accommodate. Presently, the calculus has changed to the point that demands are approached (or have already exceeded) capacity, leading to stress and an increased risk of error. Lean approaches can reduce the demands and increase the capacity (by reducing waste). (Reproduced with permission from Marks et al., *PRO*, 2011.)[9]

deletions). This may lead to stress/frustration and incomplete/erroneous documentation within the EHR, negatively affecting safety.

Within radiation oncology, electronic data systems (e.g., record-and-verify systems) have had tremendous benefits. These systems have largely eliminated the errors related to data transfer from the planning system to the treatment machine. They provide an unambiguous record of the treatment delivered, and facilitate standardized means of communication between team members. However, if an error is introduced into the system, there is a danger that this could affect multiple fractions (for a single patient) or even possibly multiple patients. The volume of information included in the EHR can be daunting, and it is sometimes difficult to identify key data elements in the electronic record. The often-bland appearance of the information displayed and the inability to readily annotate a key item can make it challenging to view key data in the record. For example, one cannot "circle" or "underline" a usual item in the electronic record as we could in the paper chart. Reviewing the chart, a routine QA step that physicists have performed for decades, can be more challenging to perform and track in the EHR. Additional issues related to understanding the context of the information within the EHR are discussed in Chapter 7.

EHRs afford the opportunity to standardize the manner in which information is displayed to avoid confusion and ambiguity. However, we have not optimally exploited this ability in our field. For example, the radiation oncology prescription (a fundamental component of our practice) is depicted in *different* formats within a single record-and-verify software package (e.g., Figure 2.5). Intervendor variations are even greater, and there is a need for broad societal standardization in this and other areas (discussed in the Appendix). This is a particular problem for clinical practices that now span across several treatment sites and where tools and techniques are not necessarily consistent between sites.

In the balance, there is no question that EHRs are a benefit to medicine and radiation oncology. However, we should be aware of their potential limitations and their associated impact on clinical care. Robust collaborative relationships between software developers and users should lead to reasonable approaches to address these types of challenges (see Chapter 7, Section 7.6).

2.4.2 Sicker Patients

People are living longer with more comorbid diseases; thus, the patients we are evaluating/treating are older and often sicker. A recent review of our patients at UNC demonstrated that about 20% had an unplanned admission to the hospital within 90 days of initiation of their radiotherapy.[12]

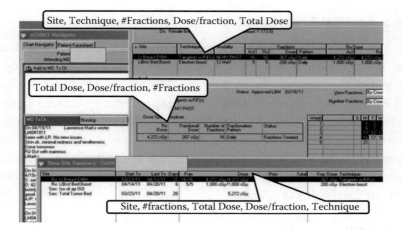

FIGURE 2.5

Our field's lack of a standard format to our radiation prescriptions is illustrated. This screenshot is taken from a commonly used "record-and-verify" system. The three separate windows each describe the radiation treatment given/prescribed for the same patient. Note that the order in which the prescription is described (e.g., treatment type, total dose, fraction size, dose per fraction, etc.) is different in each of the three windows. Each window is factually correct, clear, and readily interpretable. However, the lack of standardization likely requires an increased level of mental effort by those who input or review information from these different displays. The "callout balloons" were added to emphasize the point. (Reproduced with permission from Marks and Chang, *PRO*, 2011.)

2.4.3 Combined-Modality Therapy

There is an increasing use of induction (i.e., preradiation) and concurrent chemotherapy for a variety of diseases. This tends to increase the acute side effects of therapy and increases the number of handoffs between providers. The increasing use of "nurse navigators" and other assistants is (at least in part) a reflection of the increasingly complex nature of the combined-modality therapy we deliver.

2.4.4 Guidelines

There are an increasing number of clinical guidelines and dose, volume, outcome data, and standards that are available to help guide treatment decisions. These are useful and help to reduce practice variation and it is hoped improve patient outcomes. Nevertheless, care must be taken not to blindly follow these documents as interpatient variations influence their appropriateness/applicability.

2.4.5 Societal Expectations

The increasing affluence of our society, the rising costs of healthcare, and the competitive/entrepreneurial nature of healthcare (leading to the wide use of advertising to promote medical care) increase the hype and expectations of our patients. People expect efficacy for this expense. Unfortunately, the utility of many parts of our healthcare system have been overstated. People are willing and want to accept "more" and "more expensive" care with the expectation that it is "better." This promotes overutilization and unaligned incentives and can increase demands on an often-strained delivery system.

2.4.6 Administrative Concerns

The administrative burdens of our healthcare system are large and seem to be worsening. Increasing and often-changing regulations (from government, insurers, accrediting agencies, etc.) continue to strain operations and add work that often appears to be of little value.

2.5 SUMMARY

In summary, the increased concerns for patient safety and quality within radiation oncology result from multiple factors, such as the rapid adoption of advanced technologies; changes in work flow (e.g., multiple handoffs); the relative loss of some traditional end-of-the-line QA and control tools (e.g., port films, light fields, more difficulty performing chart checks); changes in fractionation schedules; and perhaps an underappreciation for the physical limitations of imaging-based diagnosis and treatment. Technology can also promote complacency: "It must be right; the computer said so." Further, there are other broad issues within healthcare and society (e.g., regulatory, insurance, unrealistic expectations) that strain our systems and may influence patient safety and quality. Healthcare is changing rapidly, and change is a major source of risk. As stated by Youngberg and Hatlie, "How change is creating new paths for failure and new demands on workers. ... and how revising their understanding of these paths is an important aspect of work on safety; ... missing the side effects of change is the most common form of failure for organizations and individuals."[13] Measures to enhance patient safety and quality should recognize the multifaceted nature of changes in our field and the associated challenges. Enhanced safety mindfulness at all levels (organization, workplace, and people) is needed to maximize safety in the rapidly changing and somewhat-unpredictable field of medicine.

REFERENCES

1. Dansereau RE. *Misadministrations—Event Summaries and Prevention Strategies.* Troy, NY: State of New York Department of Health; 2010. BERP 2010-1.
2. Donaldson L. *Towards Safer Radiotherapy.* London: British Institute of Radiology, Institute of Physics and Engineering in Medicine, National Patient Safety Agency, Society and College of Radiographers, the Royal College of Radiologists; 2007.
3. World Health Organization. *Radiotherapy Risk Profile: Technical Manual.* Geneva, Switzerland: WHO; 2008.
4. Dunscombe P. What can go wrong in radiation treatment? Presented at the AAPM/ASTRO Safety in Radiation Therapy meeting; Miami, FL; June 24–25, 2010.
5. Marks LB, Light KL, Hubbs JL, et al. The impact of advanced technologies on treatment deviations in radiation treatment delivery. *Int J Radiat Oncol Biol Phys* 2007;69:1579–1586.
6. Amols HI. New technologies in radiation therapy: ensuring patient safety, radiation safety and regulatory issues in radiation oncology. *Health Phys* 2008;95:658–665.
7. Pfeffer MR, Rabin T, Tsvang L, et al. Orbital lymphoma: is it necessary to treat the entire orbit? *Int J Radiat Oncol Biol Phys* 2004;60:527–530.
8. Engels B, Soete G, Verellen D, et al. Conformal arc radiotherapy for prostate cancer: increased biochemical failure in patients with distended rectum on the planning computed tomogram despite image guidance by implanted markers. *Int J Radiat Oncol Biol Phys* 2009;74:388–391.
9. Marks LB, Jackson M, Xie L, et al. *The challenge of maximizing safety in radiation oncology.* PRO 2011;1(1):1–14; 2011.
10. Moran J, Dempsey M, Eisbruch A, et al. Safety considerations for IMRT: executive summary. *Pract Radiat Oncol* 2011;1:190–195.
11. Marks L. Misperceptions on electronic health records. *News & Observer.* October 2013. http://www.newsobserver.com/2013/10/04/3253538/misperceptions-on-electronic-health.html.
12. Waddle MR, Chen RC, Arastu NH, et al. Unanticipated hospital admissions during or soon following radiotherapy: incidence and predictive factors. *Pract Radiat Oncol* 2014; in press, 108.
13. Youngberg B, Hatlie M. *The Patient Safety Handbook.* Sudbury, MA: Jones and Bartlett; 2004.

3

Best Practices from High-Reliability and Value Creation Organizations: Their Application to Radiation Oncology

---

LEARNING OBJECTIVES

After completing this chapter, the reader should be able to:

1. Understand concepts described in normal accident theory (NAT) and high-reliability organization (HRO) theory;
2. Understand some of the key "best practices" from high-reliability and value creation organizations to enhance safety and efficiency; and
3. Understand the University of North Carolina's (UNC's) initiatives at the organizational, workplace, and people levels to drive improvements in quality and safety.

3.1 HIGH RELIABILITY AND VALUE CREATION

The term *high-reliability organizations* (HROs) was coined in the mid-1980s by a group of scholars at the University of California at Berkeley, who initiated a study in three organizations in which serious accidents were not tolerated: commercial nuclear power plants, the US Federal Aviation Administration's operation of its air traffic control system, and the US Navy's aircraft carrier aviation program.[1] In general, HROs were found to focus on systemic strategies for improving safety and reliability and therefore create value to their staff and customers, for example, in a broad sense framed around the Swiss Cheese Model (Figures 1.2–1.4

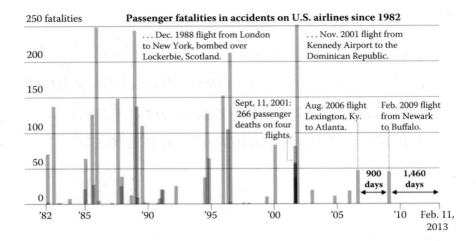

FIGURE 3.1

Time span between passenger fatalities in accidents on US airlines and number of fatalities as reported by PlaneCrashInfo.com (http://www.planecrashinfo.com). At that time (February 2013), the last commercial airline accident that resulted in deaths of passengers was four years earlier, the longest such span for decades. And, the previous span between accidents was the longest before this one. The key reasons for the reduced accident rate were ascribed to more reliable planes and engines; advanced navigation and warning systems; regulators, pilots, and airlines personnel training on the culture of safety; and a higher survival probability when crash did occur.

in Chapter 1). These industries have been extraordinarily successful in improving safety and preventing occurrence of major accidents. Sample data from the aviation industry are shown in Figure 3.1. Those unfamiliar with these concepts should read the following sections carefully as the concepts are somewhat difficult to comprehend and often misunderstood. A series of evolving figures are provided to facilitate understanding.

Sections 3.1.1 and 3.1.2 review two major theoretical models that address high reliability and value creation, each from somewhat contradictory perspectives: normal accident theory (NAT) and HRO theory (see Table 3.1 for a summary of their key elements, similarities, and differences). In each section, we attempt to project each model onto the practice of radiation oncology. Section 3.1.3 then synthesizes how we apply the fusion of concepts from both models to improve quality and safety at the organizational, workplace, and people levels within radiation oncology.

TABLE 3.1

Comparison of Two Prominent "Safety" Theories

Characteristic	High-Reliability Organization Theory	Normal Accident Theory
Views on harm	Harm can be mitigated through good organizational design, leadership, and management; and thus, this model is sometimes considered to be somewhat optimistic.	Harm is inevitable in complex and tightly coupled systems (like healthcare delivery); and thus, this model is sometimes considered to be somewhat pessimistic.
Prioritization of safety	Safety must be set as the top organizational priority.	Safety is one of a number of competing organizational priorities.
Redundancy	Redundancy of systems (i.e., multiple QA procedures) can enhance patient safety.	Redundancy often causes serious incidents as it increases interactive complexity and indirectly promotes risk taking.
Effectiveness of leadership and cultural initiatives	Leadership-inspired safety mindfulness is needed to achieve high reliability and value creation.	Organizational norms and values are not adequate to ensure the intense discipline that is needed to prevent serious accidents.
Effectiveness of planning, training, simulation	Continuous trial-and-error training and simulation for "unimagined" can create and maintain high-reliability operations (i.e., preemptively assess the likelihood of risk).	"Unimagined" operations are beyond organizational control as we do not know how systems can fail us. Highly coupled and interactively complex systems with potentially catastrophic accidents should be abandoned as they present too great a risk to societies.

Source: Modified (our interpretations) from Sagan S. *Limits of Safety.* Princeton, NJ: Princeton University Press; 1993.

3.1.1 Normal Accident Theory

Dr. Charles Perrow hypothesized that any system whose elements are tightly coupled, and interactively complex, are *impossible* to fully control, and that dangerous perturbations, leading to unexpected accidents, are inevitable in the course of normal operations.[2] In other words, such complex systems cannot be fully understood; thus, their behavior will always have some element of "chaos." He argued that only a change in their structure—from tight to loose coupling or from an interactively complex to a more linear system—can help reduce the probability of a catastrophic event. In practice, this theory has been criticized for being rather pessimistic; for example, this is exemplified by such assertions as, "No matter how hard we might try, the characteristics of complexly, interactive, and tightly coupled systems will cause a major failure, eventually."[2]

But, what do these terms mean? According to Perrow, systems can be broadly considered to be linear versus interactively complex, as well as loosely coupled versus tightly coupled.[2]

3.1.1.1 Linear versus Interactively Complex Systems

A system in which two or more discrete failures can interact in unexpected ways is described as "interactively complex." In many cases, interactively complex systems can be expected to have many unanticipated failure mode interactions, making it vulnerable to "normal" accidents. At a simple level, highly linear systems may be considered those in which one step systematically follows another, and information flow is similarly orderly, for example, A → B → C → D, and so on. With this, failures at one step typically affect the following step in a somewhat predictable manner. In more complex systems, the steps and information flow are less systematic; thus, failures at any given step, and in particular at multiple steps, may interact in unpredictable ways, leading to instability. Even very simple individual steps, if arranged in a nonlinear manner, can lead to chaos.

3.1.1.2 Loosely Coupled versus Tightly Coupled Systems

The idea of loosely coupled versus tightly coupled systems is a somewhat more difficult concept but can be expressed as the likelihood that failures (single or multiple) propagate through the system and become meaningfully manifested (e.g., lead to an accident). This might reflect the ability of a system to correct failures (to either detect them or to compensate for them). Inherent in this is the time frame/kinetics of the system, essentially the kinetics of the failure's propagation relative to the kinetics of the potential corrective actions. And, if things happen quickly (relative to human thinking times), the system is described as tightly coupled. Interestingly and importantly, tight coupling of complex systems also increases the probability that operator intervention will make things worse because the true nature of the problem may well not be understood correctly.[2]

3.1.1.3 How Complexity and Coupling Are Related to Risk?

Within this construct, Perrow argued that systems that are both interactively complex and tightly coupled are inherently more vulnerable to major accidents. Their interactive complexity is the trigger (i.e., an expected failure will occur), and their tight coupling is the propagator (i.e., the failure will be manifest as an accident). Indeed, Perrow argued that such accidents are inevitable and will occur during normal operations, hence the term normal accident theory.[2] Implicit is the acknowledgment that failures of multiple individual components *will* occur, human operators *will* make errors, and so on. The safety of the system is a reflection of *how* the failures behave within the system—in a predictable manner (linear system) or in an unpredictable manner (interactively complex system)—and how the system can (or cannot) effectively respond to the failures. The concepts and nomenclature perhaps are best illustrated through real-world examples.

a. Car manufacturing processes (assembly lines) are considered linear and loosely coupled systems. Things tend to happen in an orderly fashion (linear), and failures can often be detected and corrected in a timely fashion.

b. Water dams are thought of as linear and tightly coupled systems. A failure at one dam (e.g., a breech) typically has predictable downstream (quite literally) consequences (linear). The system is tightly coupled because this is almost certainly going to be manifest (e.g., cause a flood). Even though the breech is readily apparent, it is usually not humanly possible to prevent the flood (the timescale for corrective action is much slower than the flow of the water).

c. Universities are seen as complex and loosely coupled systems. Decisions in broad areas of the university often affect each other (interactively complex). The unforeseen impacts of these complex interactions are often detected and can be addressed and averted in a timely fashion (loosely coupled).

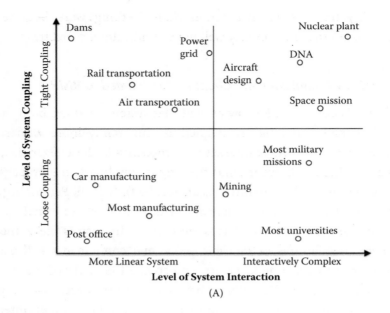

FIGURE 3.2(A)

(A) Various systems are placed within the construct of linear versus interactively complex and loose versus tight coupling (see text). (Adapted from Perrow C, *Normal Accidents: Living with High-Risk Technologies.* New York: Basic Books; 1984: Figure 9.1, p. 327.) Also, see the Appendix for an analogy related to these concepts as applied to sports.

d. Nuclear power plants are examples of interactively complex and tightly coupled systems. The interactions between the various components are hard to predict, and things can happen quickly, much faster than the response time of a human monitoring the system (tightly coupled).

These and other examples, along with related concepts, are provided in Figures 3.2A–D. As shown, linear versus interactively complex is alternatively represented as the predictability of the manner in which failures interact (i.e., probability of unexpected failure interactions). Loose versus tight coupling is alternatively represented as the ability to detect/mitigate failures and hence the probability that failures will propagate through the system and lead to an accident. Although these characteristics are presented as dichotomous, we acknowledge that, in practice, these are largely continuous variables.

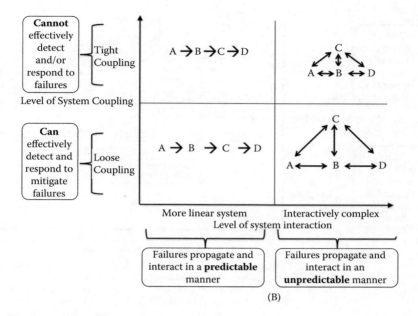

(B)

FIGURE 3.2(B)

(B) These concepts are shown schematically. System complexity is alternatively represented as whether failures behave in a predictable manner (*x* axis). System coupling is alternatively represented as whether failures can be detected, corrected, or mitigated.

3.1.1.4 Applying These Constructs to Radiation Oncology

Is radiation oncology linear or nonlinear? From the provider's perspective, work flow in the clinic might be broadly simplified as the following steps:

- evaluate the patient/records
- make treatment recommendations
- perform radiation treatment planning
- review treatment plans (often iterate)
- initiate therapy
- treatment management (i.e., monitor/continue therapy, repeat)

Similarly, on the technical side (e.g., physicist/dosimetrist/therapist), work flow for a radiosurgery case might be broadly simplified as performing the following steps:

- gather planning images
- fuse planning images with diagnostic images

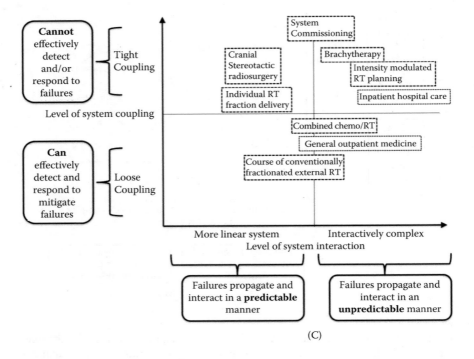

FIGURE 3.2(C)

(C) Approximate proposed placement of radiation oncology process with respect to dimensions introduced in (A) and (B). The relative positions of the entries are explained in the text. Because there is no absolute scale, groups of these entries might be translated up or down or to the left or right.

- generate some image segmentations
- review desired dose/volume parameters with the provider
- perform treatment planning
- perform plan QA
- bring patient to the machine
- perform pre-treatment QA/alignment verification
- deliver treatment

These are largely forward, or linear, processes, with failures propagated typically from one step to the next. However, these are idealized presentations of the work flow. There are many nonlinear components (e.g., iterations in the treatment-planning process and the repeats in the treatment management). Some of the newer technologies (e.g., image-guided

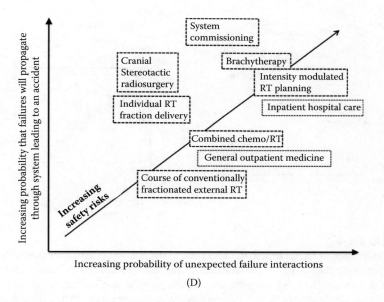

FIGURE 3.2(D)
(D) The charactersitics shown on the axes in panels A–C are presented as discrete and dichotomous for clarity but in reality are continuous.

radiation therapy [IGRT], adaptive therapy) also introduce nonlinearity and interactive complexity.

Further, information flow is not always from one step to the next. A good way to view this visually is shown in Figure 3.3. Across both axes (top to bottom and left to right) is a granular listing of our processes for patient evaluation and treatment, with the process starting in the upper left-hand corner. In each column, the flow of information from that one step to all of the subsequent steps is shown (by the shaded boxes with 1 inside them in the different rows within that column). Therefore, you can readily detect the flow of information from step 1 to step 2, from step 2 to step 3 etc. However, note that some information flow skips some of the intervening steps (e.g., in a fast-forward manner). For example, something determined in step 1 or 2 may have a direct impact on something in step 6 without necessarily having an impact on the intervening steps. An example of this might be the physician's decision to use a particular immobilization device or image guidance technique. This decision can typically be made relatively early in the planning process, and its manifestations are at multiple places "downstream."

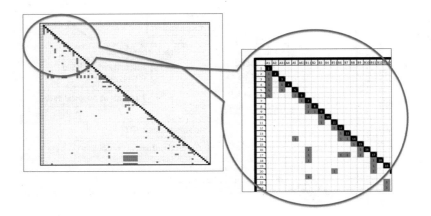

FIGURE 3.3

Representation of the treatment delivery process using a design structure matrix (DSM). The processes start in the upper left-hand corner and proceed top to bottom and left to right. A granular listing of our processes for patient evaluation and treatment are on both axes. In each column, the flow of information from that one step to all of the subsequent steps is shown (by the dots in the different rows within that column). Therefore, you can readily detect the flow of information from step 1 to step 2, from step 2 to step 3, and so on. However, note that some information flow skips some of the intervening steps (e.g., in a "fast-forward" manner). For example, something determined in step 1 or 2 may have a direct impact on something in step 10 without necessarily having an impact on the intervening steps.

Thus, for the most part, the flow of information (and the impact of associated failures) is orderly and in the forward (likely predictable) direction. However, with some of the newer technologies (e.g., adaptive therapy, IGRT) there is information flow in the reverse direction, essentially causing some procedures to be repeated. Further, some of our processes are long, with many steps (e.g., intensity-modulated radiation therapy [IMRT] planning and delivery), thus increasing the possibility of unexpected interactions of different failures.

Is radiation oncology coupled or uncoupled? Broadly speaking, we believe that most radiation oncology processes are modestly coupled (Figures 3.2C–D). The pace of much of our work is slow enough for unexpected interactions between failures to be evident. For example, suboptimal decisions about patient positioning and immobilization are typically evident early in the course of therapy and can be addressed. Physician errors in image segmentation can be detected by dosimetrists (and vice versa) during the subsequent treatment planning and plan review.

This issue of kinetics is critical. In many areas of radiation oncology (and other areas of medicine as well), the relatively slow pace tends to soften the impact of failure, that is, reduce their clinical impact. As an illustration of this, Larry sometimes wakes up in the middle of the night realizing that he made an error the prior day, and he almost always can rectify things without patient harm in the morning. An obvious corollary to this is that failures are more likely to be clinically manifest in situations for which the processes move much faster (or at least faster than the mechanisms to detect and correct the failure).

Are there parts of our practice that are tightly coupled? Yes, consider intraoperative radiotherapy, brachytherapy, and radiosurgery. These are settings for which the entire procedure is often compressed into a few hours; thus, some steps have near-immediate impacts on other steps (and Larry's nighttime realizations are less able to be rectified). Further, portions of our routine processes are very quick. Consider the setup and delivery of each individual fraction of radiation—the steps of patient identification, setup, image verification, and treatment delivery occur rapidly (and indeed many "human errors" manifest in our field occur during this rapid sequence of steps). Also, failures in some processes can be difficult to detect and may affect many treatments/patients downstream (e.g., system commissioning) and thus might be considered tightly coupled.

As we introduce more components to the processes (e.g., combined chemoradiotherapy, adaptive therapy), the number of steps and people involved increases, interactively the processes become more complex (unusual interactions between failures become more likely), and coupling becomes tighter (it might become more difficult to detect and address these failures).

Thus, our processes do not necessarily fit neatly into the boxes in Figure 3.2B. Nevertheless, overall, we submit that a course of conventionally fractionated external radiation therapy (RT) is fairly linear, modestly coupled, and relatively slow (Figures 3.2C–D). Brachytherapy, stereotactic radiosurgery, and individual-fraction treatment delivery are more tightly coupled essentially because the pace tends to be faster. Treatments involving more disciplines (e.g., combined chemotherapy and RT), more steps (e.g., IMRT), or more variables (e.g., brachytherapy) are interactively more complex as well. Several technical tasks, such as system commissioning, are likely more tightly coupled (downstream manifestations of interacting failures might be difficult to detect or the volume of data to consider may exceed human processing capabilities) and, depending on the particular task, might be more interactively complex (e.g., if various pieces of equipment are needed or data are pooled from several places).

The relative positions of the entries in Figure 3.2C and 3.2D are certainly debatable, and some of the terms are perhaps imprecise (e.g., brachytherapy for different body sites might have a different degree of interactive complexity). Further, because there is no absolute scale, groups of these entries might be translated up or down or to the left or right.

So, what is the relevance of this discussion? Can we use these constructs to guide QA strategies? Safety experts suggest that there are global optimal QA strategies that are applicable to all types of systems (e.g., leadership-driven safety mindfulness, the application of automation and forcing functions wherever able, etc.). However, there are particular QA considerations for different systems depending where they lie on this paradigm of linear versus interactively complex and loosely coupled versus tightly coupled.[2]

For example, a course of conventionally fractionated external RT (mostly linear, modestly coupled, and generally slow) might be amenable to continuous quality improvement (CQI) methodologies. The Toyota Production System[3] (TPS, often termed *Lean*) is perhaps the most powerful CQI approach ever devised to efficiently and effectively manage (create and maintain) quality and reliability in large-scale operations with these characteristics. This system helped propel Toyota Motor Corporation from a small truck maker struggling in the wake of World War II to one of the world's largest automakers. At its foundation, the TPS relies on inspirational leadership, decentralization of management, coaching and empowerment of front-line workers for CQI/safety mindfulness, and highly standardized work practices perfected to surpass the "Six Sigma levels" (3.4 defects per million opportunities) of process capability. Proposed changes to work processes are carefully considered and often subject to a formal hypothesis-driven assessment. Every employee is educated about these concepts and trained to be an active member in improvement initiatives. At the same time, Toyota adopted and operationalized many practices (e.g., automation, forcing functions, standardization, etc.) to achieve perfection in terms of reliability and value creation.

The Institute for Healthcare Improvement (IHI) believes that Lean principles can be, and are already being, successfully applied to the delivery of healthcare.[4] Hence, it makes sense to take a closer look to see how Toyota has dealt with developing high reliability and value creation. Academics and practitioners who espouse the virtues of TPS (or Lean) typically describe it on two levels. At a high level, Lean is a philosophy, a perspective that relentlessly strives to eliminate waste in a never-ending pursuit of perfection.[3] The term *Lean* has become popular and, like many buzzwords, has taken on various shades of meaning and implementation, some of which stray from the true intentions of its inventor. Most descriptions of Lean, therefore, quickly moved beyond the philosophical to an interrelated set of practices that range from overall material flow in the factory to detailed work and equipment design and human resource practices. At the operational level, Lean is equipped with two basic tools, value stream mapping and the A3 problem-solving tool.[5-7] Value stream maps graphically represent the key people, material, and information required to deliver a product or service. They are designed to distinguish value-adding from non-value-adding steps. A3 is a tool used by Toyota to help workers systematically address problems (the term *A3* derives from the paper size used for the report).

Two healthcare organizations that deserve particular recognition for their work with Lean are Virginia Mason Hospital in Seattle, Washington, led by Dr. Gary Kaplan, and ThedaCare, Incorporated, a health delivery system in Wisconsin formerly lead by Dr. John Toussaint.[8,9] Virginia Mason, by working to eliminate waste, created more capacity in existing programs and practices so that planned expansions were scrapped, saving significant capital expenses: $1 million for an additional hyperbaric chamber that was no longer needed; $1 to $3 million for endoscopy suites that no longer needed to be relocated; and $6 million for new surgery suites that were no longer necessary. Quality has improved as well, for example, facilitating a marked reduction in the incidence of ventilator-associated pneumonia, from 34 cases in 2002 to 4 in 2004. Working closely with Lean master-level experts, ThedaCare achieved $3.3 million in total savings in 2004 alone; made a reduction in accounts receivable from 56 to 44 days, equating to about $12 million in cash flow; and redeployed staff in several areas, saving the equivalent of 33 full-time positions. In 2006, when ThedaCare began changing how core lab tests were administered at its clinics, the percentage of tests whose results were provided during a patient's visit increased from 0% to 63%, and the average turnaround time for obtaining laboratory results fell from 370 minutes to 17. Both organizations, Virginia Mason Hospital and ThedaCare, have won numerous quality and safety awards, including recognition as safest hospitals in the nation by the Leapfrog Group. Lean is a particularly valuable QA strategy

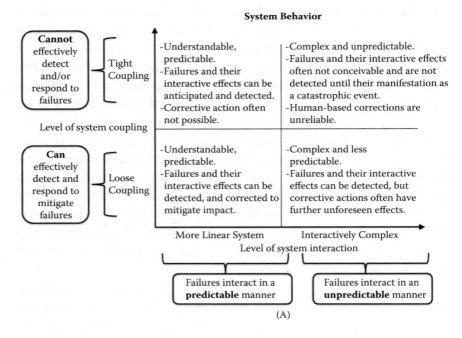

FIGURE 3.4(A)

(A) Broad descriptions of the system behaviors for systems that are characterized as linear versus interactively complex and loosely versus tightly coupled.

for systems that are linear and loosely coupled (i.e., the lower-left box of Figure 3.4A and 3.4B).

Because clinical medicine is a human endeavor, with the associated interpatient and interprovider variability, we need to educate healthcare workers to be mindful of unexplained process variations, integrate QA/QC (quality control) activities into our routine work flows, and empower all workers to be actively engaged in assessing and improving our processes. Some of this is self-evident, and many of our current practices have naturally evolved to reflect this reality. For example, the evolution and widespread use of peer review sessions within radiation oncology (e.g., chart rounds, as is commonly done in many clinics) is a reflection of the unpredictable nature of clinical medicine and an acknowledgment that human performance often needs to be checked to ensure safety. This has evolved because it was recognized that one cannot typically highly script the RT treatment decision and planning process. At the same time, we need to acknowledge the many aspects of clinical medicine that are (or that can be reasonably made) consistent across patients/providers, and

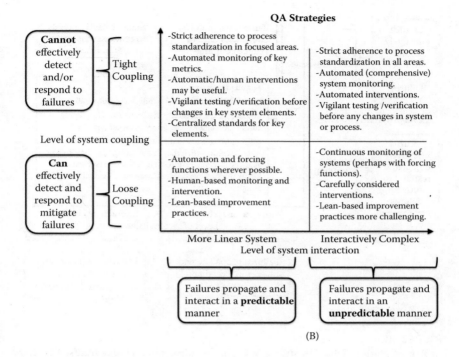

QA Strategies

(B)

FIGURE 3.4(B)

(B) Representative QA strategies are shown for the four different idealized processes. These are not intended to be exhaustive. Rather, the strategies shown in each quadrant are those that might be considered particularly pertinent to that quadrant. Within each quadrant, the principles of the hierarchy of effectiveness should be respected (e.g., automation and forcing functions applied wherever practical).

we need to highly standardize these aspects while leaving a window of opportunity for flexibility and creativity when needed, a concept that we refer to as "flexible standardization." Here, we are referring to both the processes (e.g., how a provider communicates critical information to the staff about a pending case, such as the desired patient positioning for an upcoming simulation) and the actual medical decision (e.g., in general, patients needing breast treatments should be placed in a consistent position during simulation with arms above the head in an immobilization cradle and head turned away from the treated side).

What about the three other quadrants in Figure 3.4A and 3.4B? For interactively complex systems that are loosely coupled, their behavior is less predictable than the linear systems. Failures and their interactive effects can be detected, but corrective actions often have further unforeseen effects. Thus, to ensure quality, a strategy of continuous comprehensive

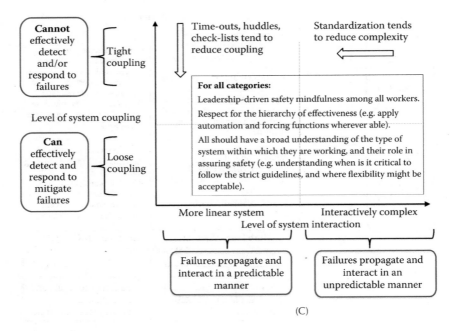

FIGURE 3.4(C)

(C) Representative global QA strategies applicable throughout all quadrants. The characteristics shown on the axes are presented as discrete and dichotomous for clarity. However, in practice these are usually continuous variables.

monitoring (perhaps with forcing functions) is best. Any changes or interventions need to be carefully considered as they can have unexpected consequences. Lean-based improvement cycles may be useful in some areas, but they can be more challenging because there are many more stakeholders, and interactive effects can be difficult to predict. Thus, these systems may appear to be sometimes chaotic, as leadership responds to continual iterations. Because their pace is somewhat slow, observers have the luxury of analyzing system behavior retrospectively and second-guessing previous actions (because interactions may seem "obvious" in hindsight). Note that Perrow placed universities in this section, and we would submit that general outpatient medical practice might also be placed in this area (inpatient hospital practice is more interactive [more "going on"] and coupled [faster]). Thus, this is the broad environment in which many of the people reading this book spend most of their time. No wonder our leaders (e.g., healthcare administrators and university presidents) occasionally find themselves in uncomfortable and difficult situations that, in retrospect, seem to have been totally avoidable.

Processes that are both interactively complex and tightly coupled can be *unpredictable*. Failures and their interactive effects are often not detected until their manifestation as a catastrophic event as their character may be unknown (it is hard to monitor and thus detect an unforeseen type of failure). Even if the effects of failures are detected, human-based corrections are unreliable as system behavior is interactively complex. Thus, quality is best ensured by rather *strict* adherence to process standardization in *all* areas. System performance needs to be *comprehensively* monitored (because the nature/type of a failure cannot reliably be predicted). Ideally, this should be automated to ensure compliance and with automated intervention (because human intervention is too slow and often misguided). Vigilant testing and verification are needed before any changes in the system or its process. Our adoption of automation and forcing functions (where possible) and of end-to-end testing, strict QA, and redundant checks for things such as IMRT planning, brachytherapy, and system commissioning reflects our field's recognition that these systems are interactively complex and tightly coupled. We *make* these processes safe for clinical use through these QA initiatives. Further, our field embraces automated technologies aimed to enhance accuracy and patient safety (e.g., automatic tracking, gating).

For the tightly coupled processes, both linear and interactively complex, experts suggested that safety and quality are optimally ensured with strict adherence to predetermined and well-defined work flows and, wherever possible, strict forcing functions and automation. Vigilant testing and verification are needed before any changes in the system or process. The scope of these interventions is different for the linear versus interactively complex systems. For linear processes, system behavior is predictable, and the manifestations of failures are often similarly predictable. Thus, the strict policy adherence, process standardization, and monitoring can be more focused *in key areas* (e.g., for cone-based stereotactic cranial radiosurgery, verification of the key elements of isocenter placement, cone size, and monitor units might be adequate to ensure quality). Centrally (e.g., governmental or professional society) based initiatives to define these key elements and the associated standards can be helpful. Conversely, for the interactively complex and tightly coupled systems, the scope of the QA initiatives needs to be far broader because the manner in which failures will be manifest is often not foreseeable (and end-to-end testing can be of particular value).

There are also differences between the linear and the interactively complex systems regarding corrective actions. In the interactively complex systems, there needs to be an increased reliance on automatic monitoring and intervention (e.g., automatic control systems) because human-based corrections are unreliable (i.e., human interventions are too slow and often misguided as the system behavior is complex). Conversely, linear systems might be amenable to automatic or human intervention or a combination of the two (i.e., the automation with human-based decisions regarding intervention are more likely to be correct), but for tightly coupled systems, implementing such interventions in an effective manner can be challenging.

Thus, applying these concepts to radiation oncology, we endorse the following:

a. automation with human oversight and forcing functions wherever possible, especially for tightly coupled processes (e.g., data transfer, dose calculation/optimization);
b. strict process standardization and monitoring of processes, supported by vigilant testing and verification before any change implementation, for tightly coupled processes for which automation and forcing functions are not possible (e.g., system commissioning, IMRT);
c. people-driven QA (e.g., huddles, time-outs, checklists, etc.); flexible process standardization; and "selective/strategic" monitoring of processes, supported by relatively "rapid" CQI methodologies such as Lean for the loosely coupled (and to some degree more-creative) aspects of our practice (e.g., treatment planning, image segmentation, clinical decisions, nursing evaluations routine, clinical care).

Above all, at the global level (Figure 3.4C), during implementation and change management efforts, leaders and staff must have a broad understanding of the type of system within which they are working and their role in ensuring safety (e.g., understanding when is it critical to follow the strict guidelines and where flexibility might be acceptable). Thus, there is a constant need for leadership to be actively involved and for **leadership-inspired safety mindfulness** for all processes because without it the probability of sustaining high reliability and value creation is close to zero.

In addition, because people are involved in all of these processes, Lean-based "people-driven" optimization initiatives are applicable throughout. For example, although it is fine to say, "We will use strict standards and forcing functions," how do we actually make that happen? *When* exactly in the process will the user be forced to do something? *How* is that requirement presented to the user, and *what* are the response options? *How* does this influence the broader work flow? *How* do we ensure that users vigilantly adhere to the processes? We need to design our systems at all levels (organization, workplace, people) to ensure that automation, forcing functions, and standards are implemented and used in the most effective manner. The deliberations related to these decisions need to especially consider peoples' safety mindfulness. For example, requiring standard checklists that are not compatible with staff work flow is a suboptimal solution. It is *not* enough to just say that the pretreatment checklist for cranial radiosurgery needs to address the key elements of isocenter placement, cone size, and monitor units. Rather, all of the stakeholders need to be involved in creating a system that is conducive to this being done in a reliable and effective manner. Therefore, we also endorse people-driven initiatives to determine *how* these QA initiatives are implemented and how they are modified over time.

We also recognize that the study of failures is difficult, and that there have been decades of efforts aimed to better understand their origins, reduce their incidence, and mitigate their effects. The concepts that we present here are certainly somewhat idealized and the analogies presented are imperfect. Further, much of the theoretical work cited is aimed at preventing catastrophic accidents and thus might not be applicable to the more mundane practice of clinical medicine. Nevertheless, we believe that presenting our recommendations in the context of this theoretical framework is useful as it provides a construct and rationale (albeit imperfect) for our approaches. In clinical medicine, we certainly share the goal of preventing catastrophic accidents but also want to minimize the risks of "weak" signals of failures as these can have meaningful clinical consequences. Indeed, while many failures in medicine (and radiation oncology) affect a limited number of patients, occasional failures affect larger numbers of patients.

Thus, the concepts presented may not be totally applicable to radiation oncology practice. Nevertheless, we have found these to be helpful in planning our safety and quality improvement initiatives. For example, there is a potential advantage to dividing interactively complex processes into multiple smaller processes that are less interactively complex. Within loosely coupled processes, moving from the lower right-hand side to the lower left-hand side of Figure 3.4B increases the utility of Lean-based methods for CQI. This realization is consistent with the general opinion that Lean-based quality initiatives need to be "local" and driven by the front-line staff rather than top-down initiatives. They need to be supported by leadership but not conducted by leadership. Within the tightly coupled processes, moving from the upper right- to the upper left-hand side of Figure 3.4B reduces the number of critical variables that need to be managed and tracked. Within this overall framework, processes can be moved to the left through standardization (e.g. limiting the number of ways something can be done reduces the number of components for possible interactions), and moved downward through "timeouts" (e.g. slowing things down to reduce coupling).

3.1.1.5 An Additional Sobering Realization: Feta vs. Swiss Cheese

The holes in the slices of cheese in Dr. Reason's Swiss Cheese model highlight the role of errors within "individual layers" in "global system failures." This perspective naturally leads to a focus on increasing reliability of individual layers. This certainly has value. Unfortunately, this focus may be somewhat misguided in complex systems. Reason suggested, and Dr. Sidney Dekker has emphasized, that even if every individual layer of a complex system functions perfectly well, that "global system failures" can (and almost certainly will) occur due to unforeseen interactions between well-functioning layers.[10] Thus, reliable/robust components do not guarantee overall system reliability. This is both interesting and sobering, and emphasizes the need for safety mindfulness among workers; i.e. to notice unforeseen behaviors and interactions within 'well-functioning' systems. Further, system failures can best be identified if there is diversity among the workers, such that processes can be viewed from various persepctives. Dekker also adds the warning that too much focus on sub-unit reliability can have a negative impact as each "improvement" (aimed to increase reliability) introduces additional opportunities for unforeseen interactions. Thus, adding layers of quality assurance/safety steps to existing practices may be detrimental.

This broader perspective suggests that Swiss Cheese may not be the ideal metaphor for complex-system failures. Holes within the cheese are not a prerequisite for system failure. A block of Feta Cheese, or nested blocks of cheese (as in Figure 1.3) may be a better dairy analogy. Stresses applied to any portion of the block can cause the block to fracture in an unpredictable manner.

3.1.1.6 A Related Construct: Mechanical-Based versus Software-Based World

Dr. Nancy Leveson presented related concepts in her book *Engineering a Safer World*.[11] She argued that the movement from a "mechanical-based" world to a "software-based" world has led to the design and implementation of multiple complex systems that interact in ways that are beyond human comprehension and that overall system behavior cannot be accurately predicted. Thus, safety can be achieved only through *monitoring* to ensure that systems operate within predefined constraints. "Safety can be viewed as a control problem. Accidents occur when component failures, external disturbances, and/or dysfunctional interactions among system components are not adequately controlled."[11] This is somewhat similar to the upper right-hand corner of Perrow's figure (Figure 3.2A) and is reminiscent of the complexities of IMRT. Further, she argued that the movement from "mechanical control" to "electronic control" of systems has moved the operators physically away from the processes that they are managing, thus reducing direct physical stimuli regarding system performance. This is reminiscent of the radiation therapists who (in the "mechanical era") used to place physical blocks on the treatment machine to define the beam aperture and manually move the table, gantry, and collimators and thus could readily check the "treatment light field" on the patient's skin. Now, in the "electronic era," therapists remotely control the position of multileaf collimators to define beam apertures and other setup or treatment parameters, often without entering the treatment room (thus losing potentially valuable visual, tactile, etc., information to prevent error propagation).

3.1.2 High-Reliability Organization Theory

The HRO theory focuses on processes and identifies organizational initiatives that can prevent incidents. Thus, it is often viewed as an *optimistic* approach (compared to NAT, by which failures are considered inevitable) as it emphasizes organizational willingness to reduce the probability of serious incidents (Table 3.1).[12]

The HRO theory is not an improvement methodology such as Lean or Six Sigma. Rather, it promotes concepts regarding how to think about organizational change and how to eliminate safety issues. At the core of HROs are the following five hallmarks[13]:

- *Sensitivity to operations:* Leaders and staff need to be constantly aware of the state of the systems and processes that affect patient care to detect and prevent risks.
- *Reluctance to simplify:* Simple processes are good, but simplistic explanations for why things work or fail are risky. We need to avoid accepting overly simplistic explanations of failure (e.g., "unqualified staff," "inadequate training," "communication failure," etc.) to understand the true reasons patients are placed at risk.
- *Preoccupation with failure:* The identification of a near miss should not be taken as evidence that the system works and has effective safeguards. Rather, near misses should be viewed as evidence of systems that can be improved to reduce potential harm to patients.
- *Deference to expertise:* Leaders and supervisors need to be willing to listen and respond to the insights of staff who know how processes really work and the risks that patients really face. This will facilitate a culture in which high reliability and value creation are possible.
- *Resilience:* Leaders and staff need to be trained and prepared to know how to respond when system failures do occur.

In general, HRO acknowledges that organizations may be interactively complex and tightly coupled, and that there may be some degree of uncontrollability (and potential chaos), but that one can still define systems to monitor and reduce risks. *Conceptually, we embrace this approach.* We acknowledge that portions of clinical medicine are interactively complex and tightly coupled, that the behaviors of patients and providers cannot be fully controlled or predicted, and that there will thus always be some chaos and risk in healthcare. However, we can still structure our organization, workplace, and people to minimize these risks (by embracing concepts presented in Figure 3.4A, 3.4B, and 3.4C). Our interpretation of key elements needed to initiate and promote high reliability and value are described in more detail in the following section. We reject the often-stated belief that patient harm occurs because of a single human error or even a chain of specific human errors. Rather, we broadly embrace the concept that patient harm reflects the confluence of several contributing latent and active "failures" (e.g., preexisting policies, work flows, environmental issues, human decisions) spanning the organizational, workplace, and people levels. Thus, initiatives to improve safety should address all three of these levels.

3.1.3 Broad Overview of Our Application of These High-Reliability and Value Creation Concepts to Radiation Oncology

We acknowledge that the procedures conducted within the field of radiation oncology span a range with regard to system complexity and coupling. As described, multiple strategies need to be pursued to comprehensively address safety challenges. The concepts and strategies described in the following material should be interpreted with caution as they might not be generalizable to all systems presented in Figure 3.2C and 3.2D. Broadly speaking, the following discussion and that in the following chapters focuses largely on processes that involve people and their environment (rather than the aspects that are purely technical and totally segregated from people). Nevertheless, even aspects deemed "purely technical" essentially always have a human component.

a. *Organizational level:* Here, we strive to have leaders who do not take high reliability and value creation for granted, and who instinctively consider these factors during decision making. They recognize that high reliability and value creation is not a segregated activity, but rather is integrated into all aspects of daily operations and oversight. Leaders have to appreciate that our systems are not perfect, so surprises and human errors are inevitable. Further, they should know and accept that no one understands all of the technology, processes, decisions and behaviors of staff completely and upstream failures are possible; thus the organization requires robust process improvement strategies that require *everyone's* input. Because medicine is a dynamic field with ever-changing clinical challenges, leaders need to acknowledge that improvement is a continuous, never-ending process. Thus, we expect our leaders to promote a culture of safety so that we continually improve our processes and bounce back from unexpected incidents quickly and in an improved state (i.e., safety events are opportunities to find improvements). We further discuss the concepts of leadership, the culture of safety, and improvement cycles in Section 3.2. Our experiences at UNC at the organizational level are detailed in Chapter 4.

b. *Workplace level:* At the workplace level, we strive to have an infrastructure for reporting events and to continually improve processes using concepts of error prevention. We know that reliance on policies or procedures and training is not enough. Thus, we try to hardwire the systems for success using automation and forced functions whenever possible, and when this is not possible, we focus on simplification, standardization, QA, and the creation of work flows and systems that support people's work. We discuss our approaches to drive improvements at the workplace level in Section 3.3 and detail our experiences in this area at UNC in Chapter 5.

c. *People level:* Although we expect people to adhere to some critical policies and procedures, at the people level we strive to motivate all our employees to identify, resolve, and positively change the processes and fundamental cultural values and beliefs that govern decision making and behaviors. To accomplish this, we try to ensure that individuals engaged in improvement efforts feel psychologically safe to share their opinions in an open and honest manner, have access to valid information, and are provided with sufficient time to solve problems. In Section 3.4, we discuss the concepts of how we define, develop, and sustain behaviors and decision making needed for high reliability and value creation, with detailed examples of our experiences at UNC provided in Chapter 6.

3.2 ORGANIZATIONAL LEVEL

The key challenges at the organizational level are to develop leadership styles and behaviors that promote a culture of patient safety and robust improvement cycles that can anticipate and address unexpected failures.

3.2.1 Leadership Style and Behaviors

The safe delivery of RT requires the concerted and coordinated efforts of many individuals with varied responsibilities. Each member of the team "deep down inside themselves" knows that optimal approaches are not static and will necessarily change to accommodate evolving practices. Thus, often, the long-held traditional approaches must be challenged and possibly modified.

However, people may be hesitant to change, often for good reasons. Good clinical practices usually evolve over years, if not decades, so change should be carefully implemented. Nevertheless, even when the need for change is evident, people can be reluctant (momentum is a strong force of nature). So, how do we go about change management in our department?

We acknowledge that our department chair (Larry) and our quality and safety director (Bhisham), both physicians, are the primary forces behind change management efforts. They are both active practitioners of high-reliability and value creation principles. We see them as leaders and expect them to actively work together to promote safety and efficiency. It is well accepted in the literature that successful change management in health-care requires trusted physicians with a high level of urgency for change, charisma, vision, and so on.[14]

From the view at 30,000 feet, Larry and Bhisham both focus on their relationship and interactions with employees. They act as transformational leaders, knowing that it is crucial in early stages of implementation to promote, encourage, motivate, and coach staff toward this transformation. All this is contingent on staff having strong levels of trust, admiration, loyalty, and respect for both of them. Experts tell us that transformational leaders are those who inspire followers to achieve extraordinary outcomes and, in the process, develop their own leadership capacity.[15] Both Larry and Bhisham are largely respected, admired, and trusted in our department. Similarly, they respect individuals' desires and needs, and they tend to be good listeners, which allows for constructive two-way communications. They are persistent and determined to reach patient safety and quality goals. They are willing to take risks when needed, but they always try to do the right thing, displaying high moral and ethical standards. They are not afraid of criticism. They actively help create an atmosphere of commitment to organizational vision, mission, and goals.

A few more things must be said about Larry. He is outgoing, is an effective communicator, and is passionate about improvement work. He effectively inspires others, both individually and as a group, and he has created a vision for our department to embrace safety and improvement as a central theme. He also exhibits strong consideration for the professional or personal needs of staff and intellectually excites them to strive above and beyond the norm.

Departmental leaders must learn and practice leadership styles that promote a mindset focused on high reliability and value creation principles. It does not necessarily come naturally, and leaders need to be consistent in their promotion of these principles. Leaders' behaviors, actions, and words can carry great weight as others will emulate them. A leader who does not consistently and overtly espouse these principles, in word and deed, may be inadvertently discouraging others from embracing these concepts. Leaders need to continuously inspire people to go beyond their regular job duties and identify ways to improve quality and safety. It is easier said than done.

3.2.2 Infrastructure for Culture of Safety

An organizational infrastructure supportive of high reliability and value creation is necessary to create a culture of safety. Let us take a quick look at the commercial aviation industry to see how it has set up its infrastructure for a culture of safety. First, the commercial aviation industry acknowledges that human error will happen and thus emphasizes training initiatives focused on mitigating secondary serious or catastrophic incidents that may result from these errors.[15] So, although they certainly train employees to prevent errors, they also train employees how to address and cope with (what they see as inevitable) errors. Most commercial airline carriers encourage, reward, and pay staff to ensure that they receive the quality/safety training required. If an employee misses or fails training or proficiency checks, the employee usually faces restrictions until this underperformance has been rectified. When employees adhere to safety guidelines or go beyond what is required, appropriate rewards are granted. One popular training program for pilots is called Crew Resource Management (CRM). CRM is a training program focused on culture, teamwork, communication, the inevitability of errors, and ways to detect, trap (i.e., contain), and mitigate the hazards (resulting from the errors) before they lead to serious or catastrophic harm. In most developed countries, pilots must now demonstrate their competency in CRM as part of their annual reaccreditation.[16]

Next, commercial aviation implemented policies and standard operating procedures that enforce safe operations. For example, there must always be two physiologically and psychologically sound pilots to fly a plane. This minimum safety requirement always applies. No exceptions are granted. This is often audited by random drug and alcohol tests. Further, during the safety-critical phases of a flight, such as flying below an altitude of 10,000 feet, the pilots and cabin crew must adhere to strict standard operating procedures and refrain from all nonessential activities (e.g., reading newspapers or chatting idly). This safety requirement is known as the sterile cockpit rule. Crew members are taught how to call, without awkwardness, for the sterile cockpit rule to be implemented at additional times when particular concentration becomes necessary. The entire crew is informed about when the rule is in force through warnings or alert systems. Adoption of comparable policies in radiation oncology centers would be controversial, but it might better ensure patient safety.

Such highly specified policies and standard operating procedures can be easily audited for compliance. Scholars suggest that highly reliable and value creation organizations encourage their staff to conform to work procedures and create a culture of safety that is based on positive feedback and reward systems to facilitate consistent behavior.[17–19] Work standard procedures are an integral part of the broader organizational system and its professional culture. Workers understand the need for hierarchy, and respect their leadership, and thus view the policies and standards put forth by this hierarchy and leadership as critical to ensure consistent performance.

In our journey toward high reliability and value creation, we learned that rules and formal work procedures are essential for ensuring quality, but we also quickly realized that providers often resist such formalities as infringements on their professional standing and autonomy. Rigidity in enforcing standards can lead to frustration and burnout. A common refrain heard is: "We are not flying planes or making cars; people are much more variable, and I need to do what is best for MY patients. Cookie cutters do not work." These comments are valid, but they do not obviate the utility of standardization where possible. We try to address this by using "flexible standardization"—designing a highly standardized process that allows for flexibility and creativity when needed—rather than dictating how providers should conduct all of their work procedures.[20] If there is no good reason to deviate from the standard, we expect the standard to be followed. However, we recognize that the variability of clinical medicine requires some flexibility. We know that our reliability depends on providers' autonomy and ability to deviate from standard work procedures when they are inappropriate in a specific circumstance. Like high-reliability and value creation organizations, we know that formal procedures are fallible. Because we have not experienced all the ways in which things can fail, we continually strive to question and examine our formal procedures. We do not want our staff to do *routine jobs*. We expect them to be mindful of the work they do. This is discussed further in Section 3.3. The balance between standardizing actions for safety yet maintaining workers' mindfulness of their actions can be challenging.

We must emphasize the distinction between standardizing "processes" versus "medical decisions." For example, at an initial level, one wants to standardize *how* a physician communicates to the simulation therapist the desired patient positioning or to a dosimetrist their desire to treat or not treat the pelvic lymph nodes in a patient with prostate cancer. This is distinctly separate from the *medical decision* regarding the optimal positioning or whether the nodes need to be treated. The former (i.e., the processes) are easier to standardize and should be more readily accepted by providers. There is certainly also some utility in standardizing some medical decisions in order to standardize work flow (e.g., generally position certain groups of patients in a consistent manner). For both the processes and the medical decision spheres, there must be some flexibility, but the need for flexibility is easier to conceptualize for the medical decisions certainly. Thus, we suggest that such standardization initiatives focus *initially* largely on processes and only later on medical decisions.

Another example from aviation of an infrastructure component that enhances the culture of safety is the use of flight recorders. These recorders monitor key flight parameters throughout each flight, and these data are analyzed by computers after every flight. Parameters outside predetermined acceptable ranges trigger warning signals that can initiate an investigation. The full exploration of flight recording (also known as black boxes) is only conducted in catastrophic circumstances, but pilots and staff know that all their actions are being monitored and that everything they do and say is being recorded.

So, how do we build an infrastructure to support a culture of safety in radiation oncology centers? Where do we start? It is not with flight recorders. In our center, we have started with a series of improvement initiatives that have been through multiple cycles based on Plan–Do–Study–Act (PDSA); actual initiatives are described in more detail in Chapters 4, 5, and 6. Next, we built a robust set of tools and policies to drive improvements in patient safety and efficiency (described in more detail in Section 3.2.3). This allowed us to build our improvement infrastructure piece by piece, along with persistent cultural emphasis supported by constant "podium pounding" by Larry and Bhisham to make this work. Our building process is *not* complete as constant adjustments and improvements must be introduced over time.

The manner in which the various components of our improvement infrastructure interact, support, and reinforce each other is shown in Figure 3.5. Taken individually, each component is not particularly effective; the whole structure is far more effective than the sum of the individual parts. Because each component has taken years to create and because they

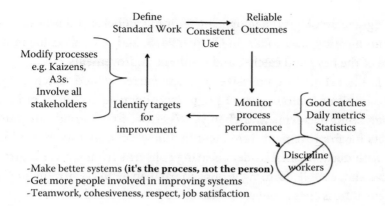

FIGURE 3.5
High-level summary of our processes and infrastructure to support high reliability and value creation. Our systems are never complete as we constantly adjust and improve them to solve problems and innovate. As each element is not as useful in isolation, the period of construction of the entire system can be frustrating (see text).

cannot all be created simultaneously, the construction period is particularly vulnerable to failure. Opponents of the initiatives can readily identify the weakness of the individual components. Proponents of the initiatives can be easily frustrated. Thus, building this structure requires time, patience, and persistence.

3.2.3 Improvement Cycles

Improvement cycles typically start with an employee being willing to report an event, defect, or concern. Our reporting and analysis infrastructure offers full anonymity and potential immunity to staff who report. We call it the Good Catch program. We think of it as our organizational learning system. The phrase *good catch*, rather than an event, defect, or concern, is used to provide a positive connotation and emphasize to the staff that we engage in a "no blame" culture. We systematically analyze each reported good catch to identify (1) where a failure has started or was caught in the process; (2) the number of safety barriers that it has crossed; (3) the root causes of failures (if possible); and (4) the actions to be taken for preventing future occurrences. Employees are encouraged to actively report good catches. More detail about the program is provided in Chapter 6.

Since the start of the program in June 2012, over 600 good catches have been reported. This has led to many improvements in processes, space redesign, technological deployment, training, policies and procedures for communication, and so on. In Chapters 4, 5, and 6, we describe in detail some of the key good catches and resultant improvements.

It is important to emphasize that our current Good Catch program is the result of several years of progressive iterative evolution of how we manage improvements and change. When we first started our journey, targets for improvement were identified in a somewhat haphazard manner, with departmental leaders hearing concerns from a diverse group of people and, as able, forming groups to participate in improvement activities to address these concerns. The more formal Good Catch program is a more systematic and streamlined way to keep track of safety and quality concerns. For example, each new good catch is discussed in a weekly meeting dedicated to this process that is attended by stakeholders from all professional subgroups.

Our improvements are based on the PDSA cycle with an overarching goal to increase employees' knowledge of the issues (e.g., the upstream and downstream factors related to any worker's individual perspective) such that more optimal global solutions can be defined. In addition, participation in formal improvement activities furthers employees' own knowledge and skills in the improvement processes themselves. Our expectation is that people's ability to effectively participate in these processes will improve with each iteration, just as the targeted processes should continually improve as they are continually addressed iteratively as well.

But, what exactly is PDSA? The concept of the PDSA cycle was originally developed by Walter Shewhart, the revolutionary statistician who developed statistical process control for Bell Laboratories in the United States during the 1930s, and is thus often referred to as the Shewhart cycle. It was used and promoted effectively in the 1950s by W. Edwards Deming and is consequently known by many as the Deming wheel. The PDSA cycle consists of four stages that the investigator must go through to get from "problem faced" to "problem solved." In summary, at each stage, the investigator performs the following activities:

- *Stage 1:* **P**lan to improve operations by identifying problems and identifying ideas for solving these problems.
- *Stage 2:* **D**o changes that are designed to solve the problems on a small or experimental scale.

- *Stage 3*: **S**tudy if the experimental changes are achieving the desired result.
- *Stage 4*: **A**ct to implement changes on a larger scale if the experiment is successful.

If the experiment was not successful, investigators skip the Act (A) stage and repeat the cycle, going back to the Plan (P) stage to define alternative new ideas for solving the problem. At times, the failure of the initial solution perhaps helps the investigators to better refine their understanding of the crux of the problem, enabling them to define improved solutions on subsequent iterations. This iterative process makes the PDSA approach flexible, dynamic, responsive to increasing knowledge as it becomes available, robust, and "realistic" (i.e., success is not expected necessarily on the initial attempt).

How does one successfully perform a PDSA cycle? There are many ways and tools to conduct an effective PDSA cycle. Our group has embraced the A3 tool for addressing problems, adopted from the Toyota Motor Company (Figure 3.6; a completed A3 is discussed in Chapter 6). The PDSA cycle is embedded within the A3 tool.

A3s serve as an interface between different stakeholders to analyze and solve problems. They do not necessarily contain sufficient details to be understandable by all stakeholders, yet they serve as a point of mediation and negotiation around the analyzed problem. The success of A3 problem solving often depends on the relationships and shared understanding developed between the individuals involved (as well as the formalism and structure afforded by the A3 tool). Scholars studying the application of A3s for problem solving in healthcare find that A3s help establish a common language and meaningful indicators to analyze and measure progress on the problem; provide mechanisms for linking process issues with human behaviors and decision making; and supply a platform for analyzing underlying cultural aspects of quality and patient safety issues. We have learned, however, that no matter how robust the methods and tools are to conduct PDSA cycles, some of our improvement cycles still fail because some stakeholders did not sufficiently understand or agree to the proposed change. Thus, we now require all stakeholders to agree to the proposed changes by physically signing an A3 form summarizing the planned improvement efforts.

We have found the A3 tool is reasonable to help manage improvement activities in the department. It helps our radiation oncology professionals better appreciate the multidisciplinary and interactive nature of their own work and develop a deeper understanding of the *process* of process

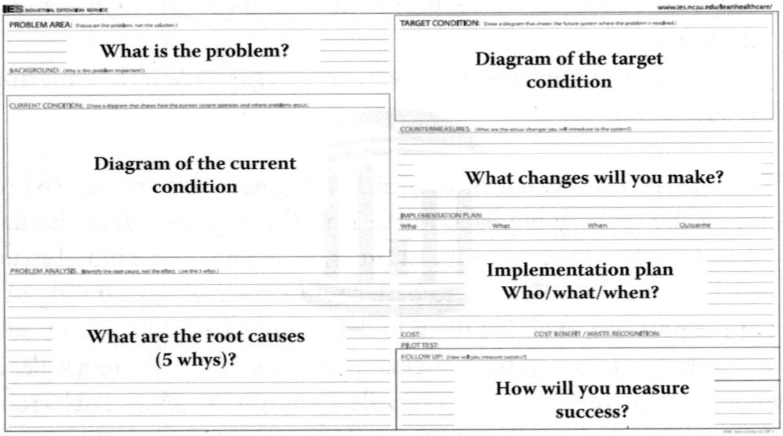

FIGURE 3.6
Our conceptual approach for conducting PDSA based on the A3 thinking. In planning stages, we first define problem and background and capture a current state of the system. This can be done by specifying current processes and key performance indicators for the system under investigation. Next, we perform a root cause analysis procedure (often asking ourselves the 5 Whys to dig deeper into root causes), while taking into consideration issues related to processes, technologies, and human factors. Next, we identify a desired future state; describe countermeasures (or improvement actions [what needs to be done?]); describe an implementation plan (how and when it needs to be done); and finally prepare and describe an improvement measurement plan (how to compare the current system vs. the new system).

improvement—increasing their competencies in analyzing and improving care delivery processes. The ability to analyze processes is absolutely critical to the evolution to a high-reliability and value-creating radiation oncology department. The ready accessibility of the A3 tools to our staff serves as a reminder of their empowerment to be involved with, and our desire for, improvement activities. Further, it is a reminder that changes in processes require the input of all of the stakeholders.

3.3 WORKPLACE LEVEL

At the workplace level, we try to create an environment and associated work flows that optimize human performance. We rely heavily on the application of concepts from Human Factors Engineering to address this challenge.

Hierarchy of Effectiveness

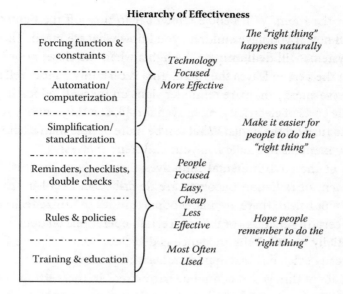

FIGURE 3.7

Hierarchy of effectiveness. Different approaches to modify behavior have different expectations for success, as shown. (Adapted from Dr. Joseph Cafazzo, Healthcare Human Factors. Presentation at the Miami Safety Meeting, June 2010.)

3.3.1 Hierarchy of Effectiveness

We endorse the concept of the hierarchy of effectiveness (Figure 3.7). The most effective way to facilitate reliability and value creation is to hardwire it into processes. For example, some light fixtures are wired to illuminate only when, for example, the door to that space is open (e.g., a closet) or the light is linked to a motion sensor to detect if anyone is in a certain space. In an airplane lavatory, the lights usually automatically become illuminated when you lock the door. These are examples of "forcing" the desired outcome. This is not a great example because the people involved in these activities will typically flip the switch on themselves because of their own desire for light (i.e., to meet their personal needs), and if they do not flip the switch, no one downstream is affected. However, what if the person's vision was not good enough to visualize the light switch, if the switch were not in a convenient location, or if their hands were full? Then, these automated approaches may be useful.

How about other situations? What if we want the person to do something that is not necessarily required of them to meet their own personal needs? Consider the exact same scenarios, but with the person *leaving* the closet or the room. Will people remember to turn off the lights? Maybe they will not. If you have children, you know what we mean. These automatic systems will deilluminate the lights when the closet door is closed or when the person leaves the room. This is certainly a more reliable way to conserve energy than are reminder signs on the wall, educating people about the costs of electricity, or, heaven forbid, creating a policy requiring people to turn off the lights. What can be more useless than placing copies of policy manuals in binders on your children's shelves?

Some of the environmental initiatives that we have instituted in our department of radiation oncology are described in detail in Chapters 5 and 6. In our field, there are many opportunities to utilize technology to control certain functions or to force certain operations on operators when a potentially harmful circumstance is detected. Some of these functions may already exist, but vast opportunities still present.

What about things that cannot be hardwired? In that setting, one wants to create an environment in which we optimize the probability that things will be done correctly. A favorite example in everyday life stems from the automatic teller machine (ATM). Everyone remembers to put their card into the machine. People are motivated to do that because the machine will not dispense any money without the card. How about removing the card from the machine? It depends on the work flow at the machine. As shown in Figure 3.8, if the machine dispenses the money prior to returning the card (see left-hand side of Figure 3.8), the customer might leave immediately after the money is dispensed (because the person came for the money and now has it) and forgets to take the ATM card. If, however, the work flow is modified (see the right-hand side of Figure 3.8), the customer is much more likely to retrieve the ATM card because the money is dispensed only after the card has been dispensed. This is a great example of how the design of the work flow has an impact on performance. Notice that the customer becomes "less forgetful" in an environment that supports the desired behavior.

Within radiation oncology, an analogy might be the following: If we want providers to convey specific sets of information to the simulation therapists, we should define work flows that enable that information to be sent as easily as possible, for example, via *one* tool within the electronic health record (EHR) rather than several tools. Indeed, if the tool within the EHR can be configured to prompt the provider to specify the necessary information, that is even better.

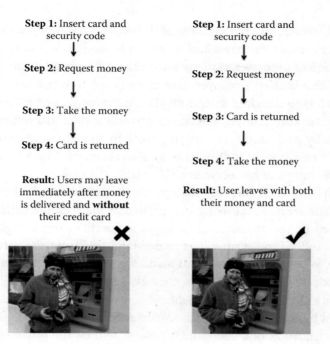

Step 1: Insert card and security code

↓

Step 2: Request money

↓

Step 3: Take the money

↓

Step 4: Card is returned

Result: Users may leave immediately after money is delivered and **without** their credit card

Step 1: Insert card and security code

↓

Step 2: Request money

↓

Step 3: Card is returned

↓

Step 4: Take the money

Result: User leaves with both their money and card

FIGURE 3.8
Example of "hardwired" functionality with automatic teller machine (ATM). Left, "poor" design leading to human error (sad user leaves ATM without card). Right, "improved" design protecting human from error (happy user leaves ATM with card).

3.3.2 Standardization

People are creatures of habit. Faced with a consistent set of inputs (e.g., environmental stimuli, requests for specific tasks), people will largely respond in a relatively consistent manner. This is with regard to the content itself and the manner in which content is presented. Thus, high-reliability and value creation organizations try to minimize occurrences of abnormal situations (i.e., with aberrant inputs) even while acknowledging that they are unavoidable. This is not to say that patient care is cookie cutter—not at all. Interpatient variations are expected and are the essence of clinical medicine. However, we can design processes to minimize alterations in the manner in which inputs are delivered and in how the providers are expected to respond. For example, the manner in which the patient's vital signs are presented to the provider should be consistent, for example, on a standard form *or* in a consistent location in the EHR, but *not* either choice.

Similarly, the *fact* that the patient has a pacemaker needs to be conveyed to the physics staff in a consistent manner (e.g., in a consistent location in the EHR, e-mail, etc., but not "any of the above"). Such standardization of processes reduces surprises and increases reliability. Without such standardization of processes, staff are more often rushed and hassled. Because stressed and hassled employees are more prone to error, we try to support work with standard operating procedures, huddles, or checklists, as appropriate. For example, checklists provide a standard foundation for sequentially performing or verifying work in an attempt to ensure that a series of items is fully addressed or to detect failures. Checklists facilitate cross-checking and can serve as a QA tool.

Patients and their families are also creatures of habit. If the patient is greeted and treated repeatedly in a particular manner, the patient will be comforted by the consistency. Changes in routine can be frightening to patients. Indeed, most providers understand this from the patient's perspective. What is often lacking in medicine is the understanding that the same concepts apply to all staff; they also appreciate, and will function better in, a consistent environment.

It must be emphasized that standardization of processes is not enough. The sanctification of a suboptimal process will be the target of ridicule. Standard processes must be made to be as efficient, and as usable, as possible to facilitate "buy-in" from the stakeholders. Leaders need to push for this to gain, and retain, credibility among their staff. If the leader promotes a particular process or work flow as the standard, the staff need to have the confidence to believe that what they are being asked to do is both necessary and as efficient as possible. This is similar to the concepts discussed in Section 3.2.2 regarding the willingness of pilots to comply with standard procedures that they understand to be critical to their organization, its professional culture, and its consistent performance. Examples that are more in depth regarding this concept applied to radiation oncology are provided in Chapters 4, 5, and 6.

3.3.3 Workload and Situational Awareness

Highly reliable and value creation organizations ensure that desired performance is consistent with the operator's workload and their situational awareness. Workload is a hypothetical construct that represents the overall "cost" incurred by a human operator to achieve a particular level of performance.[21] Situational awareness is a hypothetical construct that represents the perception, comprehension, and projection of the elements, their meaning, and their status in the environment within its volume of time and space.[22] For example, ensuring that all pilots work under optimal workload is one key priority of the Federal Aviation Administration.[22] As engine technology has evolved to enable airplanes to fly virtually 24/7 and much further than in the past, including nonstop, ultra-long-range flights, the Federal Aviation Administration continues to evaluate the latest research on the effects of time zone changes on circadian rhythm and time zone changes to mitigate pilot fatigue.[23] Workload levels have been shown to be important contributors to suboptimal situational awareness and thus human errors (Figure 3.9).[24-25]

Understanding workload and situational awareness is central to Human Factors Engineering. The processes we ask staff to adhere to, and the environment that we place them in to perform these tasks, can dramatically affect workload. Thus, it is important to consider the hierarchy of effectiveness as a means to "optimize" workload and performance.

The concepts shown in Figure 3.9 have been demonstrated in multiple settings, including high-reliability industries. Indeed, HROs have performed extensive research to define safe workload levels to ensure the optimal situational awareness and individual performance.[26] This information is used by policy makers, leadership, management, and unions to guide work duty hours and work assignments as a means of ensuring reliability and safety.

Within radiation oncology, our group has performed preliminary work to measure workload levels, situational awareness, and individual performance among radiation oncology professionals. Our data suggest that there is marked variation in workload levels among different categories of workers, and that workload levels of many EHR-based and image-based tasks often approach or reach "unsafe levels," as quantified by decrements in situational awareness and individual performance.[27] Interestingly, the specific tasks within radiation oncology that we found had the highest workload levels were the tasks most often associated with serious incidents reported to an international registry of radiation oncology events maintained by the World Health Organization (WHO).[27] Thus, our work supports the contention that decrements in individual performance that result from excessive workload can lead to adverse patient safety consequences. A more complete review of our research program in this area is given in Chapter 7.

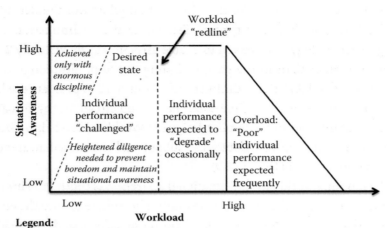

Legend:
- **Workload** is a hypothetical construct that represents the overall cost incurred by a human operator to achieve a particular level of performance.
- **Situational Awareness** is a hypothetical construct that represents the perception, comprehension, and projection of the elements, their meaning, and their status in the environment within its volume of time and space.

FIGURE 3.9

The association between workload, situation awareness, and performance. Individuals exposed to a very high workload are subjected to reduced situation awareness and a resultant poor performance. At the other extreme, with very low workload, situational awareness can only remain high *if* the individual is disciplined. However, there is a risk of boredom, multitasking, reduced situational awareness, and reduced performance. Individuals exposed to relatively moderate workload are expected to operate under adequate situational awareness and thus achieve optimal performance. Operating with suboptimal workload and situational awareness typically would be dangerous, so Reid and Colle (1988)[28] proposed that a workload limit (or "workload redline") should be set at the transition from the optimal performance region. (Figure slightly modified from original figure proposed by Endsley MR, 1993.)[29]

3.3.4 Electronic Health Records

Given the rapid and nearly ubiquitous adoption of EHRs, it is important to consider their impact on workload, situational performance, and individual performance in medicine. At the workplace level, the use of EHRs and advanced medical technologies has provided unparalleled opportunities for improved patient care (e.g., ready access to patient-specific information, data integration, visual representations of anatomic/metabolic abnormalities, imaging-based interventions, etc.). Nevertheless, the use of EHRs and imaging technologies raises new challenges; for example, locating key data elements for specific tasks within a rapidly enlarging sea of electronic data can be difficult. Clinicians need to readily review and interpret text (e.g., clinical notes), quantitative data (e.g., laboratory measures), and medical images during routine clinical tasks. However, multiple notes cannot be easily viewed concurrently or in rapid sequence; thus, the "clinical context" can often be difficult to appreciate. Notes typically cannot be annotated, and data entry/retrieval can be cumbersome. Systems that store and display medical images can be similarly challenging to navigate, and they often do not interface with the nonimaging EHRs. The rapid adoption of EHRs has, to some degree, outpaced changes in the work flows. In other words, traditional work flows that evolved over many decades to be "functional" in the era of paper charts might not be as functional in the era of EHRs. A good example in the field of radiation oncology is in the area of physics "chart checks." In the paper chart, a physicist's work could be tracked by a series of dated initials, typically adjacent to each calculation and item that they checked in the chart. There is no analogous construct in the common radiation oncology EHRs.

Going forward, we must be careful not to become overwhelmed with the technical safety considerations that are unique to our field (e.g., defining standards for complex procedures such as IMRT). These issues are certainly important and need to be addressed, but we also need to broaden our scope. It is important that we recognize the broader challenges that influence radiation oncology practice and that we learn from our colleagues in high-reliability and value creation organizations. Defining better policies is not enough. Consideration of "human factors" in the design of workspaces and processes is a powerful tool to improve patient safety. It is critical that all members of the team understand these concepts, and that they be involved in the design of their work to maintain safety. For example, defining clear systems to communicate the technical standards for IMRT, and designing workspaces that facilitate adherence to these standards, is probably just as important (if not more important) than are the details of the standards themselves.

3.4 PEOPLE LEVEL

3.4.1 Transitioning People to Safety Mindfulness

Leaders need to create an environment and infrastructure to allow all individuals to develop an understanding of safety mindfulness. Leaders need to nurture their staff to promote and sustain that active participation in the continuous creation of a high-reliability system. Similarly, employees need to be open to changes and be willing to be active participants in improvement activities. Leaders and staff need to have mutual trust and respect and share the same core values and vision for the organization.

Chapter 1 organized five behaviors into logical schema (Figure 1.6).[30] In summary, when the system is compromised by defects, individuals will typically either quickly fix the problems without addressing the underlying root causes or try to identify and initiate efforts to eliminate the root causes of problems. Alternately, when the system is running smoothly (and not compromised by defects), individuals will typically (1) continue to conform to standard procedures and processes; (2) deviate from standard procedures and processes by taking shortcuts to get work done without explicitly degrading operating performance or patient safety; or (3) in the spirit of continuous improvement and high reliability, seek to make permanent enhancements to work processes and activities. The consequences of the five different behaviors are different (Figure 3.10).

When defects occur, *Quick-Fixing* behavior is effective at resolving immediate crises, but such efforts are not captured, validated, and disseminated by the organization to prevent recurrences. Unfortunately, in much of medicine, this *Quick-Fixing* behavior is rewarded (e.g., "That

	Self-perceptions of the person (short term)	Risks to the person (long term)	Organizational risks	Perceptions of coworkers
Quick Fixing	• "Can do" gratification sense from problem solving	• Burn out: "I'm tired of dealing with this over and over again"	• Underlying operational issues not addressed	• "A real go getter" • "Hard worker" • "Gets things done"
Conforming	• "I obey the rules"	• Stagnation (organization, workplace, people)		
Expediting	• Sense of efficiency • "Got away" with something	Increased risk for human error		• "Sloppy" by the informed • "Clever" by the skeptical
Initiating & Enhancing	• Self-development mode (exploring and learning) • "Doing something different" feeling • Satisfaction	• Perceived as not competent in improvement work (if not successful) • Ridicule by skeptical colleagues	• Minimal (if improvements are supported and monitored)	• "Ambitious" vs. • "Complainer"

FIGURE 3.10

Summary of behaviors and their potential consequences. These are not unique to radiation oncology.

nurse was terrific; things were not running smoothly but the nurse made a bunch of phone calls, called in some favors for us, and now everything is back on track"). Thus, the challenge is to transform *Quick-Fixing* behavior into *Initiating* behavior by calling attention to defects and creating an infrastructure for staff to take preventive action.

In the absence of defects, individuals can *conform, expedite,* or *enhance.* The most desirable behavior is *Enhancing* because this type of individual focuses on growing the organization's capabilities for high reliability and value creation. In contrast, *Expediting* behaviors involve shortcuts and deviations from standard operating procedures to make individuals' jobs easier or seemingly more productive. *Expediting* behavior is to be expected—that is human nature. Indeed, if a worker identifies an improved way to do something that is great, the standards should be changed accordingly to reflect this improvement. Unfortunately, people practicing *Expediting* behaviors (which includes almost all of us [authors included] at least some of the time) often do not recognize the upstream or downstream consequences of these shortcuts. Such shortcuts and "favors" can cause problems of their own by introducing variability and uncertainty into the system, which can cascade and cause downstream quality and safety problems. Further, within an expediting culture, departing from the norm becomes the norm.[10] As numerous deviations accumulate, there is a progressive erosion of "standard operating procedures," increased operational variations, and increased opportunities for unforeseen interactions. Expediting behaviors can be particularly challenging to prevent since they are self-reinforcing. For the most part, people usually get away with cutting corners, thus providing an unfortunate positive feedback tending to encourage additional drifting. This phenomenon might be best expressed as an ironic twist on Murphy's Law that appears to be true, "Everything that can go wrong usually does not."[10,29]

How do we transform the safety mindfulness of people? We next outline two strategies that we believe are key during the individual transformation to safety mindfulness aligned with organizational vision for high reliability and value creation (Figure 3.11).

3.4.1.1 Transitioning from Quick Fixing to Initiating

Developing *Initiating* behavior is the responsibility of both the individual and the organization. The individual needs to be open and motivated to take on this role. Leaders need to create a supportive physical environment

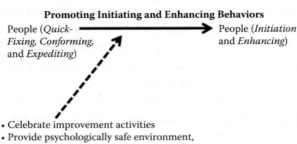

Promoting Initiating and Enhancing Behaviors

People (*Quick-Fixing, Conforming,* and *Expediting*) → People (*Initiation* and *Enhancing*)

- Celebrate improvement activities
- Provide psychologically safe environment, rewards & recognition, feedback
- Allocate time for improvement activities
- Setting examples by their actions

FIGURE 3.11

Key concepts needed to make the desired transition to *Initiating* and *Enhancing* behaviors.

(see Section 3.2). On the people level, we try to accomplish this transition by focusing on the following concepts:

- *Focus on safe patient care:* We ask staff to operate first and foremost with the objective of safe patient care. We place patient safety above all other organizational goals, such as efficiency, productivity, satisfaction, and so on. We emphasize that the defined processes were created to optimize safety.

- *Meaningful feedback*: We do our best to provide meaningful feedback to staff on every submitted good catch and A3. Employees need to know their efforts to report issues and make improvements are valued, both by their direct supervisors and by more senior leaders. If this feedback is clear and unambiguous, employees are more likely to invest in the effort of initiating and making improvements that, by attacking the root causes of the defects, are significant and result in long-term improvements.

- *Rewards and recognition*: Employees need to see that *Initiating* behavior is rewarded. We provide public recognition and monetary reward for good catches and implemented A3s. The exact nature of the reward, whether money, title, or other nonmonetary recognition, is not as important as the fact that the reward is meaningful to the recipient and valued by the organization. This creates tangible examples for others to emulate and aspire to.

- *Dedicated time for initiating behaviors*: If employees are to become initiators of improvement when defects become apparent, they first must have the time during their workdays to take the necessary actions for initiating real improvement. If patient volumes are high, the perception is that there is not sufficient time to work and institute real improvements. Thus, making quick fixes and moving on is more likely to happen. We plan CQI events (e.g., Kaizen events) well in advance with the intention to provide people with the dedicated time to meaningfully participate.

- *Psychological safety*: We recognize that employees' ability to think and act freely without fear of negative consequences to self-image, status, or career is critical. This is a major hurdle, and being associated with change efforts can be difficult. Many people have much invested in the status quo, and people most often opposed to change are often more senior/established (and often influential/powerful). Advocating for change can damage one's reputation or social standing. This is particularly true if the attempts to make positive changes are not successful. Further, even if change is successful on the broad level, dissenters might still apply a negative interpretation (i.e., "spin") to the change. Therefore, we do our best to protect our staff from such backlashes. Nevertheless, the social and personal relationships in the workplace can be complex and beyond control of the leadership. The leaders need to recognize this and try to overtly demonstrate support for the PDSA cycle (and other change/improvement activities), and for the staff involved, as described throughout this section.
- *Gratification*: When an individual employs a quick fix approach to dealing with defects, he or she is naturally going to find some satisfaction in making the immediate instance of the problem to go away. Although the problem may reappear in the future, for now it is solved. This feeling of instant gratification can be a powerful motivator for continuing to use *Quick Fixing* to obtain rapid resolution of problems. Further, as noted, others who work with the "quick fixer" might similarly celebrate the quick fixer's "can-do" attitude. We view these feelings of personal gratification and the can-do esteem as potential latent errors. Although the goal is not to eliminate all *Quick-Fixing* behavior, as it is a necessary behavior to deal with day-to-day issues, we tend to think critically of potential negative consequences of repeating such behaviors in the long run. We acknowledge, however, that this is not reasonable unless leadership provides a rational alternative (i.e., nurtures and supports the *Initiating* behavior).

- *Burnout:* Gratification comes immediately from undertaking quick fixes. However, we believe that continued *Quick Fixing* can lead (over time) to the more insidious latent failure of personal burnout. Depending on the employee's personal history of attempting to initiate real, long-lasting improvements, he or she may have a history filled with frustration and failure (e.g., "How many times am I going to have to do this myself? Can't so-and-so get their act together and do their job?"). If the employee's past is negative in this regard, he or she may have already given up trying to initiate substantive improvements in operating conditions. Instead, the employee is resigned to putting patches on problems and dealing with defects on a one-off basis as they occur. Thus, we recognize that firefighting behavior can easily become the norm, and the desire for true improvement can be dampened.

3.4.1.2 Developing Enhancing Behavior

Promoting *Enhancing* behavior can be challenging for leadership. When systems are working reasonably well and work processes are being followed, how can staff be motivated not to "cut corners" and, better yet, take action to make further operational and safety improvements?

- *Moving away from **Conforming** behavior*: Employees need to be given broad autonomy in thinking about their work, and how to improve their work, as well as some degree of autonomy in how they perform their work. Without this, employees tend only to "follow the rules," especially if the rules are perceived to be good enough and not openly causing harm. Without job autonomy, compliance is seen as a safe choice. Higher levels of job autonomy, combined with support from the employee's direct supervisor, can create an appealing work environment for safety mindfulness. Thus, we do our best to remove excessive bureaucracy and unnecessary rules and procedures that are not aligned with objectives of safety mindfulness.
- *Moving away from **Expediting** behavior:* To eliminate *Expediting* behaviors, employees need to be continually reminded of the interconnected nature of their work. They need to be mindful that if they "cut this corner," something unfavorable can happen "downstream." This is achieved by aggressive monitoring of the performance of our systems and feedback to the staff. This can serve as a continual reminder of the importance of adhering to standard work flows.

For example, in our department, it is important for the simulation therapy staff to have the completed physician directives prior to the patient arriving. It is important to the physicians that the clinic schedules in our various EHR systems are consistent. Thus, these two items are monitored and reported publicly each day along with other metrics (see Chapters 5 and 6 for more details).

Further, we encourage all staff to aggressively report all defects noted during their work. This is used to provide feedback to upstream staff and serves to reinforce the importance of their work to someone downstream (e.g., "Gee, if I forget to do this, someone downstream notices. What I do is important for our operation to run smoothly."). Through workers' participation in improvement activities, they learn the concepts of A3 thinking—again something that emphasizes the interconnectedness of everyone's work. We also emphasize the need for role models as they provide guidance by example, offer advice and feedback, and serve as visible examples of the type of organizational behavior that is valued.

- *Transitioning to **Enhancing** behavior*: If staff have not been exposed to a safety and quality improvement philosophy at work, they are less likely to know the mechanics of *Enhancing* behaviors. Although radiation oncology employees are skilled and experienced in their medical and clinical specialties, this does not necessarily mean they are proficient at process and systems improvement. Thus, we train our staff on methods, tools, and mindset required to succeed at CQI. We do this in several ways. First, A3 training promotes critical and creative thinking whereby an individual skillfully conceptualizes and assesses situations, questions assumptions, determines options for responding to the situation, and makes intelligent decisions. In the context of day-to-day operations, A3 thinking includes the ability to continuously analyze operating conditions with a "special eye" for any form of waste and potential failures. Second, the leadership tries to promote this at all levels so that the employees see themselves in an environment in which they can actively improve things. By instilling a sense of personal responsibility in their work flow and workplace, staff likely will respond by wanting to improve things not only because their supervisor tells them to do it but also because their internal pride leads them to want to do it. This internal

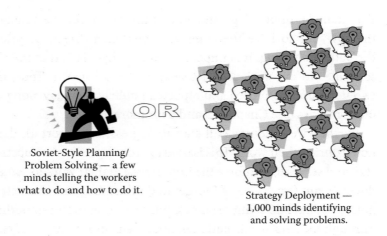

Soviet-Style Planning/
Problem Solving — a few
minds telling the workers
what to do and how to do it.

Strategy Deployment —
1,000 minds identifying
and solving problems.

FIGURE 3.12

Problem-solving strategy. Left, "Soviet-style" leadership (or dictatorship) in which a few leaders decide what problems exist and how to solve them. Right, strategy deployment via active engagement and empowerment ("1,000 minds identifying and solving problems"). (Adapted from Lean Six Sigma teaching of Dr. Blanton Godfrey, North Carolina State University, 2009.)

motivation, coupled with a nurturing and supporting environment, can unleash the power to bring "a thousand minds" to better the organization (Figure 3.12).

Third, for staff to exhibit *Enhancing* behavior, they need continual reminders of how their work processes are connected to the larger operating system. As noted, our reporting of performance metrics (e.g., on a daily and monthly basis) serve as opportunities for staff to be reminded of these connections; data are presented verbally and visually and are posted publicly as further reinforcement. Fourth, we aggressively report and follow up on defects. For each, we link each defect to a detailed process map so that all of the employees understand how each step is part of the larger process. These process maps are posted throughout our department. Fifth, the employees who have already made the transition to *Enhancing* behavior (or are in the process) need continued nurturing, reassurance, and positive feedback.

This is hard work, and it is easy for staff to revert to *Conforming* or even *Expediting* behaviors. Just as well-defined systems will decay over time (if they are not continually monitored and improved), the same is true for well-developed *Enhancing* behaviors. Employees who effectively practice *Enhancing* behaviors need to be personally and publicly thanked and celebrated. Indeed, the accolades that these employees receive serve as a motivational tool for the employees who have not yet embraced these *Enhancing* behaviors. In the true spirit of high reliability and value creation, it would be advantageous to devise systems in which public recognition of enhancing behaviors can be made on a regular basis. An employee-of-the-month program, or a similar award system for improvement activities, affords a natural venue to celebrate behaviors that have a positive impact on the organization.

Perhaps here, at the people level, lies a critical step in the journey toward high reliability and value creation: the need for leaders to recognize that they are responsible for developing organizational safety mindfulness. Through word and action, leaders need to promote the positive values (e.g., *Initiating* and *Enhancing* behaviors) discussed in this chapter. Chapter 6 presents in more detail how we engage individuals in improvement initiatives and thus transform their safety mindfulness.

3.4.1.3 Beyond Formal Leaders: Who Does All of This Apply to?

This section outlines the many efforts that must be expended by leadership to cultivate safety mindfulness among the staff. Who must expend this effort? Broadly speaking, we believe that this applies to most people, even those who lack a formal leadership title. Almost all people are seen by others as a leader. For example, each physician in a multigroup practice is seen as a leader by the nonphysician staff. Most physicists are viewed as leaders by their dosimetry and therapy colleagues. Most more experienced employees (in any job description) are seen as leaders and role models by the less-experienced employees. Indeed, through their actions, all employees have an impact on other people's attitudes, behaviors, and interest in improvement activities. All people (especially "senior personnel") who embrace the positive behaviors discussed here send a signal to others that these behaviors are important and can help cultivate positive change. Conversely, people who shun such improvement activities make it that much more difficult for others to develop these favorable behaviors. This can have a chilling impact on broad improvement initiatives, in particular those that require worker-based initiative (as is the case for the development of *Initiating* and *Enhancing* behaviors discussed in this section). Our experiences at UNC in applying the concepts described are detailed in Chapters 4–6.

REFERENCES

1. Roberts K. Some characteristics of high reliability organizations. *Organization Sci* 1990;1:160–177.
2. Perrow C. *Normal Accidents: Living with High-Risk Technologies.* New York, NY: Basic Books; 1984.
3. Liker J. *The Toyota Way: Fourteen Management Principles from the World's Greatest Manufacturer.* New York, NY: McGraw-Hill; 2004.
4. Institute of Healthcare Improvement. Going Lean in health care. Innovation Series; 2005. (Available on www.IHI.org).
5. Womack J, Jones D, Roos D. *The Machine that Changed the World.* New York, NY: Rawson Associates; 1990.
6. Ohno T. *The Toyota Production System: Beyond Large-Scale Production.* New York, NY: Productivity Press; 1988.
7. Sobek D, Smalley A. *Understanding A3 Thinking: A Critical Component of Toyota's PDCA.* New York, NY: Productivity Press; 2008.
8. Kenny C. *Transforming Health Care: Virginia Mason Medical Center's Pursuit of the Perfect Patient Experience.* New York, NY: CRC Press, Taylor & Francis Group; 2011.
9. Toussaint J, Gerard R. *On the Mend: Revolutionizing Healthcare to Save Lives and Transform the Industry.* Cambridge, MA: Lean Enterprise Institute; 2010.
10. Dekker S. *Drift to Failure.* Surrey, England: Ashgate Publishing Limited. 2011.
11. Leveson NG. *Engineering a Safer World: Systems Thinking Applied to Safety.* Cambridge, MA: MIT Press; 2011.
12. Sagan S. *The Limits of Safety.* Princeton, NJ: Princeton University Press; 1993.
13. Weick K, Sutcliffe K. *Managing the Unexpected: Resilient Performance in the Age of Uncertainty.* 2nd ed. San Francisco, CA: Wiley; 2007.
14. Weingart S, Morath J, Ley C. Learning with leaders to create safe health care: the executive session on patient safety. *J Clin Outcomes Manage* 2003;10:597–601.
15. Bass B. *Transformational Leadership: Industry, Military, and Educational Impact.* Mahwah, NJ: Erlbaum; 1998.
16. Leiden K, Keller J, French J. *Context of Human Error in Commercial Aviation.* Report prepared for National Aeronautics and Space Administration system-wide accident prevention program. Moffett Field, CA: Ames Research Center; 2001.
17. LaPorte T. High reliability organizations: unlikely, demanding and at risk. *J Contingencies Crisis Manage* 1996;4:60–71.
18. Rochlin G, LaPorte T, Roberts K. The self-designing high reliability organization: aircraft carrier flight operation at sea. *Naval War College Rev* 1987;40:76–90.
19. Weick K. South Canyon revisited: lessons from high reliability organizations. *Wildfire* 1995;4:54–68.
20. Toussaint J, Berry L. The promise of lean in health care. *Mayo Clin Proc* 2013;88(1):74–82. http://dx.doi.org/10.1016/j.mayocp.2012.07.025.

21. Hart G, Staveland L. Development of NASA-TLX (Task Load Index): results of empirical and theoretical research. In: Hancock PA, Meshkati N, eds. *Human Mental Workload.* Amsterdam, the Netherlands: North-Holland Press; 1988:139–183.
22. Endsley M. Toward a theory of situational awareness in dynamic systems. *Hum Factors* 1995;37:32–64.
23. Wilson G. An analysis of mental workload in pilots during flight using multiple psychophysiological measures. *Int J Aviat Psychol* 2001;12:3–18.
24. Rasmussen J, Pejtersen M, Goodstein L. *Cognitive Systems Engineering.* New York, NY: Wiley; 1994.
25. Wickens C, Hollands J. *Engineering Psychology and Human Performance.* 3rd ed. Upper Saddle River, NJ: Prentice-Hall; 2000.
26. Wildavsky A. *Searching for Safety.* New Brunswick, NJ: Transaction Books; 1991.
27. Mazur L, Mosaly P, Jackson M, et al. Quantitative assessment of workload and stressors in clinical radiation oncology. *Int J Radiat Oncol Biol Phys* 2012;83:e571–e576.
28. Reid GB, Colle HA. Critical SWAT values for predicting operator overload. In proceedings of the Human Factors Society 32nd Annual Meeting. Santa Monica, CA, 1988.
29. Endsley MR. Situation awareness and workload: Flip sides of the same coin. In proceedings of the 7th International Symposium on Aviation Psychology. Columbus, OH, 1993.
30. Mazur L, McCreery J, Chen S-J. Quality improvement in hospitals: what triggers behavioral change? *J Healthcare Eng* 2012;4:621–648.

Section II

Based on the beliefs outlined in Chapters 1 to 3, we describe our journey to high reliability and value creation at the University of North Carolina.

TRANSITION TO PART 2

In Chapters 4–6, we present a review of the initiatives at the organizational, workplace, and people levels, respectively. Many of these initiatives span several levels, so ascribing some of these initiatives to any one level is somewhat arbitrary. Table S2.1 provides a summary of many of our initiatives and the work needed for their successful implementation at the organizational, workplace, and people levels.

TABLE S2.1

Cataloging of Initiatives and Associated Work at the Organizational, Workplace, and People Levels[a]

Initiative	Organizational Chapter 4	Workplace Chapter 5	People Chapter 6
Elevating the stature of improvement work	Consider improvement work in faculty and staff evaluations (e.g., for promotion, incentive payments); public celebration and recognition*	Public display of Good News boards, Trophy Case, daily metrics, good catches, etc. to celebrate/ recognize improvement work	Active participation via Good Catch and A3 programs; developing improvement behaviors
Regular operations meetings (e.g., part of standard work for managers)	Active participation of key stakeholders (e.g., departmental managers)	Space and time allotment, infrastructure to tackle ongoing issues	Respect for managers, coworkers*
Hierarchy of effectiveness (automation, forcing functions, standardization, etc.)	Resource allocation, enforcement of automation, forcing functions, standardization, etc.	Software tools adjusted to support initiative*	Active participation and respect for the system
Safety rounds	Active participation of key leaders*	Flexibility to consider improvements in workplace	Empowerment to report system defects
Systematically gather and analyze input from all stakeholders regarding system performance (e.g., our Good Catch program)	Elevate the stature of this initiative; resource allocation, public support, and celebration of participation	Create an easy-to-use system to report events (e.g., good catches) and to analyze/ monitor resultant improvement initiatives	Active participation and respect for the patients, coworkers, and system*

(Continued)

TABLE S2.1 *(CONTINUED)*

Cataloging of Initiatives and Associated Work at the Organizational, Workplace, and People Levels[a]

Initiative	Organizational Chapter 4	Workplace Chapter 5	People Chapter 6
"Lean" training and work (A3s for problem solving and Kaizen events for "rapid" change)	Resource allocation, including time to attend classes	Educational materials provided throughout the department	Open minded to consider "Lean thinking" as a medium for safety mindfulness and waste reduction*
Daily morning huddle	Active participation and resource allocation (e.g., time for staff to attend)*	A large enough room for broad participation; facilities to support peer review (e.g., monitors, computers, ready access to needed data)	Active reporting of "how was yesterday" and "how is today looking" metric
Physician of the day and physicist of the day	Resource allocation, active engagement, and recognition	Publicly posted signs designate the responsible parties and demonstrate the importance of this role and initiative	Willingness to be a part of the system and take the responsibilities seriously (physicians and physicists); respect for the system and for coworkers (all)*
Patient engagement (e.g., patient self-registration, etc.)	Vision to involve patients in processes; resource allocation	Hardware and software*	Respect for patients, support for the program

[a] Many of these initiatives are discussed, to some degree, in each of the chapters. The * denotes the chapter in which this initiative is described in greatest detail.

4

Driving Change at the
Organizational Level

LEARNING OBJECTIVES

After completing this chapter, the reader should be able to:

1. Understand Larry's personal motivation to deliver safe patient care in radiation oncology;
2. Understand how we promoted high reliability and value creation throughout the organization; and
3. Reflect on things we would do differently.

4.1 LARRY'S PERSONAL REFLECTION: A SELFISH DESIRE FOR ORDER AND RELIABILITY

This chapter addresses activities at the organizational level that we use to create, maintain, and nurture high-reliability and value creation initiatives in our department. This is hard work: It is time consuming and emotionally draining. Organizational leaders need to be actively and persistently dedicated to promoting this agenda. Department chairs typically have the leeway to define their own agenda, and choosing to take on this particular challenge was Larry's personal decision. Given the "costs" (e.g., time, effort, emotion, opportunity costs) of pursuing this type of agenda, leaders need to understand their own motivations. Therefore, this chapter starts with Larry's reflection on his core beliefs, followed by an overview of organizational activities that promote high reliability and value creation: leading, motivating, and empowering the people; sustaining the spirit (of the group and leadership); nurturing the culture of safety; and developing infrastructure for continuous improvement.

4.1.1 Order and Reliability

Larry is enamored with the physical sciences. As long as he can remember, he has been fascinated with the workings of the world around him and much appreciates the way that math and physics bring "order" and understanding to our world. As a child, he loved making things like toy car race tracks or "Erector set bridges" that exploited these physical principles to yield desired outcomes. He was particularly fond of a coin sorter he made from small plastic bricks. The coins were dropped into a hole on the top and would slide via gravity through a series of branching tunnels. The variable diameters of the tunnels segregated the different-size coins into different tunnels. He was frustrated when it did not work reliably as he liked things to be organized and predictable. The coins used to get stuck on the edges and irregular surfaces of the plastic bricks, so he would try to use "roofing blocks" because those were smoother and the coins slid in a more predictable manner. Larry also enjoys looking at the planets; maybe he is comforted by their consistent behavior.

As an undergraduate in college, Larry studied chemical engineering, and his favorite classes involved physics. Within medicine, he was drawn to radiation oncology based largely on its application of physics and math to real-life human problems. Through his more than 25 years in medicine, he has been repeatedly bothered by clinical processes that are sometimes inexact, disorganized, and (ironically) predictably unreliable. The differences between his experiences in engineering and medicine are striking. For example, as a summer student engineer at DuPont, there were processes and procedures for everything. The company had successfully promoted a culture of "safety first" with multiple standardized processes and open dialogue about safety-related concerns. The company had signs throughout the facility (Figure 4.1) to remind workers about safety and the need to adhere to predefined processes.

Within medicine, radiation oncology is one of the more process-driven disciplines. We do have well-defined quantitative standards for much of what we do. Nevertheless, this information is not always well managed and thus not always uniformly applied. Further, Larry continues to see the need for improved leadership, processes, and work spaces in our field to

SAFETY FIRST

WEAR YOUR SAFETY GLASSES

FIGURE 4.1
Sign that is reminiscent of the signs seen more than 30 years ago at DuPont Chemical. (This image taken from a Google search for "DuPont safety signs.")

reduce waste and improve quality, efficiency, reliability, and patient safety. To Larry, this need appears to be increasing as the interactive complexity or coupling of various aspects of care (e.g., concurrent vs. sequential chemoradiotherapy or intensity-modulated radiation therapy [IMRT] vs. conventional radiation therapy [RT]) are increasing. The concepts of complexity and coupling are discussed in detail in Chapter 3.

Although Larry perceives engineering and medicine to be very different, he believes that we can exploit the lessons learned in engineering to create better systems and processes within medicine. Fortunately, Larry has been able to apply his interests in the physical sciences to address clinical problems (e.g., using three-dimensional imaging to improve radiation treatment planning or using functional imaging to study radiation-induced normal tissue injury). For most of his career, Larry's focus has been on improving outcomes by expanding *what* we can do (e.g., better tumor targeting or normal tissue risk assessment). He sees our application of high-reliability and value creation approaches in clinical radiation oncology as a parallel journey, now trying to better outcomes by improving *how* we do things. In both areas, he has applied lessons from engineering to medicine.

4.1.2 Rediscovering Human Factors Engineering

Larry spent most of his academic career at Duke University Medical Center, and one of his enjoyable responsibilities was to serve on the quality assurance (QA) committee. He enjoyed the multidisciplinary discussions about operations and how he could help reduce risks to the patients.

He enjoyed reformatting prescription sheets and simulation directives to enable the faculty to more easily and reliably convey needed information to the dosimetrists and therapists. He had strong intuitive opinions regarding every detail (e.g., the layout and font) in these communication tools; he wanted it to be easy for providers to input information, and easy for "consumers" to extract that information. He enjoyed studying the work flows to better understand why things happened and then trying to modify processes to reduce waste and error. He did not know the formal language of improvement, but he was using Lean and Human Factors Engineering principles to create reliable systems.

Kim Light, the lead dosimetrist at Duke at the time, kept meticulous records of "deviations/errors" in the clinic for the QA committee. In 2005, in the midst of a technology upgrade to machines with a MLC (multileaf collimator), there was a suspected subtle *increase* in the rates of deviations in the clinic. An in-depth analysis revealed an initial slightly increased deviation rate on the newer machines (attributed to unfamiliarity with the newer technology); this declined over time (attributed to a "learning curve"). This made intuitive sense. However, an unexpected increased deviation rate on the older machines was also seen (Figure 4.2).[1] Please note that the deviation rates shown in the figures largely reflect incidents with no meaningful clinical consequence. In addition, care should be taken in overinterpreting these data because attribution can be uncertain.

Of particular note, there were changes in the *types* of deviations. Incidents that appeared related to dosimetry-based tasks were reduced, while incidents that appeared to be related to delivery-based tasks were increased. In either case, the bulk of incidents appeared not to be directly linked to the new technology. Even the incidents on new machines were not necessarily related to the new technology itself. Instead, it appeared that changes in the work flow, and in particular inconsistencies in the work flow between machines, was leading to a sizable fraction of the incidents (e.g., a therapist forgetting to do something on one of the older machines that had become "automatic" on the newer machines). Therefore, processes were modified (e.g., standardized colors for skin markings, standardized checklists and time-outs for dosimetrists and therapists, and pre-RT film QA procedures) that successfully reduced incidents (Figure 4.3).[2]

This sparked a transformative experience for Larry. He had witnessed firsthand that changes in the environment affect performance. As Larry read more about errors in general, he was surprised at the depth and richness of the study of errors and human behavior. He was overwhelmed

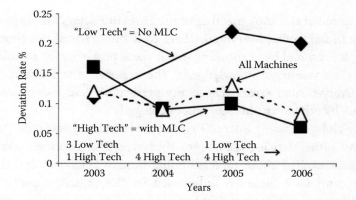

FIGURE 4.2

Rates of treatment deviations over time during a transition in equipment and work flows at Duke University. The introduction of newer machines (i.e., with multileaf collimators [MLCs]) was associated with an increased rate of deviations on the older machines (see text for details). (With permission from Marks L, Light K, Hubbs J, et al. *Int J Radiat Oncol Biol Phys* 2007;69:1579–1586.)[1]

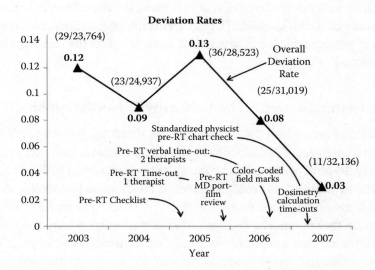

FIGURE 4.3

A reduction in deviations seen over time with the institution of multiple additional standardized processes at Duke University (see text for details). (Adapted from ASTRO presentation; Marks L, Hubbs J, Light K, et al. *Int J Radiat Oncol Biol Phys*, 2008;72:S143.)[2]

and inspired at the 2007 meeting of the Human Factors and Ergonomics Society in Baltimore, Maryland. There were hundreds, if not thousands, of people who had been thinking about these problems for decades, and there was a wealth of knowledge.[3-5] The experience at Duke regarding the delivery-related errors was totally predictable and indeed had been reported by others within radiation oncology.[3]

Larry's long-standing interest in safety and efficiency was reinvigorated. However, rather than just focusing on the physical (i.e., work space) aspects, he became excited about understanding human behaviors and decision making and how these are influenced by the organizational culture, workplace, and worker mindset (e.g., information processing, workload, situational awareness), that is, the essence of Human Factors Engineering. Larry began to give talks about these issues and organized a panel at the 2008 American Society for Radiation Oncology (ASTRO) meeting, "Improving Safety for Patients Receiving Radiotherapy: A Human Factors Engineering Approach" (other speakers included Eric Ford, Eric Klein, and Melanie Wright). This was followed by similar panels in subsequent years, such as a 2009 panel, "Towards Defining Best Practices to Improve Clinical Care in Radiation Oncology" (other speakers included Robert Adams, Todd Pawlicki, and James Hayman).

In 2008, Larry moved from Duke to become the department chair at the University of North Carolina (UNC). In his job negotiations, he asked for funds to perform quality improvement work based on the Human Factors Engineering principles.

4.1.3 Getting Started at the University of North Carolina

When Larry arrived at UNC in 2008, he was struck by the sense of responsibility to the people of North Carolina that permeates the institution. It is a busy hospital, with many chronically ill patients coming from all over the state to address their complex medical conditions. The diverse patient population is often faced with financial, insurance, and social challenges that strain the system. The dedication of the staff was (and remains) inspiring. He noted that people worked very hard, usually well beyond their regular shifts, and everyone seemed to want to "bend over backward to get it done" for the patients. Patients were receiving the care that they needed. On the other hand, people seemed to be working too hard. There were too many "special cases," and there seemed to be "work-arounds" for everything. The reliability and predictability of the processes were suboptimal.

Patients often waited, providers were frustrated, and everyone seemed to have accepted some level of chaos as "the norm." Further, the situation appeared to have been worsening with the increased complexity and coupling of care related to treatments such as IMRT, image-guided radiation therapy (IGRT), stereotactic body radiation therapy (SBRT), and concurrent chemoradiotherapy.

Larry saw the need to improve and standardize processes. He received initial guidance and help from our local experts in operational improvement at UNC, for example Glen Spivak and his group, Celeste Mayer, Larry Mandelkehr, Iris Dickinson and Dr. Sam Weir as part of UNC's Patient Access and Efficiency (*PAcE*) initiative and Dr. Tina Willis in the pediatric ICU. Drs. Dean and Hoffman in the business school provided advice on how to promote change within the department. Larry also reached out to people in industrial engineering at North Carolina State University in Raleigh. Through an arrangement with the Industrial Extension Service at NC State, one of their young faculty (Dr. Lukasz Mazur) and several of his students (Dr. Marianne Jackson, Kinley Taylor, Dr. Prithima Mosaly, and others) began work in our department in approximately 2009. Through these many contacts, we initiated numerous activities to better our operations.

Larry wishes he could say that he had a well-thought-out plan to implement a comprehensive high-reliability and value creation improvement culture. He did not. Rather, he broadly knew where he wanted to take the department and broadly understood the concepts of high reliability and value creation, but he relied heavily on the continuous advice from others. The help from the NC State group was profound and yielded long-term critical benefits.

Because several of the NC State team focused largely on our department, they had the time to become familiar with our operations, personnel, and needs. They provided a rational systematic framework to our improvement activities, helped to gather data to justify changes, and provided the department with an "outside opinion" on what to do. Thus, rather than most of the improvement activities being "Larry's crazy idea," they could be (and largely were) the result of expert opinion, often based on objective data. Thus, the NC State team provided credibility to the overall process. One of the students, Dr. Marianne Jackson, was particularly helpful in this regard. Marianne had worked as an obstetrician-gynecologist doctor for more than 20 years and, at the time Larry met her, had gone back to graduate school and was working with Lukasz. As a physician, she was (and is) able to speak with physicians as a colleague and in a productive manner.

Personally, Lukasz and Marianne provided Larry with advice on how best to address difficult improvement challenges. Equally important, they provided him with needed encouragement to continue to push forward with the Human Factors Engineering and Lean improvement agenda. This was especially helpful when there was departmental resistance. At times, this was difficult for Larry. Larry was adjusting to a new role (department chair) at a new institution (UNC) and was trying to change long-standing processes and attitudes, both in general and toward how we should approach quality improvement. Larry still painfully remembers a few instances when he lost his temper with some of the faculty, such as when he was unable to effectively engage them to assist with a problem. Indeed, one of the faculty had told him, "Just tell us what you want us to do." Later, when several faculty did not like Larry's solution, Larry was criticized by the faculty for not seeking their input or communicating with them about the problem. He learned the hard way that communication is a common touchstone, and that leaders need to be sure that they repeatedly discuss pertinent issues with their staff (e.g., sharing information or seeking input, etc.).

A particular low point related to Larry's desire for the faculty and staff to go through some formal "Lean training." The introductory Lean class at UNC is called Yellow Belt. It is a seven-hour interactive/participatory session, given off site, with a pace and level conducive to diverse learners from throughout the health system. For about two to three years, Larry had been asking all of the departmental staff to go to the Yellow Belt class and asking all managers to give their staff the time to attend. Larry wanted the faculty to attend as a sign to the department of their commitment, and for the potential educational value. Indeed, one of our departmental goals was for us to reach 100% training; this goal was discussed and agreed to by the faculty (or at least no one openly disagreed with the goal). In our monthly department-wide QA meetings, the data for percentage of people trained by group (e.g., nursing, therapy, physicians) is routinely shown publically (updated version in Figure 4.4).

In mid-2013, it was becoming clear that the faculty were not being trained at the desired pace. After repeated prodding, Larry managed to have two of our somewhat more doubting faculty to sign up for the Yellow Belt training. As it happened, seven of our departmental staff also signed up on that day, as had two of the health system's senior leaders. The outcome was not ideal. Our faculty attended but left the class early because they found the pace too slow and the content too simplistic. Their early

Group	A3		Yellow Belt	
Administration	100%	(8/8)	88%	(7/8)
Dosimetry	100%	(6/6)	100%	(6/6)
Nursing	100%	(10/10)	100%	(9/9)
Performance Improvement	100%	(4/4)	100%	(4/4)
Physicians/NPs/Residents	100%	(16/16)	75%	(12/16)
Physics	100%	(13/13)	50%	(6/12)
Research	100%	(5/5)	40%	(2/5)
Support Staff	100%	(10/10)	80%	(8/10)
Therapy	100%	(18/18)	100%	(18/18)
% Department Trained	100%	(91/91)	78%	(71/91)

FIGURE 4.4
Rates of completing A3 and Yellow Belt training (as of March 2014).

departure was disappointing to the class instructors and organizers (especially as they had increased capacity to accommodate our department) and sent a potentially negative message to the other approximately 30 participants (including our seven departmental staff). Indeed, several of our participating staff expressed to Larry (and others) their disappointment that "their faculty" did not think it worth their time to stay for the entire training. Larry was hurt.

For their part, our faculty was equally disappointed, and indeed they had a point. The educational content for the faculty was maybe limited (perhaps they had been exposed to many of the concepts through the departmental initiatives and conferences). Larry attended Yellow Belt training several years earlier, and while he enjoyed it, he acknowledged that the pace was at times slow.

In retrospect, Larry had not set the expectations and rationale adequately for the faculty. He had become so focused on the metric of "attending the training" that he had lost sight of the *reasons* for attending the training (e.g., educational, enhancing the group experience via interprofessional participation, team building, etc.) and had not provided enough clarity to the faculty regarding these reasons. Larry wishes that the faculty would have appreciated the value in actively participating in the training (even if they were not learning new material), such as sharing their prior experiences and knowledge with the group, team building, and so on. But, that was not the expectation that Larry had set. Larry tried to turn this into a learning experience to provide feedback to the class instructors and asked them to consider if there were alternative ways to provide the faculty with the necessary background training.

Over time, Larry overcame this episode and many similar hurdles. Some of Larry's strategies for retaining motivation and spirit are given in Section 4.2. Generally, Larry takes comfort from talking with others, recognizing the long-term nature of the task, and making small incremental improvements where possible. He is motivated by the realities of our operations and the continual reminders that we can be doing things better. On some level, the Yellow Belt training episode was just another realization of something that we could be doing better. Some additional thoughts regarding this circumstance are provided in Section 4.3.

4.1.4 Timing and Serendipity

Just when we were starting to get some traction and real first-hand experiences at UNC, a series of articles in the *New York Times* by Walt Bogdanich sent shivers through our field.[4–7] These articles recounted serious injuries resulting from incidents in the delivery of RT. Suddenly, the work that we had done at Duke and UNC, and on several committees at ASTRO, became more broadly relevant. Invitations to speak about our work increased (e.g., to the Food and Drug Administration [FDA], at various group conventions/meetings, and for hospital/departmental visiting professorships). ASTRO and the American Association of Physicists in Medicine (AAPM) responded to the *New York Times* articles with a multifaceted approach (see Section 1.1 in Chapter 1). Larry was invited to help organize an ASTRO/AAPM-sponsored meeting dedicated to quality and safety in 2010 and to help write several "white papers," reports, and reviews about this issue.[8–10] Larry also became more active in some of ASTRO's quality-related activities, and when the committee structure at ASTRO was modified to create a council dedicated to clinical affairs and quality, Larry was elected to serve as the vice chair. The work that he had done at Duke and in his early years at UNC positioned our group well to help our field respond to the challenges raised by the *New York Times* articles. In summary, these articles came at a fortunate time—providing validation and lending greater justification to our work (both locally and nationally). They provided uncontestable evidence of the importance and seriousness of preventing errors at a time when some were trivializing the safety and quality concerns.

4.1.5 Reliability versus Autonomy

One of the most commonly raised objections is: "Standardization does not allow me to do what is right for my patient. Each patient is unique, with their own set of clinical issues that requires me to highly individualize what I do. Planes and cars are infinitely simpler than people and just because this approach may work in industry does not mean it applies to my medical practice." This is certainly partially true, and we are not suggesting that providers compromise care. Nevertheless, the majority of processes that support medical decision making and treatment *can* be standardized. Further, many medical decisions can also be standardized, especially if there is no particular medical reason for provider-defined variations. In our specialty, for example, physicians in a group practice should agree on dose-volume guidelines for common situations to enable dosimetrists and physicists to more readily do their work. This is not to say that the provider must, in every case, use these same dose-volume guidelines. That would be silly. The bowel dose-volume constraints for a patient with Crohn's disease likely should be modified. But, the fact that "special cases" exist should not prevent us from using the power of standardization for the majority of patients. Indeed, adapting standards, and standardized processes, is a more reliable means to identify that special case. Considering a patient with Crohn's disease that needs special attention, which approach do you think is more reliable?

Option 1: A clinic has no formal dose-volume guidelines for the bowel, and the providers are expected to give the planners patient-specific constraints. We know what happens. Because providers generally over time use similar dose-volume constraints, there will be a "de facto" standard. In short order, the communication between providers and planners becomes "use our usual constraints." Indeed, over time, there is no formal communication between provider and planner but rather an implicit assumption that "our usual" is acceptable. But, what happens to the rare patient with Crohn's disease? Here, the provider needs to remember to notify the planner. Relying on short-term memory is not ideal. And, if one does remember, how will that information be conveyed? Perhaps it may be conveyed verbally or maybe via e-mail, text message, sticky note, or owl. This is not a reliable system and is actually labor intense.

Option 2: A clinic has default dose-volume guidelines for the bowel that are applied to all patients, and the providers are required to answer a question such as, "Does the patient have Crohn's disease, ulcerative colitis, or other medical conditions that may alter their gastrointestinal tolerances?" This can be done as part of a checklist ideally applied at the beginning of the planning process (e.g., at consultation or simulation). It can be "hardwired" into the plan approval process as well (e.g., a hard stop applied at the time that the bowel dose-volume histogram [DVH] is approved).

With this approach, the checklist/hard stop prompts (and forces) the provider to consider the possibility of medical conditions that might alter tolerance. There is less reliance on the provider's memory and much less variation in how information is communicated to the planners. The planners have now only one place to look to identify if they can apply the usual bowel dose-volume constraints and do not need to call or page the doctor for clarifications. The system is more robust and reliable.

Yes, the providers need to accept a standard process of communication with the planners and are relinquishing some autonomy. Is this unreasonable? Should a planner be realistically expected to acquire information from different providers via different means? Should it be OK for Dr. Smith to send a text message about patients, Dr. Howard to send e-mails, Dr. Fine to use sticky notes, and Dr. White to send nothing at all? We do not think so.

Further, adapting to some standardized processes should be liberating to the providers. Why should a provider have to think about how to convey this information about the patient's Crohn's disease and to worry about whether a dosimetrist received an e-mail or text message? In a larger practice, why should a provider even have to worry about knowing which dosimetrist will do the calculations for a particular patient? The provider has more important things to think about. Defining a standard approach thus liberates the provider from having to think too much about the mechanics of how to convey this information. On the flip side, this only works if the planners reliably receive the information. The providers

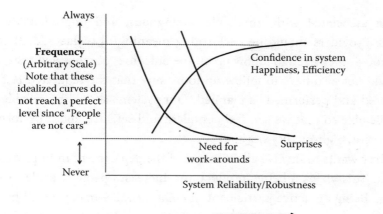

FIGURE 4.5

Building reliable systems will have multiple benefits as shown. Nevertheless, as medicine is a human endeavor, the application of "Lean systems" (initially promoted in the automobile industry) will never eliminate all uncertainties, surprises, and unhappiness (i.e., "people are not cars").

need to have confidence in the system. Building reliable systems will have multiple benefits (Figure 4.5).

Obviously, these issues are much easier to address in smaller clinics with a limited number of providers, but even there, these concepts are important.

We have adapted in our clinic a similar approach to identify patients who have had prior RT, who have a pacemaker, or who might be pregnant. For each patient about to undergo simulation, the provider is required to answer three questions within the electronic health record (EHR) addressing these issues. This approach forces the provider to consider these issues, and there is no ambiguity regarding where the planners look to ascertain this information (see Chapter 5 for more details about this initiative).

4.1.6 Altruism versus Selfishness

Larry's desire to improve operations is fueled by a desire to make the practice of radiation oncology safer but is not totally altruistic. Certainly, he wants to improve the patient/family experience and improve clinical outcomes. However, he is equally driven to make his and his coworkers' lives better. Larry wants to eliminate the frustration of wasted time and effort associated with unreliable, ambiguous, and unpredictable systems. Providers should be performing meaningful (value-added) work. Although they need to follow up on the outcomes of requested tests, they should not also have to follow up to be sure that the requested test was ordered and performed as planned. Our systems should be reliable and predictable so that we can feel confident and satisfied about performing pertinent, high-quality work.

Larry wants to involve all members of the department in improvement work. This yields a better product and increases people's pride in their work. Being an active participant in creating value makes us all happier and actualizes our contributions and creative ideas. This is a positively reinforcing loop that increases investment, pride, and motivation to continually improve reliability and efficiency.

It seems obvious that patients directly and indirectly benefit. Nevertheless, Larry is often challenged on this point. When asked, "How does the patient benefit from me [i.e., a physician] having to adopt operational standards? We can all still make errors," he responds by asking the person to consider this issue from the "consumer's" perspective. Isn't the experience in a restaurant, retail store, or airport better if their systems are reliable? Isn't it better when things happen as expected and with as few needs for "improvised work-arounds" as possible?

In multiple settings, objective assessments of patient outcomes have improved when processes are standardized to promote reliability and value creation.[11] Nevertheless, standardization alone is not sufficient. Even with standardized and reliable systems, the interactive complexity and human involvement in essentially all aspects of healthcare make our systems inherently unstable, and they thus can (and will) behave unexpectedly. The same is true even when automation addresses some aspects of our work and when forcing functions are in place. Thus, throughout the continuum of systems/work flows with variable degrees of interactive complexity and coupling, there is usually a need for various types of QA strategies, including those that are human focused (see Chapter 3, Section 3.1). It is critical that as many people as possible embrace the culture of safety, help to build better systems/work flows, and maintain a sense of safety mindfulness to detect the unexpected.

4.2 PROMOTING HIGH RELIABILITY
AND VALUE CREATION

4.2.1 Promoting a Leadership Infrastructure
for Formal Improvement Activities

Initially, Larry created a departmental operations team consisting essentially of the department's managers (e.g., leaders of nursing, physics, educational programs, clerical support staff, therapy, etc.) who have been meeting regularly twice per week since Larry joined UNC. The basic agenda for the operations meeting has largely remained unchanged: review ongoing activities with a focus on operational challenges, discuss possible solutions, implement, refine, and repeat. The frequent meetings are necessary to instill a sense of urgency and self-discipline to continually address our challenges and be proactive in seeking problems and having accountability for resolutions. In the early years, Larry personally kept lists of challenges and monitored progress. Larry's active participation in these meetings reflects his commitment to improving all aspects of our department and his support for the managers. Continuing these operational meetings reflects the reality that the operations need to be continually monitored and adjusted based on changes in staffing, clinic volumes, finances, new technologies, clinical care, and so on.

In the early years, the operations team identified many of the targets for our improvement activities. Over time, the entire department identified these targets via a systematic analysis of the "good catches" (see Chapter 5 for details).

This operations team became ambassadors for our high-reliability and value creation program (or what we refer offline to as our "Lean" or "Quality and Safety" program). As respected leaders of their individual groups, their "buy-in" was needed to help foster broader participation among the staff. Larry tries to continually celebrate their active participation in this work in order to thank them and to keep them enthusiastically engaged.

Larry urged members of the operations team to learn more about Lean. After reading a good book about Lean or operational improvement, he often distributed copies to the leadership team. An early example included *The Goal* by Drs. Eliyahu M. Goldratt and Jeff Cox,[12] which uses an entertaining novel to explain many interesting operational concepts. The book had been given to him by a Duke colleague, Dr. John Kirkpatrick (also a chemical engineer turned radiation oncologist) as a present when he went to UNC. Larry's later offerings to the managers included *Switch: How to Change Things When Change Is Hard* by Chip and Dan Heath,[13] *Safe Patients, Smart Hospitals* by Dr. Peter J. Pronovost and Eric Vohr,[14] *On the Mend* by John Toussaint and Roger A Gerard,[15] and *Transforming Health Care* by Charles Kenney.[16] These are all good books that provided much-needed motivation and encouragement. The last two books are particularly good because they are Lean focused and well describe the frustrations and experiences at two hospitals that have had successful Lean transformations (ThedaCare and Virginia Mason, respectively). Most recently, Larry distributed *Thinking Fast and Slow* by Dr. Daniel Kahneman.[17] Larry also encouraged the group to attend meetings about quality and safety to gain knowledge, meet like-minded people, and maintain/gain enthusiasm.

Broadening participation among faculty physicians was an important milestone for Larry personally and for the department. At the start, Larry was the primary physician involved, aided by Dr. Ellen Jones, our clinical director. Over time, we were fortunate that one of our young physicians, Dr. Bhisham Chera, developed a strong interest in this area. However, he was initially somewhat reluctant to devote much effort because it would detract from the time he could spend on research and other activities that are usually most celebrated in academic institutions (and that usually lead to promotion). As a young faculty physician with drive and academic aspirations, this was a totally logical and reasonable concern. However, given the increased interest in quality and safety that Larry was seeing nationally, Larry was convinced that Bhisham could make important contributions to our field in this area, and that there would be associated recognitions. Larry promised Bhisham that his efforts in the area of quality and safety would be considered during evaluation for promotion.

We created a research program linked to our improvement activities within our department (details are given in Chapter 7). We might be the only radiation oncology department in the country with industrial engineers on our faculty. Our research program provides "academic validity" to our work and academic opportunities for those interested and involved, such as Bhisham, some of our residents, and others.

Larry created a departmental position of director of patient safety and quality and named Bhisham to this role. This was intended to send a clear signal to the department of the importance of this issue and Larry's confidence in, and support of, Bhisham in the role. With the appropriate assurances from Larry, Bhisham actively engaged.

This was a "tough job" that Larry had given Bhisham. It is one thing for the chair to encourage faculty to embrace change. It was (and is) certainly more challenging for a young faculty to lead these initiatives. Larry coached and encouraged Bhisham, gave him opportunities for leadership training, and got him involved with national initiatives as well.

Larry tries to publicly thank all of our departmental staff for their activities in all areas; celebrating people's achievements is important. Thus, just as Larry celebrates and thanks people for their accomplishments in clinical care, research, and teaching, Larry repeatedly acknowledges and celebrates people's involvement with improvement activities. It was Larry's goal to make it clear to the department that participation in improvement activities is an important part of our work that should be celebrated. Indeed, Larry tries to "have the backs" of all people involved with these initiatives, as we all can face "pushback" and skepticism from resistant faculty and staff.

It is critical to emphasize the strong foundation that our operations team had built before Bhisham stepped into his new role. All of our departmental managers had worked for years to create the infrastructure (both processes and culture) that has facilitated Bhisham's success. This includes the broad acceptance of Lean principles among the staff; the infrastructure for A3s, good catches, and so on; as well as the associated information technology (IT) support. Bhisham was provided with a good framework within which he could work. If he had to start from ground zero, this would have been much harder, if not impossible.

There are so many people who have been instrumental, it is hard to acknowledge them all. Nevertheless, it is useful to describe them briefly so that the reader can appreciate the scope of this effort. First, as noted, we had people with specialized training in operational improvement and Lean. Marianne and Lukasz provided Larry (and then the managers and later Bhisham) with continual enthusiasm, encouragement, and guidance. Marianne brought her expertise, experience, and credibility as a physician. Lukasz brought his expertise in *Engineering Management* and a research overlay to our initiatives (see Chapter 7). Prithima brought her research skills and knowledge regarding Human Factors Engineering. Kinley brought energy and enthusiasm and a passion for A3 thinking and Lean improvements. Together, they provided the knowledge of how to "do" the Lean work, that is, how to organize and prepare for improvement events, monitor and build the supportive infrastructure, coordinate the A3 and Good Catch programs, and so on. In the first two years, Marianne led ten

Kaizen events, concurrently training people in Lean principles. This was an enormous effort that helped to kick-start our program.

Plus, we had our dedicated staff from within radiation oncology. Kathy Burkhardt, Dr. Sha Chang, and Dr. Mich Price brought their clinical expertise as experienced organized medical physicists. Kathy has been particularly instrumental and has taken a leadership position in defining our clinical pathways and in supporting the Good Catch program. Dana Lachapelle brought similar skills in the area of RT; and Lesley Hoyle brought her expertise in dosimetry and Mosaiq®. Robert also helped these areas and incorporated our therapy and dosimetry students into our work. Together, they were the "subject matter experts" for many of our "technical" initiatives. We had similar enthusiastic support from Ken Neuvirth and Lauren Terzo in nursing; Patty Saponaro, John Rockwell, Lori Stravers, and Diane Coffey from administrative support; and Tim Cullip, John Dooley, Gregg Tracton, and Liyun Yu from computing. Gregg was particularly helpful in creating several IT-based tools to facilitate our work (see Chapter 5). Our hospital leaders were supportive of our work as well (e.g., John Lewis, Marlene Rifkin, Glen Spivak, and Drs. Brian Goldstein, Ian Buchanan, Bill Roper, Tony Lindsey, Michael Pignone, Tina Willis, and Allen Daugird). It is worth noting the number and diverse skill sets of the managers involved. Given the complex, multifaceted nature of radiation oncology clinical care, a broad team as described is most helpful, if not required.

Thus, it was critical to build a respected departmental operations team of smart, articulate, motivated people to oversee and promote these initiatives. Plus, it was necessary to continually reinforce our support for their activities to bring sustainability and credibility to our efforts.

Engaging our resident physicians was also critical to promote a leadership infrastructure. As residents are deeply involved in all clinical activities, their participation is critical to any improvement initiative. They often best know the deficiencies of our systems because they are often given the tasks to create work-around solutions to our operational challenges. Equally, if not more important, as physicians, our residents are leaders, and through their actions, they are setting an example to the staff (just as is the case for faculty physicians). We were (and are) fortunate to have a dedicated group of residents who are largely positively engaged. We appreciate the involvement and support from the residents because they must have been getting mixed signals from the faculty physicians (some of whom were not as supportive of this work). A particularly memorable moment occurred during one of our monthly departmental QA meetings.

We were having a fairly open discussion, and there were pointed questions being raised about the utility of several of our initiatives, in particular some recent Kaizen events. One of our senior residents, who was the physician representative at a Kaizen, stood up and said, "Truthfully, I was skeptical and did not think it would be worth the time. But, to my surprise, it was really valuable. I have a better appreciation of the specific challenges of our patient flow through the clinic and more broadly understand and appreciate the Lean approaches we are taking." It was a powerful, positive, and validating statement. That event might have encouraged others to be less skeptical and to become involved. These sorts of experiences helped to build the leadership infrastructure to support our initiatives.

The physicians and managers fill obvious leadership roles and are usually held responsible for quality improvement. However, by broadly educating everyone about concepts of Lean, safety, and reliability and then empowering the managers to empower all of their workers to proactively address opportunities for improvement, we are (in essence) trying to diffuse this responsibility more broadly. In this way, everyone can enjoy the gratification of improvement work, thus enhancing the capacity for formal improvement activities (Figure 3.11).

4.2.2 Promoting a Process Infrastructure for Formal Improvement Activities

Much of this book is a description of the systems that we have put into place to support this initiative. One can argue that you can do improvement in an ad hoc fashion: "A problem comes up, we discuss, we deal with it." This is unlikely to be helpful. Clinical departments are interactively complex, and one needs a systematic approach to monitor performance, create improvement initiatives, assess impact, and iteratively repeat. As outlined in the previous chapters, the multiple components of our high-reliability and value creation infrastructure are mutually reinforcing. Alone, any of these components can be helpful, but in concert, they are much more powerful. For example, defining standard work flows is really only helpful if one (1) monitors the "system's performance" (e.g., performs QA, (2) listens to the users (e.g., our Good Catch program), and (3) reassesses systems and implements changes as needed (e.g., A3s, Kaizens; see Figure 3.5 in Chapter 3).

An example of a formal process infrastructure to support this work is based on Kaizen events. A Kaizen (Japanese for "improvement," "change for the best," "good change") event is a several-day meeting at which all stakeholders for a particular process thoroughly analyze that process, define its true value stream (i.e., its essential components), and eliminate waste (e.g., redundant or unnecessary steps). In the beginning, our advisors (e.g., some of the improvement people from UNC and later NC State) participated and helped lead several of our initial Kaizen events to more formally address some of our challenged processes. In our second year, Marianne trained several managers in Lean principles and techniques so that they were able to lead their own Kaizen events. Kaizen events require participants to dedicate a meaningful block of time to formally consider the process in detail. Traditionally, these are five-day events. Given the importance of physician participation, and recognizing their time constraints, we structured several two-day Kaizen events, with a fair amount of prework before the event to maximize productivity during the event. Larry participated in several of the earliest events. These were generally successful, but we stumbled when we hurriedly made superficial assessments of complex processes or failed to have enough physicians involved. For example, one of our Kaizens without a fully engaged physician led to implementation of a work flow that did not address the physicians' concerns and committed them to processes to which they had not agreed. Several of our Kaizen events are described in more detail in Chapters 5 and 6. Additional examples of our infrastructure are given in Chapters 5 and 6; these include examples of automation, forcing functions, and standard processes worked into our normal work flows.

4.2.3 Promoting High Reliability and Value Creation by Leadership Actions

a. *Walking the leadership talk*: As a leader promoting Lean-based improvement activities, it is important for Larry to be actively involved in these initiatives for several reasons. First, participation is educational. Larry has learned a lot about quality improvement and about how challenging this work can be by being directly involved. Defining value streams, analyzing processes, rooting out waste, and so on is hard work and not always intuitive. Second, such first-hand experiences enable Larry to be a more credible advocate for this sort of work. Larry is able to reflect and speak much more knowledgeably about improvement initiatives having worked on many improvement projects. Third, we think that a leader should generally be willing to do what the leader is asking of his or her staff. Larry is much more comfortable asking others to do improvement work knowing that he has done it as well. Last, Larry's participation brings added credibility to our global improvement program. Larry's commitment sends a clear message to the department that he thinks this is important. Many of the managers, and now Bhisham as well, are similarly walking the talk.

b. *Banging the drum and sending a persistent message*: We try to publicly thank and celebrate those who are involved in improvement work. We do this through announcements at any and all of our departmental meetings. Our departmental daily morning huddle is Larry's favorite venue for such announcements. Indeed, one of the benefits of having regular meetings is that they provide a routine venue for such announcements. Our morning huddle is regularly attended by more than 20 people, including most of the faculty and residents (physician and physics), staff physicists, dosimetrists, students in our dosimetry and therapy programs, and representatives from nursing, therapy, and clerical support staff. For example, we might thank someone who had a particularly helpful suggestion or good catch, participated in a Kaizen event, attended a class about quality, gave a presentation about improvement, presented a poster at the hospital Quality Expo, and so on. Accolades are frequently repeated on several occasions to send a consistent and persistent message, for example: "Thank you to Bill and Mary for participating in the Kaizen event later this week"; "Bill and Mary will be working on a Kaizen today"; "Thanks again to Bill and Mary for their Kaizen efforts yesterday." We want to emphasize that we thank people for big and little things because it is the thousands of little things that improve operations. Similarly, in our smaller groups (e.g., committees), we will similarly publicly thank people for their activities that promote our culture of safety.

In addition, we use our departmental Good News board, Trophy Case, Employee of the Month, and Good Catch Recognition boards (Figure 4.6). We believe in the power of advertising, such as billboards. Commercial interests know that it works, and that is why they use it. We often think of these displays as our departmental billboards, and these are strategically placed in high-traffic areas to maximize visibility.

FIGURE 4.6
Examples of "recognition" displays in our departmental hallways and conference room. Good News Board (top left); Trophy Case (top right); Employee of the Month (bottom left); Good Catch Recognition (bottom right). The basketball in the trophy case is signed by the "winners" of the Good Catch initiatives (see text for details).

These public venues are also used to congratulate and thank people for their accomplishments in other areas, such as clinical care, education, and research (e.g., opening a new clinical program, teaching a class, having a paper accepted or published, submitting a grant proposal or receiving grant funding, etc.). Celebrating improvement activities in the same venue used for clinical, educational, and research accolades sends a message that these are *all* valued by the department.

c. *Validating our approach*: People should understand the importance of continuous quality improvement and that the approach we are taking has a track record for success. Wherever possible, Larry publicly highlights lessons/initiatives about quality and safety from elsewhere in medicine and more broadly from a societal perspective. For example, when there is a report in the newspaper about the importance of the safety culture within the US airline industry or an obituary for Mr. Toyoda that espouses the virtues of Lean in creating reliable automobiles, Larry brings the newspaper to our morning huddle and will read excerpts to the group.[18-19] These articles are often copied and distributed or posted on bulletin boards in our conference room. If there is an article about an accident whose cause has been ascribed in part to a suboptimal work flow or imprecise communication between well-meaning people, we talk about it. This applies to reports from within and outside healthcare. We believe this tends to validate the utility of the multifaceted initiatives we are promoting at UNC.

Perhaps more important, Larry continually highlights the results of improvement work within the department. There are posters and graphs outlining the improvement activities in the department, along with associated supportive data, all over the department (but strategically placed in high-traffic and high-occupancy areas). The results from Kaizen events, Good Catch awards, and others are proudly posted in multiple areas.

d. *Building pride*: We also try to place our departmental initiatives in a broader context so that people know that they are an important part of larger improvement efforts. For example, we discuss improvement initiatives elsewhere at UNC and encourage people to participate in, and attend, the hospital's Quality Expo (a poster session at which people from around the institution present their work). The posters from our own department's prior presentations remain on display in several of our break rooms. We celebrate the fact that some of our initiatives are being emulated elsewhere at UNC and nationally. We note ASTRO's initiatives and highlight journal articles from our field about quality improvement and our participation in these initiatives.

We want people to know that our department is respected in the field for our approach to quality improvement, and that they should be proud. When one of us is invited elsewhere to give a talk about our quality improvement programs or serves on a national or international committee related to this work, we celebrate that with announcements and postings. However, we always try to remember to say (truthfully) that we are merely ambassadors speaking on behalf of the entire department, and that any accolades directed at us are a reflection of everyone's work. Larry is particularly proud when we have visitors come to the department to see our processes. Their visits are announced and celebrated and reflect external validation for our work. We have had visitors from several other clinical areas within UNC, from the provost at UNC's main campus, and from individuals from other institutions.

e. *Elevating the level of respect for improvement work*: Performing improvement work is often viewed as less valuable than the three usual pillars of an academic practice: research, clinical care, and education. We have made a concerted effort to elevate the level of respect for improvement activities by repeatedly stressing their critical role in making all of our lives better—physicians, staff, and patients. Developing high-reliability and value-creating systems through improvement work supports the aims of research, clinical care, and education by freeing faculty and residents to attend to meaningful (not wasteful) work and by raising the level of expectations for safe, effective, and efficient practices in all spheres of the department (the labs, the classrooms, the exam rooms). For example, if the clinical systems are reliable and efficient, the physician-scientist is less likely to receive a page on a nonclinical day. We have found this argument to be helpful in encouraging others to support improvement activities.

f. *Sustaining leadership spirit and self-help*: This has been a challenging and rewarding experience, but often frustrating and seemingly too slow. Larry took comfort in the books (e.g., those from Virginia Mason and ThedaCare discussed previously) that emphasized the long-term nature of their transformation. Their words of frustration and occasional failure resonated with us. Larry in particular would read books and articles and scribble words such as "yes" or "so true" in the margins, sometimes even writing details from the analogous situations at UNC. Larry keeps many of these books on a file cabinet just inside his office. Their prominent location serves as a constant reminder to Larry of their lessons (Figure 4.7).

More important, we were continually motivated by the eventual successes. We drew further encouragement from our colleagues at UNC (both within the department and beyond) who were similarly minded. We became active in UNC's quality-related activities (e.g., joining committees, helping to organize educational sessions about Lean principles and methods) and have met and now know many dedicated and thoughtful people driven to improve quality. Beyond UNC, we were rejuvenated and felt validated by attending meetings such as the IHI (Institute for Healthcare Improvement) and visiting centers that had embraced Lean.

FIGURE 4.7
Books in Larry's office reminding him of the principles of quality improvement work, and the struggles and achievements of others.

Larry was honored to speak at Virginia Mason, invited by colleague Dr. Kas Badiodamazi. Larry was inspired by their ubiquitous embrace of Lean principles to improve operational reliability. He was particularly inspired by a meeting organized by Jeff Spade at the North Carolina Hospital Association dedicated to Lean whose guest was Don Berwick (an internationally recognized leader in this area and founder of the IHI).

It is not only Larry, but also the whole leadership team that needs to remain motivated, optimistic, and inspired. Therefore, as noted, they share many readings and books, seek out other like-minded people at UNC, involve themselves in local and national committees, and attend or present at national meetings if able. We have been fairly successful in this regard. Drs. Chera, Adams, and Mazur are active in various national or international quality/safety initiatives (e.g., through ASTRO and the International Atomic Energy Agency), have written papers, and have given many invited talks in the mainstream radiation oncology venues (e.g., ASTRO, ASCO, the *Red Journal*). For example, through Dr. Mazur's contacts in the broader field of Industrial Engineering, we have presented our work at the Industrial and Systems Engineering Research Conference, Human Factors and Ergonomic

Society, and IHI. We obtained grants from the UNC Innovation Center, Elekta, Accuray, Agency for Healthcare Research and Quality (AHRQ), and Centers for Disease Control and Prevention (CDC); a more detailed description of this work is provided in Chapter 7. It is fitting that we are all writing this book together because the optimal approach to improve quality and safety in radiation oncology is to leverage diverse skills and knowledge.

4.3 IF WE COULD DO IT OVER AGAIN

We are most proud of all that we have done. Nevertheless, there is way more to do, and in retrospect, there are several things that we would have done differently.

a. *Be more assertive*: Leadership is about influencing the beliefs and actions of others. Many books about change management emphasize building consensus, team building, setting the vision, and inspiring others to follow. Nevertheless, there are times when the leader needs to set a mandate. By nature, Larry tends to want to get along with people and sometimes shies away from mandates. In retrospect, Larry thinks that some of our initiatives could have been moved along more quickly if he was more assertive. For example, Larry should have set clearer expectations for participation in Lean/improvement activities and in attending Lean training. Our improvement initiatives would have been better (e.g., better solutions instituted faster and more sustainably) if we had had more stakeholder involvement in Kaizen events and improvement activities. There remain members of the department who are skeptical of our approach and thus participate only to the "minimum degree necessary." For example, they may attend our monthly QA meeting but not actively participate. Or, they might attend a Kaizen event but arrive late and leave early. It is challenging because one really wants the participants to "want" to participate. Forcing participation also may not yield a good outcome. Had we set the expectations for participation higher and more clearly (perhaps with more objective "rewards and penalties"), we might have had broader active participation. With regard to Yellow Belt training, Larry should have made the expectation to attend it more strictly at the start and better explained the multiple rationales for attending the Yellow Belt training that is offered to all of the staff. For the physicians in particular, a better clarification of the expectations for the training (i.e., the goals beyond the physician's own education) would have been helpful (see Section 4.1.3 for more details). Alternatively, we could have considered creating formal focused Lean training to be given to our departmental staff, including physicians, rather than relying solely on the hospital-provided classes. We did not formally do this because we think there is good value in attending training with people from other departments and because the educational program that they provide is good.

b. *Training while doing*: We initiated the first ten Kaizens (led by Marianne) without sufficient readiness or training. This was done intentionally as Marianne was promoting a "do-and-learn" experiential approach because it seemed impractical to obtain widespread formal Lean training for all of the participants in the Kaizen events. In retrospect, some of the staff did not fully understand the iterative nature of Lean improvement activities and were somewhat disillusioned when the first Kaizen for a particular work flow did not yield a "perfect" result. This led to some sustainability and disillusionment issues. We had not set expectations properly, and perhaps we should have done better staff education prior to the improvement initiatives.

c. *Embrace "improvement" jargon*: Initially, Larry was reluctant to embrace the jargon of improvement because he was worried that the indistinctiveness of the words (e.g., quality improvement vs. quality management vs. QA) would turn people off. However, over time, this has been a hindrance to clear communication and a lost opportunity for the staff to appreciate the nuances of improvement work. Further, it is challenging to effectively use tools such as control charts and daily metrics without clearly understanding the jargon. Over time, we are using the formal improvement jargon more often as we find it is needed to foster communication and the improvement work itself.

d. *More rapid and widespread implementation of initiatives*: We continue to struggle with defining good daily metrics (How was yesterday/today?) and robust QA procedures for some of our processes. This is not for lack of desire. Rather, our processes are complex, and these initiatives require input from all stakeholders; thus, a large effort is needed. As much as we have done, we need to be even more focused and persistent in driving these initiatives. Too often, we become distracted by other concerns (e.g., the ASTRO deadline, the new IT rollout or update, etc.). It is sometimes too easy for the improvement work to be delayed or pushed off the agenda altogether. For example, if we had done a better job at defining, recording, and displaying daily metrics, maybe it would have been easier to maintain focus on our improvement work. The more that this work can be spread within the department, the more that it can be seen as "integral" rather than an "add-on."

e. *Better defining standard work for managers*: This is a difficult transition for managers who have been trained and promoted for creative work-arounds and managing by jumping in. Standard work for managers requires constant monitoring of employee behaviors, process measures, and safety indicators that have been developed and agreed on by leadership. We have done this to some degree, but not to the degree that we need. We should have made this more of a priority at the start, dedicating time and resources to retrain managers. More time should be allotted to enabling managers to track, manage, and visually display improvement activities in their areas. In addition, they need to learn how to coach their staff to really do two jobs: (1) their job and (2) improvement work, but also to engrain the latter in the former.

f. *Knowledge management*: We should have set up a system to prospectively record our Lean journey and keep track of what we have done, have accomplished along the way. We are writing this book somewhat like "historians," retrospectively, with all of the biases of memory in recalling the good, the bad, and the ugly.

4.4 SUMMARY

Change management is difficult. This is evidenced by the numerous books, seminars, and self-help programs on this issue. Bringing change to medicine is particularly challenging given its traditions and hierarchical structure.[20] Nevertheless, the experiences described in this chapter demonstrate that change is possible. We encourage you to be inspired and to inspire/support others so that we together can make healthcare a high-reliability and value creation industry.

REFERENCES

1. Marks L, Light K, Hubbs J, et al. The impact of advanced technologies on treatment deviations in radiation treatment delivery. *Int J Radiat Oncol Biol Phys* 2007;69:1579–1586.
2. Marks L, Hubbs J, Light K, et al. Improving safety for patients receiving radiotherapy: the successful application of quality assurance initiatives. *Int J Radiat Oncol Biol Phys* 2008;72:S143.
3. Huang G, Medlam G, Lee J, et al. Error in the delivery of radiation therapy: results of quality assurance review. *Int J Radiat Oncol Biol Phys* 2005;61:1590–1595.
4. Bogdanich W. Safety features planned for radiation machines. NY Times. 2010;A19.
5. Bogdanich W. VA is fined over errors in radiation at hospital. NY Times. 2010;A20.
6. Bogdanich W, Ruiz RR. Radiation errors reported in Missouri. NY Times. 2010;A17.
7. Bogdanich W. Radiation offers new cures, and ways to do harm. NY Times. 2010;A1.
8. Marks LB, Adams RD, Pawlicki T, et al. Enhancing the role of case-oriented peer review to improve quality and safety in radiation oncology: executive summary. *Pract Radiat Oncol* 2013;3:149–156.
9. Moran JM, Dempsey M, Eisbruch A, et al. Safety considerations for IMRT: executive summary. *Pract Radiat Oncol* 2011;1:190–195.
10. Marks LB, Rose CM, Hayman JA, Williams TR. The need for physician leadership in creating a culture of safety. *Int J Appl Clin Med Phys* 2011;79:1287–1289.
11. Chassin M, Loeb M. The ongoing quality improvement journey: Next stop, high reliability. *Health Aff* 2011;30:559–568.
12. Goldratt EM, Cox, J. *The Goal: A Process of Ongoing Improvement*, Great Barrington, MA: North River Press; 2004.
13. Heath C, Heath D. *Switch: How to Change Things when Change is Hard*, New York, NY: Broadway Books; 2014.
14. Pronovost P, Vohr E. Safe Patients, *Smart Hospitals. How One Doctor's Checklist Can Help Us Change Health Care from the Inside Out*, New York, NY: Hudson Street Press; 2010.
15. Toussaint J, Gerard R. *On the Mend: Revolutionizing Healthcare to Save Lives and Transform the Industry*. Cambridge, MA: Lean Enterprise Institute; 2010.
16. Kenny C. *Transforming Health Care: Virginia Mason Medical Center's Pursuit of the Perfect Patient Experience*. New York, NY: CRC Press, Taylor & Francis Group; 2011.
17. Kahneman D. *Thinking Fast and Slow*. New York, NY: Farrar, Straus and Giroux; 2013.
18. Mouawad J, Drew C. Airline industry at its safest since the dawn of the jet age. *New York Times* February 11, 2013.
19. Tabuchi H. Eiji Toyoda, promoter of the Toyota Way and engineer of its growth, dies at 100. *New York Times* September 17, 2013.
20. Atul Gwandu Ted Talk. http://www.youtube.com/watch?v=L3QkaS249Bc.

5

Driving Change at the Workplace Level

LEARNING OBJECTIVES

After completing this chapter, the reader should be able to:

1. Understand how we apply concepts of Human Factors Engineering and the hierarchy of effectiveness to reduce human errors and serious incidents;
2. Understand how improvements to the workplace can improve teamwork, communication, and overall job performance; and
3. Understand how we improve workload and reduce stressors to facilitate reliability and value creation.

5.1 CREATING SAFE AND EFFICIENT ENVIRONMENTS: TWO CRITICAL CORE CONCEPTS

In Chapter 3, we acknowledge that the procedures conducted within the field of radiation oncology span a range with regard to system *complexity* and *coupling*. A summary of the discussion in Chapter 3 relating the types of quality assurance (QA) approaches for the various processes within radiation oncology is provided in Figure 5.1.

In general, we endorse (1) automation with human oversight and forcing functions wherever possible, especially for tightly coupled processes (e.g., data transfer, dose calculation/optimization); (2) strict process standardization and monitoring of processes, supported by vigilant testing and verification before any change implementation, for tightly coupled processes where automation and forcing functions are not possible (e.g.,

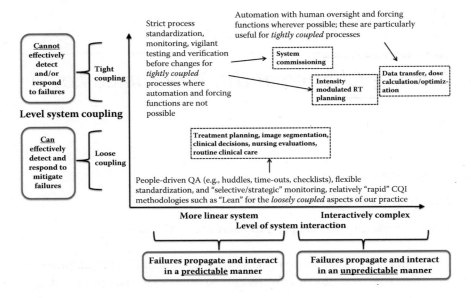

FIGURE 5.1

Summary of quality management strategies as characterized by system behavior. See Section 3.1 in Chapter 3 for details. *x* axis, linear vs. interactively complex; *y* axis, loosely vs. tightly coupled.

system commissioning, intensity-modulated radiation therapy [IMRT]); (3) people-driven QA (e.g., huddles, time-outs, checklists, etc.), flexible process standardization, and "selective/strategic" monitoring of processes, supported by relatively "rapid" continuous quality improvement (CQI) methodologies such as Lean for the loosely coupled (and to some degree more creative) aspects of our practice (e.g., treatment planning, image segmentation, clinical decisions, nursing evaluations, routine clinical care).

Above all, we emphasize the constant need for leadership to be actively involved and for **leadership-inspired safety mindfulness** because without it the probability of sustaining high reliability and value creation is close to zero.

In this chapter, we further expand the concepts borrowed from Human Factors Engineering with a focus on the hierarchy of effectiveness of error prevention to explain how we implemented changes to our workplace aimed to improve safety and efficiency. These two concepts are discussed in detail in Chapter 3, and the reader is referred there for details. A brief overview is provided here for completeness. Readers familiar with these concepts can skip to Section 5.2.

5.1.1 Human Factors Engineering

Human Factors Engineering is the recognition that a person's performance is greatly affected by his or her environment and culture. Work flows and work spaces should be designed such that people will "do the right thing" naturally. This intuitively makes sense and indeed sounds almost self-evident. Nevertheless, in our everyday lives, this is just simply not the case. Many poorly designed products or systems promote their misuse or at least inefficient, redundant, and frustrating use. Consider the difficulty in setting the alarm of many clock radios. Consider difficult-to-read instructions, poor signage, or confusing or ambiguous tools within our electronic health records (EHRs).

Therefore, a key principle to create reliable systems is to move as many of the processes as is possible and practical to the top of the hierarchy of effectiveness. Further, whenever human input is needed, apply human factors principles to design systems (work flows and work spaces) such that the most likely outcome is consistent with the desired outcome. Minimize ambiguities and redundancies, and maximize clarity and efficiency, to facilitate proper usage.

5.1.2 Hierarchy of Effectiveness

Hierarchy of effectiveness is the recognition that different approaches to error prevention have different degrees of robustness/effectiveness. In general, people-focused interventions (e.g., education, training, rules, and policies) are the least effective, and technology-focused interventions (e.g., forcing functions, automation) are the most effective (left-hand side of Figure 3.7 in Chapter 3). It is hoped that the reader finds this to be self-evident. There are countless examples in our everyday lives. For example, you are required to put money into vending machines *prior* to receiving the desired goods. This "forcing function" is essentially 100% effective and is far more effective than would be a sign reminding you to pay. Is this concept valid for radiation oncology? New York State maintains a database of radiation oncology events/errors. "Failure to follow policies/procedures" was implicated as a contributing factor in 84% of events and "inadequate policies/procedures" in 16% of events. This highlights the relative ineffectiveness of these approaches.

Sections 5.2–5.6 review the application of some of these principles within our radiation oncology department through a series of examples of our initiatives. The initiatives are grouped (e.g., automation/forcing functions, standardization, workplace) to provide a framework for the chapter. However, as some of the initiatives touch on multiple concepts, this grouping is somewhat imprecise. This is followed by discussion about the application of these principles in medicine in general, particularly in the realm of the electronic medical record.

5.2 MOVING PROCESSES TO THE "TOP" OF THE HIERARCHY OF EFFECTIVENESS: EXAMPLES APPLYING AUTOMATION AND FORCING FUNCTIONS

5.2.1 Consistent Naming of Radiation Treatment Plans

During the planning process, dosimetrists and physicians often generate alternative treatment plans for consideration/comparison. Without a naming convention, it can become difficult to remember which plan was which. Plans would often have names such as "4 field," "initial," "with extra field," "final," "really final." Sure, the knowledgeable user can figure out which plan is which by opening them or by looking at the directory to assess when the plan was made. But, that requires work. This is analogous to the challenge we face when we have multiple versions of an electronic document on our computer. It is easy to become confused if one does not use a strict naming convention.

How can this problem be addressed? Based on the hierarchy of effectiveness, there are multiple options (e.g., set a policy, train people, standardize processes, implement forcing functions, or automate the process). When we set a departmental policy (discussed with, and agreed to by, all of the stakeholders), it was only partly effective. Why? It is not because people are bad or are lazy. Rather, it is because people are human. We are busy, we multitask, we forget, we make typing errors, and we are easily distracted. Thus, in our clinic we modified our treatment-planning system such that all saved treatment plans are given a default name that includes the date, time, and name of the person who is logged in to the computer. The user often appends some additional descriptive information (e.g., treatment site or technique); e.g., "LM_040611_0935_RtBreastTangents." We have found this to be helpful in sorting through the directories with multiple plans, particularly during the iterative planning process and peer review sessions. A similar function was added to our planning system decades ago to automatically name beams based on their orientation.[1] A summary of these and examples of additional QA functions we have embedded within PLUNC, our University of North Carolina (UNC) planning system are shown in Table 5.1. Figure 5.2 illustrates features built-in to PLUNC and intended to enhance safety.

5.2.2 Goal Sheets

Review of the dosimetric parameters within an IMRT plan, and often even a conventional 3D plan, can be cumbersome and perhaps haphazard; there are many images and parameters to review. Typically, the provider will review a dose-volume histogram (DVH), identify some critical values (e.g., mean dose, V20), and compare this to some standard. This comparison is often done "in one's head," perhaps aided by some dose limits written on a piece of paper attached to the wall with a thumbtack. Alternatively, the goal sheet is a checklist where predetermined dose metrics from the plan are exported and automatically compared to departmental standards (Figure 5.3). Color coding is used to facilitate easy review of the data (e.g., parameters meeting the standards/goals are green and those out of range are red). For IMRT cases, we require that the goal sheet be signed prior to treatment initiation and have made tools in PLUNC to facilitate this signing at the time the plan is approved. Goal sheets are helpful during peer review, and their use enables harmonization of departmental standards and the rapid deployment of new or modified standards.

5.2.3 Pacemaker, Pregnancy, Prior Radiation

We had repeated incidents when information regarding pacemakers, pregnancy tests, or prior radiation (also known as the 3Ps) was either not known or not considered at the appropriate time. In many instances, the information was known at an earlier point in time, but it was just not conveyed to the appropriate person or not followed up (or not remembered) when needed. An analysis of the problem demonstrated that we had neither a uniform manner to document this information in the medical record nor a uniform manner to convey this information to those who needed to know it. For example, the physician might have

TABLE 5.1

Examples of QA Features Integrated into PLUNC

Goal		Functionality Added to PLUNC
Unambiguous beam names	→	Beams are automatically named to reflect their orientation gantry and table angles as well as use of bolus.
Unambiguous plan names	→	Plans are named automatically to reflect the treatment planner, date, and time to aid the tracking of the planning process. The user can append additional descriptive information as desired.
Ensure that DVHs are reviewed prior to plan approval	→	At time of plan approval, the associated dose-volume parameters for the plan are brought to the forefront of the computer screen.[a]
To facilitate assessment of whether the desired DVH dose constraints are achieved	→	Reference DVHs are displayed as an overlay with the treatment-plan-generated DVH.
To facilitate review of doses to multiple critical structures in a 3D or an IMRT plan	→	Dose metrics from the plan are exported to a "goal sheet," where these are compared to departmental standards (see Figure 5.3). Color coding is used to facilitate easy review of the data (e.g., parameters meeting the standards/goals are green and those out of range are red).
To facilitate review of the treatment plan within the EHR (i.e., without needing to open the planning system itself)	→	Reference documents from the planning system are exported to the document section of the EHR.
To reduce errors in isocenter placement if the treatment isocenter differs from the isocenter placed at the time of CT planning	→	The user is warned if the isocenter is changed after the simulation procedure.
To reduce errors using the incorrect isocenter for plans with multiple isocenters	→	Plans with multiple isocenters and beams of different isocenters are automatically labeled as such and are color coded on documentation.
Verify the calculated dose from PLUNC	→	The monitor unit calculation is automatically compared with an independent calculation. The user is warned if a 5% threshold difference is detected.

[a] The next-level iteration of this would require the user to "sign off" any DVH that was outside some "departmental standard," perhaps even requiring a comment regarding why the plan was being approved if it failed to meet this standard.

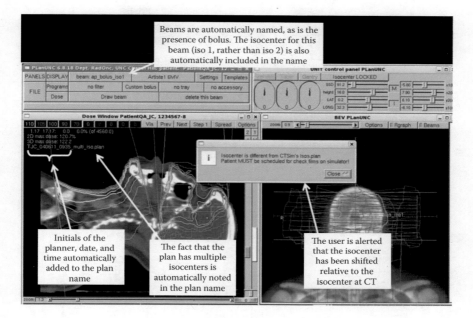

FIGURE 5.2

A screen shot of the PLUNC treatment-planning system illustrating three features aimed to enhance patient safety: (1) When the isocenter set at the time of computed tomography simulation is changed during the treatment-planning process, a warning window appears to alert the planner (the warning can prevent accidental isocenter change and remind the planner of the follow-up action needed if the isocenter was purposefully moved according to internal protocol); (2) the treatment plan is automatically named to include the initials of the planner, date, and time of the plan creation and to note if there are multiple isocenters in the plan; and (3) the treatment beams are automatically named by their orientation (i.e., gantry and couch angles), beam modifier used (e.g., wedge, compensator, bolus), and isocenter (i.e., if more than one isocenter is used). (Adapted with permission from Chera BS, Jackson M, Mazur LM, et al. *Semin Radiat Oncol* 2012;22:77–85.)

known about the prior radiation therapy and documented this in the consultation note, but this information was forgotten by the time the patient underwent treatment planning. Or, the presence of a pacemaker was known and maybe the provider told the nurse, who maybe told the physicist, who maybe gathered the necessary information, and so on. There was too much variation in the information flow. Pacemakers were sometimes identified by the therapist on the first day of scheduled treatment, leading to unexpected delays, replanning, and occasional chaos. Similar scenarios played out regarding pregnancy tests (e.g., "Is it needed?" "Was the result checked?" etc.).

Structure	Constraint	Result	Meet Goal?	N/A
PTV_SR_inskin	95% of the PTV receives 100% of the Rx	99.9 %	Yes	
	if not, does 100% of the PTV receive >= 95% of the Rx?			X
	>=99% of the PTV receives >= 93% of the Rx	100.0 %	Yes	
PTV_IR_inskin	95% of the PTV receives 100% of the Rx			X
	if not, does 100% of the PTV receive >= 95% of the Rx?			X
	>=99% of the PTV receives >= 93% of the Rx			X
PTV_HR_inskin	95% of the PTV receives 100% of the Rx	83.1 %	No	
	if not, does 100% of the PTV receive >= 95% of the Rx?	96.3 %	No	
	>=99% of the PTV receives >= 93% of the Rx	98.1 %	No	
Spinal Cord+3mm	Max 50 Gy to point dose	28.58 Gy	Yes	
Brainstem+3mm	Max 54 Gy to point dose	53.32 Gy	Yes	
Parotid_R+3mm	Mean dose <=26Gy			X
	50% receives < 30 Gy			X
Parotid_L+3mm	Mean dose <=26Gy	8.99 Gy	Yes	
	50% receives < 30 Gy	6.56 Gy	Yes	
Larynx+3mm	Mean dose <=41Gy	30.73 Gy	Yes	
	Volume receiving 60 Gy <= 24%	0.0 %	Yes	
Cochlea_R+3mm	Mean Dose < 45 Gy	31.72 Gy	Yes	
Cochlea_L+3mm	Mean Dose < 45 Gy	24.32 Gy	Yes	
Optical Chiasm+3mm	Max 50 Gy to point dose	53.74 Gy	No	
Optical Nerve_R+3mm	Max 50 Gy to point dose	63.96 Gy	No	
Optical Nerve_L+3mm	Max 50 Gy to point dose	54.22 Gy	No	
Retina_R+3mm	Max 45 Gy to point dose	65.04 Gy	No	
Retina_L+3mm	Max 45 Gy to point dose	52.78 Gy	No	
Lens_R+3mm	Max 10 Gy to point dose	45.22 Gy	No	
Lens_L+3mm	Max 10 Gy to point dose	25.76 Gy	No	
Pituitary+3mm	Mean Dose < 45 Gy	53.53 Gy	No	
Submandibular_R+3mm	Mean Dose < 35 Gy			X
Submandibular_L+3mm	Mean Dose < 35 Gy	10.89 Gy	Yes	
Oral Cavity	Mean Dose < 39 Gy			X
Constrictor	Mean Dose < 50 Gy			X
Unspecified tissue out PTV	<= 1% recieves > 110% of the Rx			X
Body	Max dose <= 110% of the Rx	106.1 %	Yes	

FIGURE 5.3
UNC head and neck IMRT goal sheet. The "Results" and "Meet Goal" columns are color coded, with red color indicating that the goal is not met ("No"; shown in enclosed box) and with green color indicating that the goal is met ("Yes").

Initial attempts to place a forcing function (also known as a "hard stop") in our work flow were not well received by the providers and staff. Neither were anxious to have yet another required step in their work (e.g., to enter or review information). The staff were worried about anticipated conflicts with the faculty if the necessary information was not provided (e.g., "Are we going to refuse to simulate the patient if the provider does not fill out the form?"). As the discussion evolved, we tried repeated attempts at education and reminders about policies and tried to standardize the flow of information. However, these were not effective, and the problems persisted.

We gathered data over many months (largely via our Good Catch program; see Section 6.3), and an assessment was performed using the A3 formalism (see Section 6.2). Armed with the data regarding persistent problems with the 3Ps, and the results of the A3, we were more readily able to institute a hard stop into our work flow to address this issue. Providers are now required to answer questions about the 3Ps in the Assessments Tool of Mosaiq˚.

- Pacemaker: No or Yes
- Pregnancy test: Not needed, Ordered/pending
- Prior radiation: No or Yes [get records]

These questions need to be answered prior to the simulation, and the simulator staff are empowered, and backed by the department chair, to refuse to simulate a patient unless these questions are addressed. This is a hard stop. The providers are encouraged to answer these three questions at the time of consultation, when the information is still fresh in their minds.

The therapists are required to review these three questions prior to simulation and to follow up pending issues if needed. If the patient is listed as having a pacemaker, they check with nursing and physics to be sure that the appropriate information about the pacemaker has been requested. If a pregnancy test is needed or was ordered, they follow up on the result. To improve efficiency, we recently instituted a rapid pregnancy test system that our nurses perform in clinic just prior to simulation. If the patient has had prior radiation, the therapist verifies that the necessary records have been requested.

From the provider's standpoint, this does require an extra step. However, overall, we believe that this is a reduction in work, and is liberating, as providers no longer need to worry about who they need to notify about the pacemaker, the need for a pregnancy test, and so on.

5.2.4 Detailed Simulation Instructions

The scenario described about the 3Ps was repeated for providers' instructions to the simulator. We were having occasional delays in the simulator and occasional rework that was associated with suboptimal communication to the simulator therapists. Initial attempts to have a formalized hard stop built into the work flow were understandably not well received by the providers. After additional data demonstrated persistent problems in this

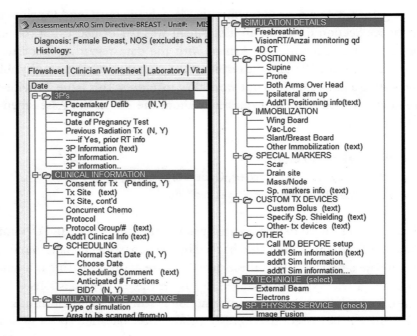

FIGURE 5.4

Portion of the Assessment Tool in Mosaiq® that serves as a checklist to be completed prior to computed tomographic (CT) simulation.

area and after several providers successfully piloted a formal "presimulation checklist" built in to the Assessment Tool of Mosaiq, we have now adopted a hard stop in our work flow. Providers are required to answer a series of questions prior to simulation. A portion of the content of the Assessment Tool is shown in Figure 5.4; it broadly addresses things such as treatment site, positioning, immobilization, oral/intravenous contrast (it prompts the provider to check the patient's creatinine value if intravenous contrast is being used), desired scan range, start date, number of anticipated fractions, image guidance, and so on.

We are basically asking the providers to give the information to the simulator that they will need to efficiently do their work. We recognize that the provider may not know the answer to all of the questions and thus "don't know" or "pending" is an acceptable answer for some of the questions. The therapists tell us that "don't know" or "it depends on the … " is preferable compared to having no communication at all. Sometimes, if the therapists understand the issues, they can be more informed regarding what to expect and plan accordingly. The questions for the 3Ps have been incorporated into the global Assessment Tool as well in order to reduce the number of checklists the providers need to address and reduce the number of places others need to go to retrieve information. In our daily morning huddle, the chief therapist reports on the number of anticipated simulations for that day and which patients have or do not have the Assessment Tool completed (further explained in Section 5.4).

5.2.5 Patient Self-Registration

Patients coming into the department for their daily treatment used to have to stop at a reception area where one of our clerical staff registered the patient into the system, essentially alerting the treatment machine that the patient had arrived. This was suboptimal. This was time consuming for staff, patients often had to wait (especially first thing in the morning), and there were occasional clerical errors (e.g., patients with similar/common names were not registered, and names were mistyped and needed to be reentered).

Therefore, we created a patient self-registration system. On the patient's day of simulation, patients are given a card with a bar code. On subsequent visits, the patient waves the card in front of an electronic scanner (much like one sees in the grocery store) that is linked to Mosaiq. This registers their arrival into Mosaiq, thus alerting the staff at the treatment machine. The patient receives audio feedback (a "beep" sounds) and visual feedback (a green light flashes at the scanner, and they can see the first few initials of their name appear on the computer screen adjacent to the scanner; see Figure 5.5). This has essentially eliminated much clerical work and patient waiting, increased the accuracy of registration, and empowered the patients to be a part of the process. A clerical staff member, positioned immediately adjacent to the scanner, greets the patient and is available to assist if the scanner is not working or if the patient has a concern.

Although this has been successful, it did raise an unexpected problem. The system was created with a focus on treatment patients (those coming in daily for repeated visits), with the notification/alert directed at the treatment machines. However, when some patients used their bar-coded cards to register for subsequent follow-up visits, the clinic staff was not alerted to their arrival. This led to some patients waiting unnecessarily. We have modified our processes to deactivate the bar code, and for the patient to discard their card, at the end of treatment (see Section 5.5.5 for more details). We have also altered signage to direct follow-up patients away from the scanner.

FIGURE 5.5
Patients self-register by waving a bar-coded card beneath the reader. This electronically notifies the machine that the patient has arrived. The patient receives audio and visual feedback of successful registration. This system saves time and is convenient and reliable.

5.2.6 Encouraging Staff to Wear Their UNC ID Badges

It is desirous for the staff to wear their UNC ID name badges so that patients and staff know everyone's name. To prevent unauthorized personnel from entering the "back door" of the department, these doors were fit with a lock and card reader. Fortunately, our ID badges also serve as the "pass" for the card reader. So, when we had the option to eliminate the locks on these doors (to make movement between the two floors of our department more fluid), we declined. This fostered an environment where most people wear their name badges (and we are maybe a tad safer as well).

5.3 MOVING PROCESSES "UP" THE HIERARCHY OF EFFECTIVENESS: EXAMPLES OF APPLYING STANDARDIZATION

For items that cannot be fully automated or amenable to forcing functions (e.g., technologically cannot be done; or some flexibility is needed for operations and improvement), standardization can be a useful approach. This section outlines several improvements along these lines.

5.3.1 Defining a Standard Way for Communication Regarding Patient Status in Our "Holding Area"

In our clinic, we have a "holding area" where inpatients are brought prior to, and after, their treatment or simulation. This is essentially an area where the patients are "handed off" from the transport staff to the machines and vice versa. We had problems with this arrangement because the nursing staff (responsible for the patients in the holding area) did not always know why the patients were there (e.g., "Is this patient on his or her way in or out of the department?" "Is he or she going for treatment or simulation?"). Communication between the nurses, transport staff, and therapists was somewhat haphazard.

To address this, we placed whiteboards on the walls behind each of the bays where the patients were placed. When bringing a patient into the holding area, the transportation staff or the therapy staff write on the whiteboard a few key facts about the patient: who they are, why they are there, and what step of the process pertains (e.g., "Mr. Smith, simulation done, ready to go back to the floor"; Figure 5.6).

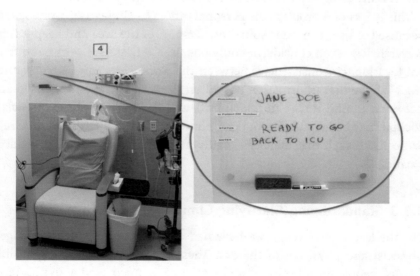

FIGURE 5.6

Whiteboards on the walls behind the bays in the recovery room where inpatients are brought before and after simulation and treatment. The staff write a few key facts about the patient to facilitate hand-offs between nursing and transportation and the simulation/treatment therapists.

5.3.2 Standard Work Space for Providers (the "Physician Cockpit")

For providers to do their work reliably and efficiently, they need ready access to information (e.g., phone numbers, instructions for various tasks). Thus, clinical work spaces are often littered with "important information" fixed to the wall. Because the important information evolves, and because different providers might share a work space, some clinical areas can become messy and cluttered, and no two workstations in a multiworkstation area are consistent.

To address this, we have designed a "core set of information" that we believe could be helpful for most providers. This information is affixed to the desktop surface of all work spaces and covered in glass. There is no reduction in the work space surface as the computer and mouse sit on top of the glass. Regardless of where the provider sits, the provider will have ready access to the same information. We hope that this aids in efficiency. We call this the "physician cockpit" because it is analogous to a pilot who is licensed to fly a particular make or model aircraft (Figure 5.7). No matter which particular plane they enter, if it is the same make and model, the controls are always in the expected (and consistent) location.

This is less of a problem for personal offices or single-user work spaces because the user can exert some "ownership" of the area and keep it tidy. Nevertheless, even considering only one user, if that user works at different locations, inconsistencies between the workplaces can be frustrating (e.g., "I have that information posted on the wall in my office, but I cannot seem to find it here in the clinic"), and the concept of the physician cockpit may be helpful. Similarly, we have tried to standardize each clinic exam room such that materials, equipment and forms are in predictable locations.

5.3.3 Standardizing/Clarifying Clinic Cross Coverage

For the last several years, we have had a formal publicly acknowledged physicist and physician of the day. These are the ultimately responsible "go-to" people for all otherwise-unassigned or uncovered activities (e.g., reviewing portal films for providers who are out of town, addressing the unexpected recalculation, addressing all urgent issues, filling in when others are not available). This system, and the general understanding of the system by all, has reduced the chaos in the clinic.

(A)

(B)

FIGURE 5.7

The clinical workspace for providers is often cluttered, with "important' information posted on the walls or on sticky notes on the work surface in a somewhat haphazard fashion (A). The "physician cockpit" (B) places often-used information in a reproducible location under glass on the tabletop, aimed to assist providers in their work.

To provide increased clarity, the "doc of the day" is prominently listed in red ink on the monthly physician's calendar that is posted throughout the department. The physicist of the day is similarly posted. Further, the physicist and physician of the day are announced during our daily morning huddle. Much of the work anticipated to "fall" to these people often becomes evident during the morning huddle. For example, as the names of patients for simulation or initiation of therapy are reviewed, the absence or presence of the responsible faculty is noted, as are potential conflicts (e.g., "Yes, I am here at 2 p.m., so I could probably cover the simulation, but there is a radiosurgery case at the same time, so I might not be able to get there."). Plans for coverage are determined at that time (i.e., to try to preempt chaos later in the day). Broadly speaking, there is wide satisfaction with this initiative. For this particular example, we do try to avoid the need for such cross coverage by synchronizing the simulation schedule with the provider's calendar. We have not yet tried to synchronize the "treatment initiation day" with the provider's calendar but that would be logical to do as well.

For example, one of the more problematic areas in our department used to be the computed tomographic (CT) simulator, specifically, the timely presence of the attending physician. This may not sound like a great problem, but when schedules are "tight" and one patient is delayed, it has a negative domino effect on several downstream processes. Often, the responsible faculty could not be found or had a competing commitment; if a resident was involved, the resident perhaps was not fully clear on what the faculty wanted. There were delays, rework, frustration, and waste. Accordingly, the CT simulator therapists began to build in cushion times in their schedule. Some therapists opted not to work in the CT simulator to avoid the conflict and frustration. The physician of the day, the morning huddle, and standardization of the presimulation orders has been a major improvement. The CT simulator therapists have the ability to do their work more efficiently and to better control their schedule. It is not unusual now for our CT simulator to serve upward of eight to ten patients per day (significantly increased from our prior limit of six). The simulation therapists stress the importance of clarity between physicians regarding what is needed or wanted in the simulator as a way to ensure smooth operations (i.e., communication between residents and attendings in the academic setting).

As it turns out, the physicists have long had a coverage system in place, but it was not codified and not known clearly to the rest of the department.

Similarly, when a faculty member had a scheduling conflict with a simulation, the person often would arrange for a colleague to cover. Nevertheless, having this coverage more overtly defined, and clear to all, helps the clinic run more smoothly.

5.3.4 Electronic Templates

Our institution recently adopted Epic as a system-wide EHR. In preparation for this, we spent a fair amount of time generating "standardized" notes for a variety of situations. The goal was to make it easier for the providers to generate the necessary documentation for different patient encounters (consultations, follow-ups, simulations, ongoing care management). Thus far, these have been of mixed utility. In retrospect, we placed too much emphasis on these template notes. We have found that for notes that are generally short (e.g., ongoing care management notes), the templates tended to make the notes too long, leading to "note bloat," thus making it harder for the subsequent reader to identify the critical patient-specific information. Generating patient-specific notes (e.g., typing or dictating) might yield more useful content and present it in a more efficient manner.

Nevertheless, "templating" some aspects of notes can be helpful as it reminds the provider to address each of the necessary areas, and this might be most valuable for the longer notes (e.g., consultations). Further, for all types of notes, standardization can provide some consistency so that providers can become accustomed to finding specific information in a consistent location within the records. For example, imagine if every posttreatment follow-up note was templated such that they all had a section called "disease status" where the provider was forced to choose one or several of these options:

- No evidence of cancer
- No evidence of progression
- Suspected recurrence or progression
- Continue current regimen
- Continue surveillance
- Consider change in therapy
- Other

A similar menu of discrete items can be used in a section called "normal tissue status," and formal toxicity grading can be applied to all patients.

These approaches are of potential value for both the creator and the consumer of these notes; indeed, many providers have adopted such standardization in their own notes. As these types of data are essentially discrete, they are more amenable to entry as discrete items or transformation into discrete data via natural language extraction, thus facilitating formal data analyses. Such discrete data elements may facilitate embedded tools in the EHR to increase contextual understanding of the content (discussed in more detail in Chapter 7).

As essentially anyone who has done a retrospective chart review can attest, most medical records are not very clear and determining even basic information is not always possible. For these sorts of items, adopting some standardization within the EHR is likely useful.

5.4 MOVING PROCESSES ONTO THE HIERARCHY OF EFFECTIVENESS: EXAMPLES OF APPLYING POLICY/ PROCEDURES AND TRAINING/EDUCATION

Formally defined policies and procedures are often necessary and helpful. First, they help to guide the creation of automated and forcing function tools and their associated work flows. For example, if the departmental policy calls for a signed treatment plan and signed prescription before treatment is delivered, software can be created to link these items (i.e., prevent treatment from being delivered unless the required electronic signatures are present). If a departmental policy calls for a signed consent prior to simulation, work flows can be structured to support forcing functions to facilitate this. Given the (often large) effort required to generate formal work flows and forcing functions, it is best if there is clarity regarding their goal (i.e., what policy they are reinforcing).

Further, a large fraction of work cannot be "automated" or "forced." Here, staff need an initial orientation to the policies and procedures to clearly set expectations. Staff are largely well intentioned and generally want to adhere to defined policies (especially if they agree with the policy). However, if staff does not agree with the policy or if the environment is not conducive to adherence education, compliance will tend to be suboptimal. Thus, we need to educate staff about the rationale for the policies and create an environment that is conducive to adherence. For example, if we require a consent form to be signed prior to initiation of therapy, these consent forms need to be readily available in the exam rooms where patients are being seen (ideally in a consistent, well-labeled location).

As staff are human, they will occasionally forget to adhere to policies (e.g., when they are busy), even if they have the best intentions. Thus, staff might need frequent, and maybe even continuous, reminders about policies and their associated expectations. One approach might be to continually monitor adherence, in real time and publicly, as part of QA. For example, our policy is that providers complete an Assessment Tool in Mosaiq prior to simulation. This serves as a checklist for the providers and as instructions to the simulation therapists. In our daily morning huddle, we display the simulation schedule, and the chief therapist will publically say, "We have XX patients on the simulation schedule today, and we have the Assessment Tool on all of the patients except the 11:00 case." The superficial goal is simply to remind the provider for the 11:00 case to complete the Assessment Tool (i.e., a form of QA). However, this is also a daily reminder, to all of the providers, of our departmental policy regarding completion of the Assessment Tool and the importance that we place on its completion (i.e., a form of continuous reinforcement of our desired optimal work flow).

It is important to recognize that we do not view the failure of a provider to fill out the Assessment Tool as an indictment of an individual staff person, but rather of our entire system (organization, workplace, and people). Have we done everything we can to make it "as easy as possible" for the Assessment Tool to be completed? Have we allotted adequate time, and provided access to the necessary information, to facilitate adherence to the policy? Only after those sorts of issues are addressed does one hold the individual primarily responsible for adherence. Even then, we recognize that providers become busy and can simply forget to perform this and other expected tasks. At UNC, we have made the Mosaiq software accessible from essentially any hospital computer (within our department, the multidisciplinary clinics, and inpatient hospital rooms) with the hope of making it easier for providers to comply with this policy.

We have a similar approach for required documentation (e.g., clinical treatment planning, simulation notes). Each week, a clerical person checks if the necessary documentation is present in the electronic record for the patients who initiated therapy during the prior week. A report is sent via e-mail to all providers noting compliance with this policy. The e-mail is sent out even if all of the documentation is present as a means of providing positive feedback and serving as a constant reminder that "this is important."

Policies are critical in guiding many of our technical procedures (e.g., treatment-planning tasks performed by dosimetrists), and in many cases, adherence is ensured through the use of checklists. For example, our dosimetrists use an extensive checklist when performing treatment planning. Supervisors spot-check these checklists as a means to promote their use. We have similar extensive policies and procedures for things such as machine calibration, IMRT QA, and so on.

We also have many unwritten, informal, policies that are created as needed in response to various system strains. These are typically agreed on by consensus of the stakeholders or are dictated by leadership, as needed. For example, if one of our treatment machines is particularly busy, we ask providers to try to limit their requests for that particular machine unless there is a clear clinical benefit. To reinforce the need for this informal policy, the chief therapist will announce the treatment volume on that machine each morning in our morning huddle. It serves as a reminder to the staff that we do care about this issue. This particular example has been the source of some interfaculty disputes because some physicians may perceive that their patients are not being allowed to access the "optimal" machine. Typically, if the providers believe that their patient will have a clinically meaningful benefit from being assigned to one machine versus another, we will comply with that request. However, they should be prepared to answer in public, "Beyond a better dose distribution, what is the prospect for a meaningfully-different clinical outcome?" These issues are often discussed in public in the morning huddle so that the staff and providers have clarity. Similar informal policies are made in response to machines being out of service for repairs (e.g., putting patients on break vs. replanning for another machine), schedule modifications due to weather or illness, and so on.

For many policies, the act of creating the policy can be enlightening; unexpected unknowns and inconsistencies in current practice are often identified. Opportunities to standardize and improve practices are often found. For example, we had a recent Kaizen event to better define the desired work flows for emergent/after-hours treatment and to create an associated policy. We addressed questions such as the following: Should emergent weekend cases have a CT simulation? Should we use blocked versus open fields? Is there a preferential machine to "turn on" during the weekend? The process unearthed marked variation in providers' understanding of what was possible, reasonable, or necessary in emergent situations and led to a good open conversation on these topics. The implications of some providers wanting access to the CT simulator on the weekend had an impact on which therapists could take call because not all of the therapists were equally comfortable in operating the CT simulator. This linkage was not previously known by most of the providers, including Larry.

Therefore, we believe it is necessary to have policies to define the desired work flows—to hardwire (e.g., automation, forcing functions) wherever possible and, for the rest, create a support/monitoring structure for the remainder that are "mission critical."

Because of tracking some of our good catches to our less-experienced radiation therapists, we are in the process of modifying our educational and evaluation policy for our radiation therapists. We are planning to add to their annual review a "check off" that the therapist has had peer review (by a fellow therapist) for setting up patients for different types of setups (e.g., clinical setups).

We will also modify some of our formal annual didactic and clinical training. A goal of this initiative is to increase safety mindfulness among the therapy staff. Among our senior therapy staff, their clinical training included an emphasis on double-checking and cross-referencing everything. There was always an assumption that anything could be wrong. From this type of training, these radiation therapists developed a skill set by which they questioned every setup for correctness. In the modern era, so much of the setup information is implemented "automatically" (e.g., field sizes, gantry angles, table positions). Given the power of the computer (e.g., "It must be right, it is on the computer"), younger therapists perhaps are less in tune to identifying potential problems in setups or that the setup could be wrong (see Section 2.3.2 for further discussion of this point). Although our therapists are all certified and complete continuing medical education for ongoing certification, we hope that these additional initiatives will be helpful. These initiatives were developed with input from the therapists, and we will similarly seek their input in assessing the utility of these initiatives. We have also tried to consistently pair more- and less-experienced therapists together, which we believe is helpful in addressing some of these issues.

5.5 WORKPLACE CHANGES INTENDED TO FACILITATE DESIRED BEHAVIORS AND OUTCOMES

5.5.1 Monitors in the Treatment Room Maze to Facilitate Patient Self-Identification

One of our safety initiatives is to ensure that we are delivering treatment to the intended patient. Certainly, our staff verifies the patient's name and a second identifier prior to treatment. However, it seems reasonable also to involve the patient. Patients have only their own treatment to worry about, and they usually are focused on that; perhaps they are less distracted and hassled than the staff. We mounted computer monitors in the mazes leading into our treatment rooms to display information from the Mosaiq chart of the patient's record that is opened on that machine at that time. The patients are instructed to look at the monitor to verify that their name and face are present on the screen (Figure 5.8).

FIGURE 5.8
Monitor in the maze to the treatment room to facilitate patient self-identification.

5.5.2 Communication among Staff and between Patients and Staff

Research has demonstrated that people are better able to communicate with each other if they know each other's names.[2] It is hard to say, "Hey you, I think you are about to make an error." Therefore, we have posted photos of all of our staff (along with their name and job title) in a public hallway in our clinic (readily available to staff and patients). Similarly, we have photos of the therapists in the hallway just outside the treatment rooms as well as in the area where gowned patients sit just prior to their treatment. We believe that the patients might be more comfortable speaking with the therapists if they know their names. We also have photos of the clinic staff (e.g., nurses and residents) at the patient entrance to the clinic and photos of the residents and dosimetrists near their offices (Figure 5.9).

5.5.3 Patient Discharge Instructions in the Rooms

We have created a one-page (double-sided) handout that is intended to assist with providing instructions to patients at the end of a course of radiation therapy. This is generic, with sections dedicated to the common issues that need to be addressed (e.g., fatigue, pain, dysuria, diarrhea, skin

FIGURE 5.9
Examples of staff photos that are posted throughout the department. This particular display has all of the staff who perform work related to the clinic. Similar photos of subsets of people are posted in other areas, such as outside the treatment rooms and in the clinic.

care, etc.). The provider can customize by circling the pertinent paragraphs for each specific patient. In this way, the handout can also serve as a reminder to the provider of the needs that should be considered as well. The handout also includes contact information for the clinic, as well as parking instructions for the follow-up visits (the parking arrangement that we have for our patients under treatment is not available for patients being seen in follow-up). These were posted on the exam room walls, with a sign encouraging patients to "Please take one if you are nearing completion of your course of radiation."

5.5.4 Color Coding Supplies in the Nursing Room

The nursing supply room for our clinic has over 50 items, all in similar size containers. It used to be hard to find things. Also, it was cumbersome for the people responsible for restocking of the bins to know what was needed. To make it somewhat easier to identify where things are located, each item was categorized by physiologic theme (gastrointestinal, genitourinary, hematology, skin care, etc.), and colored tape related to its category was added to each bin base (Figure 5.10). Although it is not "pretty," this does make it easier for the staff to locate things. We also alter the orientation of the label in the front of the container (rotating it 90 degrees) if that container needs to be restocked. We should move to a more formal Kanban card and dual-bin system to better address this challenge. These are Lean-based approaches to more readily and easily keep supply areas well stocked. For example, items in a container might be tightly stacked, and near the bottom of the stack (i.e., when it is close to being empty), there is a card that says "Restock bin X in room Y." When a user comes on that card, the user places the card in a nearby "central restocking information bin." The person responsible for restocking the bins only has to look in this central bin rather than needing to look in every bin as is commonly the case. The dual-bin system is similar. There are two bins for each item, and when one becomes empty, that empty bin can be placed in a larger "central restocking bin." Again, the person responsible for restocking the bins only has to look in this central location. These approaches are easier, faster, and more reliable than the current setup.

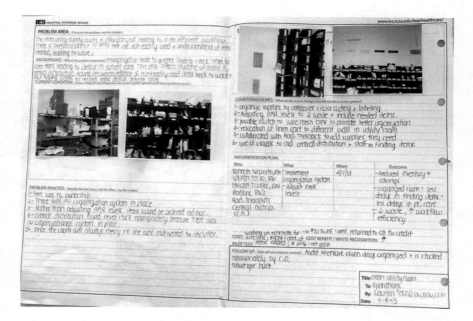

FIGURE 5.10

Completed A3 addressing our supply room. On the left are images taken before the improvement initiative. Note that all of the bins looked alike, and finding things was challenging. On the right are images taken after the improvement activity. The bins are color coded based on their category (e.g., gastrointestinal, genitourinary, hematology, skin care, etc.), making it somewhat easier to find things.

5.5.5 Retrieving the Self-Registration Cards from Patients at the End of Therapy (to Prevent Them from Trying to Use Them at a Follow-up Visit)

At the end of a patient's course of therapy, they are offered to ring the gong located in the department lobby (we like to think that it sends a sound of hope to the other patients). This is often a big deal for the patients, who frequently come in for the last day with multiple family members and their cameras. Immediately beneath the gong is a container where the patients are asked: "Place your plastic registration card in here" (Figure 5.11). This is our way of trying to avoid the problem of the patients using these cards at their follow-up visits (see Section 5.2.5 addressing patient self-registration).

FIGURE 5.11

The "gong" and the "black box." At the end of therapy, the patient is invited to hit the gong in our lobby. This is a symbolic way to end their radiation treatment at UNC. The black box on the side is intended to remind the patient to return their self-registration card (as this will not work properly when the patient returns for follow-up). This is analogous to many hotels asking for their plastic room entry card to be returned. The location of the gong in our lobby is better appreciated in Figure 5.15.

5.5.6 Lobby versus Waiting Room

The presence of a "waiting room" sends a signal to both patients and staff that waiting is to be expected and is indeed almost part of the "natural state of things." To try to eliminate this negative expectation, our signage for this area says "Lobby" (Figure 5.12). Maybe this is trivial, but we think it is important.

5.5.7 Mirrors in Hallways to Prevent Collision

Approximately every quarter, departmental leadership (e.g., the chair, administrator, safety director) visit front-line staff, at their workplace, and say, "Tell us anything that would make the area safer or make your job easier." We term these "safety rounds" (see Section 6.7.2 for details). We often receive more than ten suggestions during a one-hour safety round tour. During one of our first sessions, a radiation therapist at a linear accelerator

FIGURE 5.12
Lobby sign. We use the word *Lobby*, rather than *Waiting Room*, to reduce the expectation for waiting.

noted that there had been several "near collisions" and one actual collision between stretchers, wheelchairs, and people at a specific corner where several hallways converged. We consequently added a concave mirror on the wall at the intersection to reduce this risk (Figure 5.13). The idea for the mirror came from a front-line employee, who noticed something that happened infrequently, but that could have major detrimental consequences for the safety of patients and employees.

5.6 EXAMPLE CHANGES AIMED TO IMPROVE WORKLOAD AND REDUCE STRESSORS

5.6.1 HDR Brachytherapy Workload

Workload appeared to be relatively high for nurses assisting with high-dose brachytherapy (HDR) procedures for gynecologic cancers (because of our high volume and the nature of these procedures). In an attempt to reduce their workload, Dr. Prithima Mosaly (a *Human Factors Engineer*

FIGURE 5.13
Mirror in hallway to prevent collisions, added based on a suggestion made during "safety rounds."

in our department) observed 45 hours of activities related to 15 brachytherapy procedures. This allowed her to divide the goal-oriented procedures into various tasks, and she collected NASA-TLX scores on the identified tasks (done as part of a broader research program detailed in Chapter 7). Four tasks scored the highest level of workload: (1) CT scan and radiation delivery preparation, (2) patient identification and preparation, (3) preparation of the cervix, and (4) physician outreach and assistance during the procedure. Several errors were noted to occur during these high-workload tasks (e.g., information miscommunication, incorrect placement of catheters/tubes). These errors did not result in patient harm but did cause rework and consequentially unnecessary stress and frustration. She then used the systematic human error reduction and prediction approach (SHERPA) to classify potential errors related to high-workload tasks.[3] Based on the systematic review of the tasks and work space, changes were made to standardize the work and to improve the physical layout of the HDR treatment room (see Table 5.2 for a summary). These changes were implemented over about 16 months. Repeat NASA-TLX scores collected after the interventions (with the

TABLE 5.2

Human Factors Improvements Made to Reduce Workload for Brachytherapy Nurses

Improvements	Result
Medication table was moved next to the patient's bed.	Improved efficiency/work flow.
Additional instruments were purchased to improve efficiency.	Prior to this, only one set was available and had to be cleaned prior to each HDR procedure, causing significant delays and interruptions.
Glove box was moved from the sink to worktable/patient's bed.	Improved efficiency/work flow.
Sterile gowns and caps were moved to provide more direct access.	Improved efficiency/work flow.
An additional, portable examination light was placed in the treatment room.	Improved efficiency. Previously, one light was shared between multiple providers, limiting productivity.
Phone numbers at the nurses' desk in the HDR suite and at the patient's bedside were changed to carry the same number.	Reduced rework. Prior to this change, the nurse had to tend to two phones.
All HDR cables are now tethered together.	Improved efficiency and safety. Prior to this change, often the nurse would have to search for a missing catheter. Also, tethering them together has reduced inadvertent disconnection from the HDR unit and brachytherapy apparatus.

same nursing staff) noted reduced (i.e., improved) workloads compared to the prior measurements (see Figure 5.14). Since implementation, most changes have been sustained with some further refinements.[4,5]

5.6.2 Reducing the Frequency and Sources of Stressors

During formal monitoring in 2010, we observed that radiation therapists working on our linear accelerators were interrupted an average of four times per patient treatment (treatment times were approximately 15–25 minutes). A sizable fraction of the interruptions was phone calls to the machine area from the lobby and nursing inquiring whether they were "on time" and other nonurgent communication.

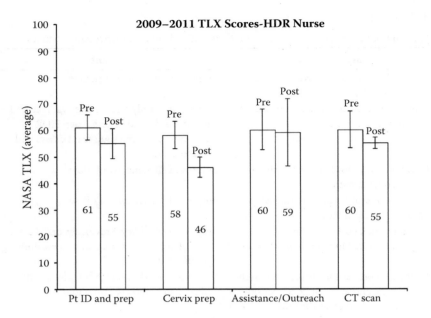

FIGURE 5.14

Impact of improvement initiatives on the workload level for the nurses performing high-dose-rate (HDR) brachytherapy procedures. National Aeronautics and Space Administration Task Load Index (NASA-TLX) scores for HDR nurses before (2009) and after (2011) interventions were implemented to standardize or streamline work-flow, remove non-value-added tasks (see Table 5.2), and improve the HDR room layout. The tasks listed on the *x* axis are those identified as having the highest workload levels. The workload levels postintervention appear to be somewhat reduced (improved) compared with the preintervention levels and are closer to or below acceptable absolute levels (NASA-TLX < 55). (Adapted with permission from Chera BS, Jackson M, Mazur LM, et al. *Semin Radiat Oncol* 2012;22:77–85.)[5]

We implemented a multiprong approach aimed to reduce interruptions, including (in increasing level of effectiveness) staff education, encouraging use of an alternative Mosaiq-based means of communication to the therapists for nonurgent matters, rerouting of some phones, and placing large electronic message boards reporting the machine status in public areas (e.g., lobby and nursing station). The last is analogous to the "on time" message boards we all rely on in airports (Figure 5.15). Following the implementation of these interventions, the mean number of interruptions was reduced from a preintervention level of 4 (range 0–11) to a postintervention level of less than 1 (range 0–3) (Figure 5.16).

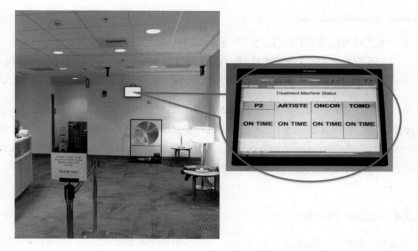

FIGURE 5.15
Monitors (present in the lobby and clinic) display the machine status, thereby reducing phone calls to the therapists (see Figure 5.16). This was instituted as part of a multifaceted strategy to reduce interruptions of the therapists on the treatment machines.

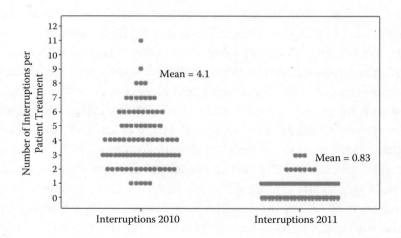

FIGURE 5.16
The number of interruptions of radiation therapists on treatment machine, per patient treatment, is shown before and after implementation of a series of operational changes (including the monitors shown in Figure 5.15). Each dot represents an observation of a single patient's treatment. In 2010, therapists were interrupted on average four times per patient treatment. Several policies were implemented to reduce interruptions, and on repeat measurement, the average number of interruptions was less than one ($P < .001$).

5.7 "GOING PAPERLESS": EXAMPLE CHANGES INSTIGATED BY OUR ADOPTION OF A RADIATION ONCOLOGY ELECTRONIC HEALTH RECORD SYSTEM

A factor in many safety events is inaccurate, untimely, unclear, and absent communication between people. Recognizing this, we have made a concerted effort to improve communication and teamwork within our department while transitioning from paper to an EHR system.

5.7.1 Clinic Work Flow

A particular challenge has been integrating a radiation-specific EHR system into our work flow. In approximately 2008 to 2009, our clinic completed its transition to an EHR system (Mosaiq) that includes scheduling and clinic support, replacing the previously used paper chart. However, the paper chart served functions that were not readily provided by Mosaiq. For example, the chart served as a visual cue to prompt staff that patients were ready for movement between stations in the clinic (e.g., lobby, simulation, treatment machines, and clinic exam room). Loss of this visual cue led to disrupted flow, unnecessary waiting, and nursing rework and overwork. Over a three-day period, we performed detailed observations of clinical operations. We identified multiple opportunities for altering processes to reduce wasted motion and wait times and to better utilize staff. We instituted a multiprong system that included the following: (1) a central whiteboard and color-coded plastic sleeves identifying patient location by physician and arrival time and (2) a flag system at each exam room to alert providers to waiting patients (Figure 5.17). We hired a unit coordinator to disseminate limited, key information from Mosaiq to the whiteboard and assist with communications. We quantified the impact of these initiatives on clinic staff satisfaction (via survey). After the initial switch to Mosaiq, only 16% of responding clinicians and nurses (3 of 19) were satisfied with the overall patient flow in the clinic. After implementation of our initiatives (e.g., whiteboard to track patients in the clinic), satisfaction increased to 85% (17 of 19). Other improvements in clinical flow are shown in Table 5.3.

FIGURE 5.17

Several of the workplace initiatives to assist with patient flow in the clinic. Left, large whiteboard centrally located in the clinic shows the names of patients who are in exam rooms, along with the time that they entered the room. Patients waiting in the lobby are noted by color-coded plastic sleeves (different colors for each provider). Each provider's work is in one column, with the names of the "team" (e.g., provider, nurse, resident/extender) at the top of each column. Personnel names are on magnetic boards readily moved as needed. Right, flag system at each exam room noting when (for example) providers need to attend to the patient.

TABLE 5.3

Metrics of Patient Flow Assessed Pre- and Postimprovements (See Text)

Metric	Pre versus Post	Improvement (%)	P Value
Time from patient registration to patient placement in a clinic room (mean)	31 vs. 17 min	45	<.01
Time from patient leaving the lobby to patient being ready to see the provider (mean)	28 vs. 20 min	29	<.01
Percentage of patients experiencing delays on the simulator	>50% vs. < 10%	≈80	<.01

5.7.2 Using Electronic Work Lists to Help Track Work Flow and Tasks

Radiation treatment-planning processes have several sequential handoffs between team members (e.g., nurses, simulator therapists, dosimetrists, physicians, physicists, and treatment therapists). Generally, each team member's completion of assigned tasks is needed for other team members to perform subsequent work. Delayed task completion (e.g., because of busyness or failure to remember to do something) can have troubling domino effects. We capitalized on our transition to a paperless chart (see preceding section) by utilizing the quality checklist (QCL) function in Mosaiq to help track our work flow and tasks to be completed. A QCL item can be created for a patient by a Mosaiq user, and the item can be assigned to another user, instructing that user regarding what and when tasks need to be completed. Users can access their personal QCL (i.e., work list), and they can see all their required tasks. Once the task is completed, it can be signed off electronically.

The QCL work list system is reliably used by all professional subgroups in our department *except* physicians. Some physicians found it cumbersome to have to navigate in Mosaiq to their QCL work list; some were confident in relying on their memory and diligence to complete tasks responsibly. To further ensure timely completion of radiation therapy planning tasks among the physicians, we developed a visual display of the Mosaiq QCL data. Gregg Tracton (a computer programmer in our department) created a visual display of the QCL data that we term the eWhiteboard. This computer program automatically extracts QCL data (which is entered into Mosaiq as part of the normal work of the dosimetrists, therapists, physicists) and displays a timeline of when critical tasks are due. The timeline counts backward from the desired date of the first treatment to determine when previous tasks would need to be completed (to meet that start date). Critical events/tasks displayed include the simulation date, image segmentation (–5 days), peer review (if IMRT) (–4 days), plan approval (–2 days), pretreatment QA date (–1 day), the first treatment date (day 0). Each patient is noted by name, along with the patient's diagnosis (a blank reminds the provider to enter a diagnosis into Mosaiq) and the responsible dosimetrist and physician. The eWhiteboard is displayed on 42-inch television monitors in the physician's clinic workroom and in dosimetry (i.e., "high-traffic areas" for the providers). Entries are color coded (e.g., tasks due for completion that day are yellow, and tasks that are overdue are red) (Figure 5.18). Thus, from a distance, one can readily assess if work is proceeding as expected for individual patients, providers, and so on. Again, this is analogous to the arrival/departure monitors in airports, where many red entries are readily interpreted as delays.

We also use the QCLs for various other functions. For example, when a patient has a CT simulation, the simulation therapist sends the following

FIGURE 5.18

Screenshot of our eWhiteboard that is displayed on 42-inch monitors within both dosimetry and the physicians' clinic workroom. This provides a visual display, by patient and provider, of the dates needed for various tasks to be completed (e.g., plan review) based on the anticipated date to start treatment. This is generated from the QCL entries in Mosaiq. Entries are color coded (e.g., tasks due for completion that day are yellow, and tasks that are overdue are red); thus, from a distance, one can readily assess if work is proceeding as expected for individual patients, providers, and so on.

QCLs: (1) to the physician for image segmentation and generation of a treatment-planning note; (2) to the list of patients needing pre-radiation therapy peer review; (3) to dosimetry for treatment planning; (4) to physics for special procedures (four-dimensional computed tomographic [4D-CT] reconstruction); and (5) to the financial counselor for IMRT preauthorization (although we recently had to modify this in response to changes in the precertification requirements).

5.8 SUMMARY

The representative initiatives outlined in this chapter summarize our work aimed to improve our workplace—to make it easier for staff to do what they want and need to do. This represents the concerted efforts of countless people, each identifying and helping to facilitate many small (and sometimes large) changes. These efforts are supported by the organization (Chapter 4) and rely on people being involved (e.g., identifying opportunities for improvement, implementing and evaluating change; Chapter 6).

To some people, some of these concepts and items discussed in this chapter may seem trivial and not worth the bother. We strongly disagree. Too often, the physical space within which we work serves as an impediment to our completion of work. Placing workers in suboptimal environments is disrespectful, increases risks, and sends the message that leadership does not really care about quality and safety.

We do not expect baseball players to perform on muddy baseball fields, bus drivers to drive with cracked windshields, or surgeons to operate in dark rooms. Then, there are the many little things as well. In baseball, we make sure that the batter's box is well marked, the grass in the far corner of right field is well groomed, and the bats have just the right amount of resin. For bus drivers, we make sure the seat is comfortable, the seat and windows are well positioned, and so on. All of these things are done (at least in part) to optimize performance.

If we value our colleagues and our patients, we need to address our work space. Even small issues can matter, and many small inconveniences or issues can add up to reduce our performance and harm our spirit (perhaps undermining transitions to *Initiating* and *Enhancing* behaviors; see Section 3.4.1). The fundamental principles of Human Factors Engineering and the hierarchy of effectiveness are powerful, and their systematic application to medical practice has tremendous potential. They can directly enhance safety, quality, and efficiency (through improvement initiatives) and indirectly as well (e.g., by promoting safety mindfulness).

REFERENCES

1. Sailer SL, Bourland JD, Rosenman JG, et al. 3-D beams need 3-D names. *Int J Radiat Oncol Biol Phys* 1990;19:797–798.
2. Hargie O. *The Handbook of Communication Skills*. 3rd ed. London, UK: Routledge; 2006.
3. Embrey DE. SHERPA: A systematic human error reduction and prediction approach. Paper presented at the International Meeting on Advances in Nuclear Power Systems; Knoxville, TN; April 1986.
4. Mosaly P, Mazur L, Banes D, et al. Interventions in standardizing work procedures and reducing stress in high-dosage-radiation nurses' work. Paper presented at the International Forum on Quality and Safety in Healthcare Expo 2012; Paris; April 2012.
5. Chera BS, Jackson M, Mazur LM, et al. Improving quality of patient care by improving daily practice in radiation oncology. *Semin Radiat Oncol* 2012;22:77–85.

6

Driving Change at the People Level

LEARNING OBJECTIVES

After completing this chapter, the reader should be able to:

1. Understand the rationale for a formalized system to have all employees involved in improvement work;
2. Understand how we apply the A3 thinking and Plan–Do–Study–Act (PDSA) to develop our people and improve systems; and
3. Understand some of the methods we use to promote safety mindfulness.

6.1 PEOPLE LEVEL

6.1.1 The Importance of "People"

In the paradigm of the nested levels (organization, workplace, and people), the "people level" is the most important component to meaningfully impact high reliability and value creation in the long run (Figure 6.1). Certainly, motivated and strong leaders, automated systems, and forcing functions can have positive impacts on operations, such as by setting organizational priorities, by defining behavioral norms (see Chapter 4 for additional concepts), and by improving the workplace and work flows (see Chapter 5). However, improvement activities driven only at organizational and workplace levels may not be that impactful. First, leaders typically do not have the necessary knowledge to optimize the workplace and work flows. That knowledge lives within the workers themselves, who are obviously closer to the work being done. Second, the capacity of an entire organization's workers is far greater than that of their leadership. Improvement is hard

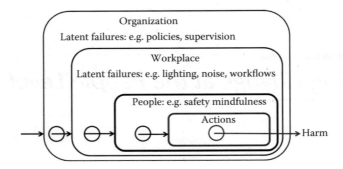

FIGURE 6.1
Nested configuration of the Swiss Cheese Model with safety mindfulness at the inner-most level of the model, representing the most important component to meaningfully impact high reliability and value creation in the long run.

work and time consuming. Just as "many hands make light work," many minds will provide more ideas for innovative improvement. Thus, empowering all people on this mission will increase the yield (see Figure 3.12 in Chapter 3).

Even if the leadership were omniscient (all knowing) and omnipotent (all powerful), improvement initiatives that do not broadly include everyone are likely not going to be sustained over time. Buy-in from the front-line workers is easier to achieve if they are the ones who are brainstorming and implementing the improvements. They are more likely to take ownership; hence, the improvements have a better chance of being sustained. Because improvement is a continuous process, a one-time "quick fix" (even if correct at that instant) likely will not yield long-term benefits.[1] Rather, one needs to motivate and empower all to be continually actively involved. A wise phrase that well addresses this point is, "If you want something done fast, do it yourself. If you want something to last, involve others" (attribution unknown).

Initiatives at the people level involve many more people than do those at the organizational or workplace levels and thus are more difficult. This is totally analogous to team sports. People need to be trained, nurtured, and managed as both individuals and as part of the team. Getting people to work constructively with each other can be tough because each person brings their own biases and preferences to any joint activity. Many of the challenges that leaders face in creating, nurturing, and managing the people level are discussed in Chapter 4.

6.2 FORMALIZING PEOPLE-DRIVEN QUALITY INITIATIVES: A3 THINKING AND PLAN–DO–STUDY–ACT

We believe that it is important to have "formalism" for improvement work. This provides a systematic manner to consider and address concerns and to monitor initiatives. It provides a mechanism for all workers, at all levels, to raise concerns and participate in improvement activities. Without such a formalism (e.g. A3s), staff largely raise issues and problems (e.g. in the form of complaints) without always thinking deeply about the causes and potential countermeasures to improve the system. Expecting to be heard, staff feel content having called attention to the problem and handing it off to managers to "fix." There is an absence of any method for prioritizing improvements. Lost are the opportunities to gain from the frontline staff knowledge of the problems and to demonstrate to them how their work is interconnected to others. Ad hoc approaches are less likely to be successful. Indeed, the current state of our healthcare system perhaps reflects the results of ad hoc approaches. A formal structure is intended to make all employees, even the most junior, feel comfortable raising their concerns and actively engaging in improvement work. Formalism also sets a framework and expectation for leadership to constantly and more readily support changes. The formalism indeed represents a public acknowledgment from the leadership that "our systems are suboptimal; we alone do not know how to optimally improve things, and we need everyone's help." This is indeed a powerful statement from leadership to their employees. The formalism that we have embraced for our people-driven improvement efforts involves the iterative Plan–Do–Study–Act (PDSA) management method supported by an A3 tool. The steps are:

1. Plan (i.e., hypothesis): establish objectives, goals, targets, and the new process to be tested.
2. Do (i.e., experiment): implement the new plan/execute the new process.
3. Study (i.e., measure): measure outcomes/monitor the new process, understand better the differences between the old and new process and their relative effectiveness.
4. Act: modify processes accordingly.

It is common (indeed expected) that the PDSA cycle will be applied several times before the optimal "future state" is defined. Further, the PDSA problem-solving method will need to be reapplied as needs evolve over time. However, for tightly coupled systems, in which the effects of any changes may propagate quickly (see Chapter 3, Section 3.1, for details), extra care must be taken to assess the system implications of considered changes. For example, changes in our planning software (PLUNC, University of North Carolina [UNC] planning system) are brought forward only in the context of strict procedural tests to assess and verify their impact.

The A3s are a formal tool for workers to systematically consider problems and possible improvements and to communicate this information to stakeholders and management. A3s empower people helping us create a cultural shift toward grassroots improvements and ownership. Perhaps this is best represented by a quote from Eiji Toyoda[2]: "One of the features of the Japanese workers is that they use their brains as well as their hands. Our workers provide 1.5 million suggestions a year, and 95 percent of them are put to practical use. There is an almost tangible concern for improvement in the air at Toyota."

Often, the success of A3s depends on relationships between individuals involved in problem solving. Researchers studying applications of A3s for problem solving in healthcare found that A3s help (1) establish a common language and meaningful indicators to analyze and measure progress on problem solving; (2) provide mechanisms for linking process issues with human behaviors and decision making; and (3) supply a platform for analyzing underlying cultural aspects of quality and patient safety issues.[3-5]

Similarly, we have created a formal system for managing the A3s. This was needed to ensure that employees have the competencies to analyze and improve their processes. This is operationalized using an "A3 management" cycle. The A3 program is run and supported by the multidisciplinary Quality and Safety Committee led by Bhisham. The committee meets weekly to (1) discuss process performance; (2) identify targets for improvement; (3) review good catches; (4) review and approve A3s (when ready); and (5) plan for future Kaizens (continued improvement efforts with dedicated time for employees). Our goal is to define a standard manner for doing and managing improvement work.

The A3 program is run by a program manager, Kinley Taylor, an industrial engineer specializing in process improvement. Managing the A3s includes training (Section 6.2.1), ongoing coaching (Section 6.2.2), approval process and implementation (Section 6.2.3), sustainability

(Section 6.2.4), visual management (Section 6.2.5), and rewards/recognition (Section 6.2.6).

6.2.1 Training

All employees (including physicians and new employees) have 1 hour of formal training. Trainees were given a hard copy of the training material, along with step-by-step instructions for completing the A3 process. Originally, training was developed and spearheaded by Lukasz. After about 1 year, leadership was transitioned to Kinley. She is a perfect fit for this job—she is dedicated to improving quality, believes in the inclusive nature of our A3 program, and thus prioritizes her time to coaching employees involved in A3 projects. Kinley works well with others and has high respect for her supervisors and teammates. We were impressed with the rapid pace that she mastered the practical essence of the A3 and how to best train people to use A3s.

6.2.2 Coaching

After initiation of an A3, people are encouraged to work with Kinley, who will coach them through the problem-solving process. Typically, staff approach Kinley with their A3 partially completed and usually seek assistance with the problem analysis (root cause analysis) and follow-up. With experience, employees require less-formal coaching. Lauren Terzo, one of our nurses-leaders who embraced the A3 program early in its implementation stages, completed several A3s (with coaching) and then became a coach herself for her fellow nurses. This led to more nurses engaging in A3s (see Section 6.2.6). The A3 owners are also encouraged to collaborate with their fellow employees and stakeholders to ensure they understand all facets of the problem and develop robust countermeasures that have group consensus. All stakeholders are required to sign the A3 as written agreements to the proposed changes.

Sometimes, A3 topics reach beyond the employee's (A3 owner's) work area. In this case, they can request that a multidisciplinary team meet to develop countermeasures. In such circumstances, Kinley usually facilitates a brief meeting or a half- to full-day Kaizen event to work out the potential improvement ideas (or countermeasures). Fifteen Kaizen event days (~120 hours) were held between 2009 and 2013. This allowed stakeholders from different groups to collaborate, understand the complexity of the processes, open lines of communication, and build a team atmosphere. After completion of the A3 (with or without a formal Kaizen event), the A3 owner presents the countermeasures and implementation plan to the Quality and Safety Committee.

The actual pieces of paper (the A3s) are kept by the owner and updated (as needed) until they are implemented. Once implemented, these A3 papers are stored with Kinley, in a binder, and are available for reference.

6.2.3 Approval Process and Implementation

The Quality and Safety Committee is the governing body for approving and supporting A3 efforts. Once an employee has done their own research and completed the first half of the A3 (problem description through root cause analysis), the employee is welcome to come to the weekly meeting held by the Quality and Safety Committee for assistance and guidance. Typically, the person might speak to the several members of the committee with particular interest and expertise in the A3. After completing the second half of the A3, the employee presents the proposed countermeasures and implementation plan to the committee for approval before implementation (an example of a completed A3 is shown in Figure 6.2).

Data are collected on a number of approved A3s, discontinued A3s, number of staff submitting A3s, number of staff with multiple A3 submissions, and number of Kaizen events originating from A3s. Overall, we have had 32 A3s initiated by 21 different "owner" staff members from all of the different department areas. Six staff initiated more than one, and three Kaizen events originated via A3s (additional Kaizen events were initiated outside the A3 structure). Table 6.1 summarizes our departmental A3-based improvements. Overall, 22 A3s have been implemented, 8 are in progress, and 2 were piloted and discontinued (see Section 6.2.7 concerning challenges).

6.2.4 Sustainability

Following implementation, the outcomes of A3s are monitored for effectiveness and sustainability for approximately three months. Typically, Kinley conducts 30-, 60-, and 90-day check-ins with the A3 owners to assess their perceptions, and if possible, data are collected over time. If the A3 was related to a specific tangible process or area, the Quality and Safety Committee might go on periodic *Gemba* (go and see) walks to assess the

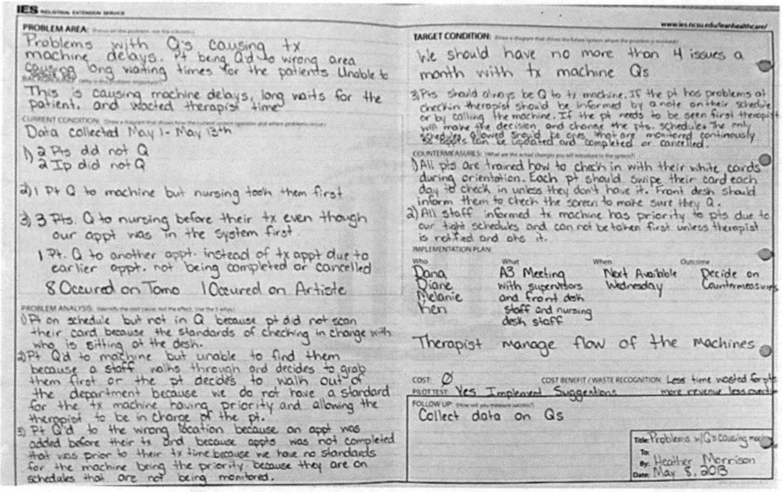
IES

PROBLEM AREA:
Problems with Q's causing tx machine delays. Pt being Q'd to wrong area causing long waiting times for the patients Unable to

BACKGROUND:
This is causing machine delays, long waits for the patient, and wasted therapist time

CURRENT CONDITION:
Data collected May 1- May 13th
1) 2 Pts did not Q
2 Ip did not Q
2) 1 Pt Q to machine but nursing took them first
3) 3 Pts. Q to nursing before their tx even though our appt was in the system first
1 Pt. Q to another appt. instead of tx appt due to earlier appt. not being completed or cancelled
8 Occured on Tomo 10ccured on Artiste

PROBLEM ANALYSIS:
1) Pt on schedule but not in Q because pt did not scan their card because the standards of checking in change with who is sitting at the desk.
2) Pt Q'd to machine but unable to find them because a staff walks through and decides to grab them first or the pt decides to walk out of the department because we do not have a standard for the tx machine having priority and allowing the therapist to be in charge of the pt.
3) Pt Q'd to the wrong location because an appt was added before their tx and because appts was not completed that was prior to their tx time because we have no standards for the machine being the priority because they are on schedules that are not being monitored.

www.ies.ncsu.edu/leanhealthcare/

TARGET CONDITION:
We should have no more than 4 issues a month with tx machine Qs
3) Pts should always be Q to tx machine. If the pt has problems at checkin therapist should be informed by a note on their schedule or by calling the machine. If the pt needs to be seen first therapist will make the decision and change the pts. schedules. The only schedules allowed should be ones that are monitered continously so appts can be updated and completed or cancelled.

COUNTERMEASURES:
1) All pts are trained how to check in with their white cards during orientation. Each pt should swipe their card each day to check in unless they don't have it. Front desk should inform them to check the screen to make sure they Q.
2) All staff informed tx machine has priority to pts due to our tight schedules and can not be taken first unless therapist is notified and oks it.

IMPLEMENTATION PLAN:

Who	What	When	Outcome
Dana Diane Melanie Ken	A3 Meeting with supervisors and front desk staff and nursing desk staff	Next Available Wednesday	Decide on Countermeasures

Therapist manage flow of the machines

COST: Ø
COST BENEFIT / WASTE RECOGNITION: Less time wasted for pts more revenue less overtime
PILOT TEST: Yes Implement Suggestions

FOLLOW UP:
Collect data on Qs

Title: Problems w/Q's causing machine
To:
By: Heather Morrison
Date: May 5, 2013

FIGURE 6.2
A completed A3. Led by a radiation therapist, Heather Morrison, and addressed problems with patient queuing (tracking).

new process. Subjective opinion-based data on the threats to A3 sustainability are also collected. The committee typically revisits projects on a yearly schedule to further assess sustainability or the need for modifications. We must emphasize and acknowledge that we have not always done as well as we could with sustainability, particularly in our early years. As a result, some of our early initiatives decayed with time.

6.2.5 Visual Management

Visual management displays are present throughout the department and are used to keep information flowing between the Quality and Safety Committee and the department (to individual employees and collectively to groups). These visual tools are used to highlight A3-related items. For example, Figure 6.3 shows a board located in the central department conference room (where we have our morning huddles). The board provides a summary of A3-related activities, and a quick glance at the display provides employees with an update of the status improvement initiatives. The presence of the board itself, posted prominently in the main conference room, is a constant reminder of the department's focus on improvement efforts.

TABLE 6.1

Summary of Improvements Related to A3s

A3 Title	Description and Results
Automatic Doors	Installed automatic doors for improved patient transport
CyberKnife Protocols	Developed standard protocols for different types of CyberKnife patients
Recovery Room	Standardized operations in recovery room
CT Simulator Phone	Implemented new scheduling phone for simulator
Quick Rx	Improved information flow for patient prescriptions
OP-IP Protocols	Improved process for inpatient to outpatient transition during course of treatment
Consent and creatinine levels	Developed a standard procedure for pretreatment consent, creatinine and IVs
CT Imaging for protocol patients	Improved notification of protocol patients and protocol guidelines
3Ps	Implemented safety barrier to screen for pregnancy, pacemaker, or prior radiation for 100% of patients
Nurse Carts	Standardized and implemented Kanban system for restocking nursing cars
New Patient Orientation	Revamped new patient orientation materials
Clean utility room	"Five S" of clean utility room
Pyxis scanner swap	Improved location of Pyxis and scanner in clinic
Overhead paging	Decreased overhead paging by ~70%
Problems with Queuing	Reduced treatment delays due to unknown patient location by ~50%
CyberKnife phone	Improved communication by installing new phone
Charge nurse role	Improved utilization of charge nurse role
Dept. phone calls	Decreased misrouted phone calls by ~85%
Late RN communication	Improved communication of late nurse transition
Sterilization for utility room	Improved sterilization safety in utility room
Organize utility room	Improved organization of utility room
IP consult requests	Improved process for inpatient consult requests
Miscommunication of Sim orders	Improve communication between MDs and simulator therapists
Clinic exam rooms 2.0	Implement phase 2 of exam room improvements
Pre-Authorization process	Improve pre-authorization process to reduce claim denials
Late Treatment patients	Improve safety and efficiency of late treatments
Skin Contours	Improve skin contour accuracy in software
DIBH process	Increase number of successful deep inspration breath hold treatments
Financial Counselor	Improve flow and communication with financial counselor
Emergent afterhours treatment	Develop standard process for emergent afterhours treatments
Chemo-Rad Coordination	Improve communication between radiation therapists and chemotherapy infusion nurses
Ordering Labs	Decrease non-value added nursing time for lab orders

The first group of rows (Automatic Doors through IP consult requests) is labeled "Implemented"; the second group (Miscommunication of Sim orders through Emergent afterhours treatment) is labeled "Approved and in progress"; the last two rows (Chemo-Rad Coordination and Ordering Labs) are labeled "Discontinued".

6.2.6 Rewards and Recognition

Employees are recognized and rewarded both individually and collectively for participating in the A3 program. New A3s are highlighted at the monthly departmental quality assurance (QA) meeting and posted on the visual management board. For each A3 that is implemented, the "area" in which the A3 owner belongs (i.e., nursing, physics, administrative, etc.) receives $100 in their "bank." Thus, the more A3s that the nurses (for example) complete that lead to an improvement implementation, the more money they will have in their bank (Figure 6.4). The nurses (as a group) decide how to spend the money, provided that the money is used

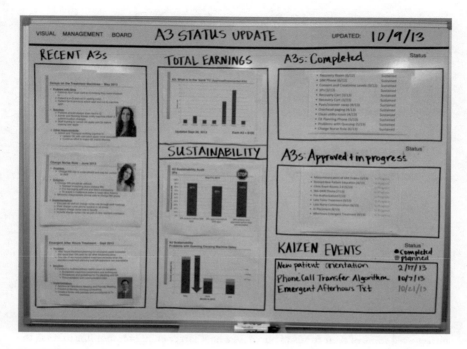

FIGURE 6.3

A3 visual management board posted in our departmental conference room (where we have our huddles). The six sections on the board are recently implemented A3s, total earnings of reward money (see Section 6.2.6), sustainability of previous implementations, a running list of completed A3s, recently approved and in progress A3s, and recent or planned Kaizen events.

toward improving quality and safety and pending approval by the Quality and Safety Committee. For example, the nurses implemented several A3s, earned \$800, and installed a monitor in the nurses' work room to display the queue of patients in the lobby so they could better monitor their patient flow and minimize patient wait times.

6.2.7 Challenges with the A3 Program

Implementing the A3 program was not "fast or easy." It took a long time for staff to buy in and become involved. To this point, only 20% of departmental staff have led an A3 effort. There were some early adopters, who have done multiple A3s, but the majority of people have not. It is a slowly evolving process.

It has been difficult for us to get physicians to initiate and own A3s. Front-line staff (e.g., nurses and radiation therapists) who deliver the actual

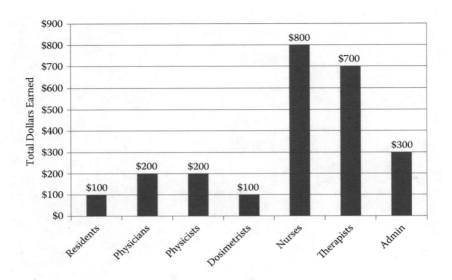

FIGURE 6.4

Rewards for implemented A3s. Each group is provided with $100 for each A3 that they complete. The group can use the funds to improve their workplace. For example, the nurses used some of their funds to purchase a new, larger computer monitor to track the patients in the clinic. Physicians=Faculty Physicians.

treatment are more willing to complete A3s. The residents were often willing to participate in A3 efforts as stakeholders but often not as owners. We imagine that the residents feel conflicted because only some of the physician faculty are involved in these initiatives. Some of the management challenges that leaders face in creating and nurturing an improvement culture are discussed in Chapter 4.

From June 2012 to January 2014, there were 22 A3s successfully implemented, to at least some degree, during their three months of postimplementation evaluations. The two A3s that were not at all sustained are discussed further as they illustrate common challenges.

6.2.7.1 Ordering Laboratory Studies

There was some disagreement among providers regarding how to best coordinate laboratories and other ancillary services for outpatients on the same day as (or just prior to) their follow-up visit. The nurses completed an A3 that led to a one-hour "mini-Kaizen" to develop and consider countermeasures and an implementation plan. The physician participating in the Kaizen agreed to the first proposed countermeasure and left the Kaizen early. Shortly thereafter, the other affected physicians were surprised with the new process as it did not address their concerns, and they stated that they had not approved it. We obviously had a communication breakdown, both between the involved physicians and between the physicians and the rest of the Kaizen team. Bhisham had an emergency meeting with involved physicians and some Kaizen team members, and the laboratory ordering process reverted to its pre-Kaizen state. Larry has also met with the involved physicians and Kaizen leaders to express his disappointment in how this all evolved. This issue continues be a source of frustration. Since this failed A3, we recognize that we need to be more diligent to schedule improvement events such that a larger number of the stakeholders can attend (e.g., if we had more physicians involved we might have come up with a better countermeasure). Further, we have requested that all stakeholders sign completed A3s to signify their endorsement.

6.2.7.2 Coordinating Chemotherapy

We were having problems coordinating concurrent chemotherapy given on the same day as radiation. Some patients were delayed in medical oncology and were late for their subsequent radiation, requiring the therapists to "work them in" to the schedule (often delaying other "downstream" patients). The reverse was also true (radiation visits delaying subsequent medical oncology visits), but most patients had the prior sequencing. An A3 was conducted with the primary stakeholders, including the radiation therapists and chemotherapy infusion nurses. Contributing causes included a lack of communication between these two groups: They did not know each other personally and there was no clarity on how they were to reach each other (e.g., via phone to discuss specific patients). Countermeasures from the Kaizen included that (1) the radiation therapist would write their direct contact information (i.e., the radiation therapist's names and the phone number at the treatment machine) in the patient's chart and (2) the infusion nurses would call the radiation therapists as needed to discuss a patient's status (e.g., if the chemotherapy was running late).

This A3 was not broadly successful, in part because the infusion nurses' high workload made compliance challenging. The current state is that if a patient is late for a scheduled radiation treatment, the radiation therapist will call the nurses' desk in the infusion center to obtain an update. Nevertheless, some infusion nurses do proactively call the radiation therapists to communicate about these issues. Further, even though not totally successful, this improvement initiative helped to build bridges and increase communication between the two different departments.

Goals for our ongoing A3 program include the following:

- Improve sustainability and develop a consistent manner to assess and report sustainability.
- Increase the stature of the A3 program to obtain more participation, particularly among the physicians.
- Increase the capacity for coaches to support A3 owners.
- Having supervisors more-consistently use A3s to manage issues within their group.

6.3 ENCOURAGING PEOPLE TO REPORT "GOOD CATCHES"

The Good Catch program is our web-based in-house incident learning system that we initiated in June 2012. All members in our department are encouraged to submit events through this electronic system (Figure 6.5); this

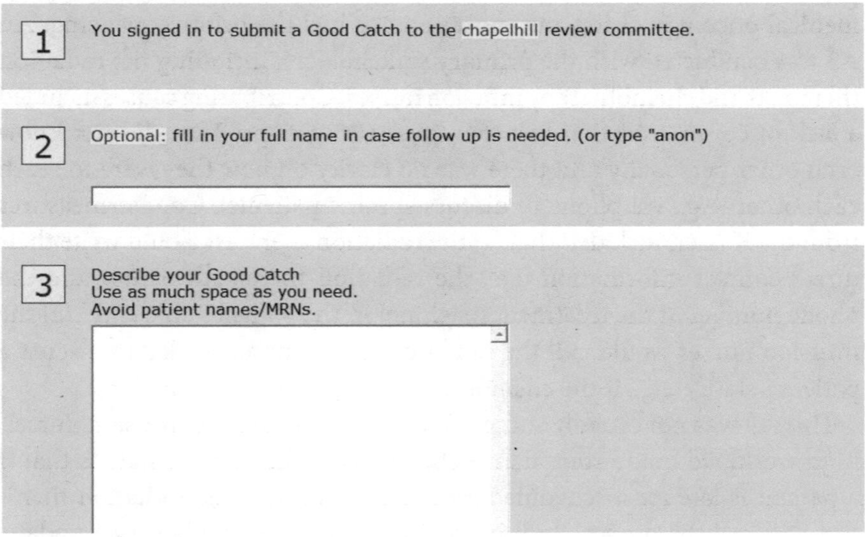

1   You signed in to submit a Good Catch to the chapelhill review committee.

2   Optional: fill in your full name in case follow up is needed. (or type "anon")

3   Describe your Good Catch
Use as much space as you need.
Avoid patient names/MRNs.

FIGURE 6.5
Good Catch submission website.

includes actual incidents that affected the patient, as well as near misses and unsafe conditions.

Submitted good catches are reviewed weekly in our Quality and Safety Committee meeting. For each submission, we use a previously defined process map (i.e., patient care pathway) to define where the "event" was initiated, where it was "caught," how many safety barriers were crossed, and (as able) the contributing (or root) causes of that event. We are thus able to monitor the performance of our processes and the effectiveness of our safety barriers. As able, we categorize submitted good catches by our initial impression regarding which "pieces of the Swiss Cheese Model" are implicated (e.g., organization, workplace design, people's performance) and whether there are contributing technology/technical factors. From the discussion at our weekly meeting, we prioritize responses to events based on their potential severity and triage them to the most appropriate "champion" on our committee (typically the supervisor most closely associated with the event's underlying causes, origins, and the associated safety barriers crossed; Figure 6.6). Sometimes, a rapid countermeasure is implemented, but most often further investigation by the champion is warranted. Champions often ask the employee submitting the good catch, or other stakeholders, to complete an A3 to help address the problem.

We use the Good Catch program to help drive improvement initiatives and as an educational/motivational tool for the department and our operations team. We use several visual aids (e.g., boards prominently posted throughout our department) to track and promote the Good Catch

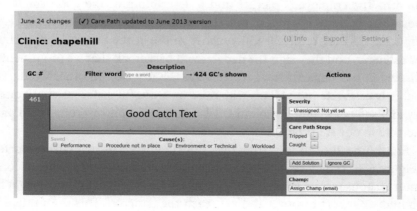

FIGURE 6.6
Good Catch analysis website.

FIGURE 6.7
Visual board in the break room recognizing an individual for submitting exemplary good catches.

program (e.g., summarizing the number and scope of the good catches reported and celebrating particularly important good catches; Figure 6.7).

Good catch data are reviewed with the whole department at our monthly quality safety meeting. Recognition is critical. At this meeting, we publically recognize an employee with the most seminal good catch for that month. The employee's picture and a description of the good catch are posted on bulletin boards in several locations within the department (e.g., Figure 6.7). They receive a $30 voucher to use at the hospital coffee shop or cafeteria, and they sign the department basketball that we prominently display in our departmental trophy case (Figure 6.8). In other words, we publicly celebrate individuals who raise meaningful concerns about quality and safety (analogous to our celebration of people or groups who participate in our A3 program; see Section 6.2.6).

From June 2012 to July 2014, over 600 good catches had been reported (Figure 6.9). When we started to ask people to report good catches, a common response was: "We catch errors all the time; it's part of our job. Why should we report errors that don't reach the patient?" This is an interesting perspective that merits consideration. As described in Chapter 3, for highly linear work flows, one could argue that an effective (and perhaps

FIGURE 6.8
UNC basketball signed by individuals recognized for submitting exemplary good catches.
Each individual receives a $30 gift card to the hospital coffee shop or cafeteria. This ball
is on prominent display in the trophy case (see Figure 4.6) in the hallway immediately
outside our main departmental conference room.

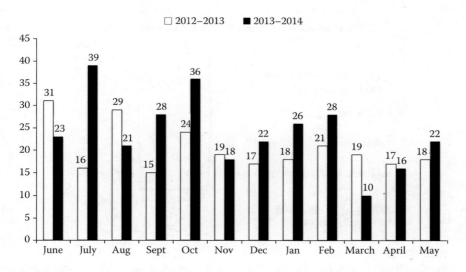

FIGURE 6.9
Number of submitted good catches per month.

efficient) manner to ensure quality is a robust "end-of-the-line" review. If our work flows were extraordinarily regimented and consistent between cases, and if our end-of-the-line reviews were always comprehensive and always performed perfectly, this might be a valid argument. However, this is not the world that we live in, at least not yet. Many aspects of our work are interactively complex, and high-quality performance throughout our processes is typically required to ensure safety. Further, a review of failures typically will reveal a haphazard collection of interactively complex events. This observation supports the notion that finding failures at the end of the line is not a reliable means to ensure quality. Further, the fact that we have errors that do reach the patient should temper our confidence in QA checks as a means to ensure patient safety and quality. Therefore, QA checks are critical because upstream processes (and the humans involved) are imperfect, and we need to optimize performance throughout the process because the QA checks are also imperfect. Alternatively stated, a good catch typically indicates a suboptimal process that likely needs to be addressed and is not indicative of a well-functioning system.

In addition, some people voiced, "I don't want to report 'errors' because I don't want to get into trouble." This apparently is a somewhat common perception. A national survey of 600 radiation therapists found that roughly 18% were uncomfortable reporting errors, and that 16% were personally reprimanded for reporting errors (Figure 6.10).[6]

Survey of Radiation Therapists (n = 600 random sample)

	Bad	Neutral	Good	Very Good
My communication with my: radiation oncologists is...	8%	11%	27%	54%
physicists is...	6%	6%	23%	65%
departmental administrators is...	19%	13%	30%	38%
My comfort level reporting errors is...	10%	8%	16%	66%

RTs <u>personally</u> reprimanded for reporting errors: 16%   ≈ 18%

FIGURE 6.10

Results from a national survey of radiation therapists illustrating communication challenges. (Data from Church J, Adams R, Hendrix L, et al. *Pract Radiat Oncol* 2013;3(4):165–170.)[6]

To address these challenges, we have tried to alter our culture. As noted, we celebrate employees' participation and successes in quality initiatives (e.g., reporting good catches, participating in A3s) and provide positive feedback. Managers thank and encourage their staff to be involved and to submit good catches. Our visual management boards that display recent good catches and subsequent actions taken (e.g., A3 requested, Kaizen, etc.), our discussions about good catches at the departmental QA meeting, and our recognitions and awards are all aimed to build our "safety culture." We believe that they are effective and are appreciated by our employees. Indeed, one month we had a low number of reported good catches and all were of minor importance, so we did not select a good catch awardee. Many employees were disappointed.

To facilitate reporting, it is the leadership's responsibility to create an infrastructure that makes it as easy as possible to submit a good catch. We have created a quick link within Mosaiq° that brings the user to the web-based reporting tool with a "single click." This is a good example of synergies between initiatives at the workplace and people levels.

The majority of good catches are reported by a core group that does include several physicians. However, most physicians unfortunately rarely formally report good catches. Those who do tend to report scheduling errors and concerns about staff performance. Low physician participation does not reflect contentment with operations. Rather, many of the physicians voice concerns directly to the staff or leadership. Although their concerns are heard, and often considered formally by the Quality and Safety Committee, many informal comments or concerns are likely forgotten. An informal complaint made by a physician in the hallway or elevator to Larry or Bhisham (which might lead to a scribbled note in one of their pockets) often lacks the details needed to be the source of meaningful change. Larry routinely encourages physicians to report many of such complaints via the Good Catch system. We are in the process of expanding our Good Catch program to our affiliated centers beyond UNC hospitals.

6.4 INTEGRATION OF GOOD CATCH AND A3 PROGRAMS: CASE STUDY WITH COMMON CHALLENGES

Several of the earliest good catches were related to (1) prior radiation and pacemakers not being considered in the radiation-planning and delivery process and (2) pregnancy tests not being performed prior to radiation in age-appropriate women. The Quality and Safety Committee asked a nurse and therapist to conduct an A3 resulting in a checklist (referred to as the 3Ps: pacemakers, pregnancy tests, or prior radiation) in the Assessment section of Mosaiq (see Section 5.2.2 for details). The nurse completes this checklist at the time of consultation. If the patient is a menstruating female with intact reproductive system, regardless of use of contraception, the nurse will order a pregnancy test to be performed prior to (including on the day of) the computed tomographic (CT) simulation. If the patient has a pacemaker, the nurse will set up a cardiology evaluation for pacemaker interrogation prior to starting radiation and denote "y" (for "yes") under pacemaker in the 3 P checklist. If the patient has had a prior history of radiation, the nurse similarly denotes "y" in the pertinent portion of the checklist. The simulation therapist will not simulate a patient unless the checklist has been completed and approved by a physician or nurse practitioner. It serves as a hard stop supported and enforced by leadership.

The information in the 3Ps is supposed to guide the work on the day of the CT simulation. For example, if the patient is noted to have a pacemaker, the simulation therapist must ensure that the pacemaker is included in the CT planning images and notify physics to measure the approximate dose to the pacemaker on the first day of treatment and verify with physics, nursing, and the physician that the necessary discussions with cardiology have been initiated. Similarly, if the patient is noted to have had prior radiation therapy (RT), the simulation therapist must discuss this with the physician; placing catheters on the tattoos from the prior RT must be considered; and prior RT records are requested as needed. If the patient needs a pregnancy test, nursing must perform a "point-of-care" urine test in our department immediately prior to the CT simulation.

Nevertheless, our system was still not perfect. We had a good catch involving a young woman being treated for a keloid. The 3Ps had been completed as required. However, as she did not have a CT simulation, her urine pregnancy test was inadvertently not completed. Two additional good catches related to prior radiation and pacemaker issues that reached patients, despite the 3P checklist, highlighted the need for a more robust system. Thus, we initiated another PDSA cycle using A3, countermeasures were implemented, and for some time it seemed we achieved a desirable level of reliability.

About ten months later, the prior radiation received by a patient was not accounted for in a subsequent treatment plan. This patient had a history of right breast cancer treated with radiation to her right breast and right supraclavicular region. During a subsequent consultation for a new head and neck cancer, the prior RT for the breast cancer was noted, and the 3Ps were correctly completed by the nurse and approved by the physician. The records of the prior radiation were obtained and reviewed, and documentation of the prior radiation was made in the hospital medical record. The patient had a two-month interval between this consultation for the head and neck cancer and initiation of radiation (she had a slow recovery from her prior surgery). At the time of radiation planning, the history of prior radiation was forgotten by the physician, and a three-dimensional (3D) conformal radiotherapy plan was created that treated bilateral necks (without consideration of the prior course of radiation). The right supraclavicular area received 45 Gy for the breast treatment and an additional 50 Gy for the head and neck cancer. Thus, while the 3Ps and prior radiation records were available, they were not reviewed again by the physician, the simulation therapist, or the dosimetrists. Review by any one of these likely could have prevented this patient harm. We are now considering more robust approaches to ensure that the 3P information is more consistently reviewed and considered by the nurses, simulation therapists, dosimetrists, and other "downstream" providers—another PDSA, another A3.

We have noted an increase in this type of "data extraction" error with the EHR. While the EHR is a wonderful repository of information, it is often challenging to extract information, and there is often not a good way to "flag" particularly important things items. With the paper chart, one could readily write in red ink on the prescription page, "Prior RT," or literally tape notes to the outside of the chart to serve this function. Granted these were ad hoc, and inconsistent, and thus not idea. However, this function has not been fully well reproduced in the EHR era.

In a similar recent incident, a patient with a pacemaker was inadvertently planned (and initiated treatment) with a 15-MV beam. The use of a 15-MV beam in this setting is against our policy because it increases the degree of neutron production that might increase the risk of pacemaker failure (compared to lower photon energies that produce lesser amounts of neutrons). The 3Ps were correctly completed by the nurse and approved by the physician at the time of consultation and denoted that the patient had a pacemaker. The patient went through treatment planning (by dosimetry), treatment plan approval (by the physician), and several other physics/clinical QA steps. At the time of the patient's first treatment, the physicist performing measurements based on MOSFET (metal oxide semiconductor field effect transistor) of the pacemaker dose noted that 15-MV beams were being used and called this to the attention of the providers. The plan was subsequently redone. Further evaluation of this incident revealed that some of the providers involved with this case did not review the 3P information. Further, several were unaware of the departmental policy against the use of 15-MV beams in this setting.

6.5 PATIENT SAFETY CULTURE: OUR PEOPLE'S PERCEPTION OF ORGANIZATIONAL CULTURE

The successful change of an organization's culture requires active leadership (as discussed in detail in Chapter 4) and broad buy-in and participation of the staff. In our case, Larry had a vision when he became department chair to implement a continuous quality improvement program such as Lean and broadly focus on quality and safety improvements. The A3 and Good Catch programs are examples aimed to empower and motivate our staff to directly participate in our quality and safety agenda. But, has this altered our culture?

The Agency for Healthcare Research and Quality (AHRQ) defines the safety culture of an organization as the product of individual and group values, attitudes, perceptions, competencies, and patterns of behavior that determine the commitment to, and the style and proficiency of, an organization's health and safety management.[7] The culture of an organization might be more simply described as its shared values or principles that are acted upon; that is, it requires both belief and action. AHRQ has an assessment tool that measures the patient safety culture for hospitals, nursing homes, ambulatory outpatient medical offices, and pharmacies.

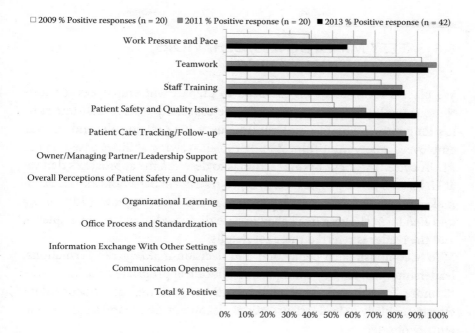

□ 2009 % Positive responses (n = 20) ■ 2011 % Positive response (n = 20) ■ 2013 % Positive response (n = 42)

FIGURE 6.11

Positive response rate to several items from the Agency for Healthcare Research Quality (AHRQ) Patient Safety Survey given to departmental employees. Note the increase in positive response rate over time. Also, note the large increase in the number of respondents to the survey, which we interpret to reflect an increased respect for QA/quality improvement activities.

The AHRQ patient safety survey measures 12 dimensions of patient safety culture. Our institution routinely administers this survey every 18 months for our outpatient clinics. Figure 6.11 illustrates our safety culture survey results from 2009, 2011, and 2013. For most of the items, the percent positive responses appear to have increased from 2009 to 2013. As these surveys are anonymous, and we certainly have had personnel changes over time, it is not certain that these changes reflect a true change in "culture." The people responding to the surveys in the different years certainly varied. Nevertheless, we find these data to be encouraging. Further, the number of people responding to the survey has increased over time, which we interpret to reflect an increased respect for QA/quality improvement activities.

6.6 SAFETY MINDFULNESS, BEHAVIORS, AND DECISION MAKING

We place a lot of focus on the need to prepare our employees for continuous quality improvement work. We especially believe that our clinic's long-term reliability and continuous value creation depend on our employees' safety mindfulness and problem-solving abilities based on the PDSA cycle. The focus of this section is to describe the approaches that we at UNC take at the people level to try to transform behaviors and decision making from *Quick Fixing, Expediting,* and *Conforming* toward *Initiating and Enhancing.*[1] These five behaviors are discussed in detail in Chapter 3, and the reader is referred there for details.

To accomplish such behavioral and decision-making transformations, leadership must lead by example and allocate appropriate time and effort to more formal and consistent initiatives. Informal and inconsistent efforts are likely to lead to frustration, disappointments, and a suboptimal culture of safety.

6.6.1 Transforming *Quick Fixing* Behaviors to *Initiating* Behaviors

People have many responsibilities in their jobs, and asking people also to focus on *Initiating* improvements may be overly burdensome. The challenge is convincing people of the broader benefits to the organization (because of higher reliability and value creation), and that these organizational improvements lead to better efficiency that will improve their own efficiency and job satisfaction (and more poignantly, the healthcare we provide patients).

The "long-standing" culture in medicine has been for people to "quick fix" suboptimal communications from physicians; for example, a pharmacist may say, "I know that it is hard to read, but I know what the doctor usually orders," or a clerk asking a patient, "I am having trouble reading this lab order sheet; do you know what tests your physician wanted?" An analogous situation in radiation oncology is when physicians provide unclear or incomplete directives. Under such circumstances, therapists or dosimetrists must often "hunt down" the physician to obtain needed information and occasionally assume what the physician wanted in order to complete their work. This certainly happened (and occasionally still happens) in our department, sometimes leading to waste (e.g., replanning of cases with alternative techniques or constraints). After several good catches directly related to miscommunication of physician directives to therapists and dosimetrists, the Quality and Safety Committee wanted to tackle these *Quick-Fixing* behaviors and asked representative dosimetrists, therapists, and physicians to work together to initiate a formal improvement effort.

As described in Sections 5.2.2 and 5.2.3, we developed more robust systems to try to address these issues. We needed to present the providers with data related to the number of these events (e.g., how often we had communication problems) and information about actual incidents (e.g., how it affected patients and workers) to actively engage providers. As a result, we implemented policies to require timely written documentation of simulation orders and treatment-planning directives in a standardized manner and location within the electronic medical record (Mosaiq). We monitor the adherence to these policies and procedures. The simulation therapists keep track of how often the simulation orders are available in Mosaiq prior to simulation and also of the accuracy of the information. At our daily morning meeting, our chief therapist reviews that day's simulation schedule with the group. She announces which patients are missing their treatment-planning directives or where the directives are incomplete, ambiguous, or otherwise in need of further clarification. At first, physicians felt constrained by the rigidity of requiring documentation prior to simulation and treatment planning. They also were threatened by the public accounting of who had delinquent treatment-planning directives and simulation orders. One of our physicians, in a faculty meeting, stated that they felt like we were running a "police state." Over time, this has been largely accepted as the routine of how we practice. We believe that the physicians saw the value of standardized communication with dosimetrist and therapists, with fewer needs for rework (e.g., replans) for themselves. Maybe it also helps that the departmental operational leadership (e.g., Larry and Bhisham) are occasionally "called out" as delinquent in this regard as well.

We want to emphasize that this discussion is not intended to "blame" physicians for "sloppy work." Physicians are busy people who work hard to try to do the right thing. However, physicians are often faced with multiple competing demands, ambiguous rules or expectations, and suboptimal systems (e.g., the computer system was running slow and the provider was interrupted twice while entering the directive into the system). It is leadership's or management's responsibility to create a culture (see Chapter 4) and work space (see Chapter 5) that facilitates the desired behaviors.

6.6.2 Reducing *Expediting* Behaviors

People often create shortcuts and opt not to follow procedures to make their job easier or improve productivity; this is to be expected as it is part of human nature to do so. However, this type of behavior often does not consider the upstream and downstream consequences.

Our record-and-verify system tracks the table position and institutes a hard stop to prevent treatment if the table is not within a given tolerance range (set by our physicists) of the anticipated position. The hard stop is intended to prompt a more careful recheck of the table position by the therapist, who can then manually override the hard stop if the table position is deemed acceptable. Initially, we had relatively tight tolerances of about 2 mm, resulting in frequent hard stops, frequent table position rechecks, and frequent overrides. This caused some people to become desensitized to these alerts, to be more comfortable with manually overriding the system, and to view the hard stop as a nuisance that slowed their work.

Some of our patients have a treatment isocenter that is different from the simulation marks. For example, in many patients with head and neck cancer, reference setup marks are placed on the head mask, but the treatment isocenter is often located in the neck, thus requiring a manual shift (often up to 10 cm) during each treatment. We had two patients whose manual shift was inadvertently not done prior to one of their fractions. The record-and-verify system alerted the therapists to the incorrect table position, but the therapists assumed that the hard stop was "the usual" and expedited treatment by overriding the system without double-checking the table position. Interestingly, both patients were midway through their course of treatment, so the manual table shift was not a new procedure for these therapists. After these incidents, several countermeasures were discussed. One suggestion was to create a position of lead therapist who would have override privileges. At a meeting of the therapists, this proposal was not favored because it promoted hierarchy. We later modestly relaxed the table tolerances, thus reducing the number of hard stops, but added a requirement that the therapist document the table coordinates in the electronic health record (EHR) if an override was performed—basically forcing verification that the override was justified. However, small errors in table position no longer trigger an alert. The number of overrides has been markedly reduced, and we hope that this approach reduces *Expediting* behaviors. Another consideration raised by this case is whether the systematic shift between the reference setup marks on the head mask and the treatment isocenter is optimal, and if an alternative approach might be better. Other technologies can also be used to try to address this type of error (radio-frequency- or imaging-based tracking of patient positioning).

6.6.3 Transforming *Conforming* Behaviors to *Enhancing* Behaviors

Recognizing *Conforming* behaviors might be difficult as they are often embedded deeply into the fabric of our daily organizational lives. Further, as they are long standing, there is much resistance to change, and it is thus challenging to transform *Conforming* behaviors to *Enhancing* behaviors. A good example of such a transformation in our clinic occurred during an episode of cross coverage.

Cross covering for a colleague is a situation when one might feel inclined to conform to colleagues' directives for patient care, perhaps out of respect or experience or seniority status. Our policy is that a physicist be present for each radiosurgery treatment. For one of our patients, the physicist who did the planning and pretreatment quality checks could not be present for the initial treatment. Under this circumstance, the cross-covering physicist thought it would be prudent to redo the pretreatment physics QA check to become more familiar with the patient's case. This behavior is not required. Nobody asked the cross-covering physicist to redo the pretreatment physics QA check. The cross-covering physicist found that only two of the three implanted fiducial markers had been identified during treatment planning. The covering physicist replanned the patient, resulting in more robust treatment delivery plan.

Another example of *Enhancing* behavior originated from one of the senior faculty members noting the suboptimal manner in which we were interpreting and using maximal intensity projection (MIP) images processed from 4D CTs of the liver. Interestingly, he had noted this issue in an informal manner previously, but his concern had gone unaddressed. As happens with many informal efforts, we did not listen carefully and kept *Conforming* as the status quo. This submitted good catch and follow-up exemplifies *Enhancing* behaviors and was recognized in our monthly departmental QA meeting. This faculty member's photo is now on the wall and his signature on the department basketball with those of others who have submitted the most meaningful good catches. We hope having our senior faculty involved in these initiatives helps to promote broader participation.

Enhancing behaviors require some sort of intrinsic motivation (a desire and belief that they can individually make a difference) that can be encouraged or cultivated by external factors (e.g., Larry and Bhisham beating the drum, multiple public recognitions). Once people experience the pride and self-satisfaction of meaningfully impacting their environment, they likely develop increased intrinsic motivation (i.e., a positive-feedback loop). Thus, although the recognitions or rewards (e.g., name on the Good Catch board, $100 for the A3, etc.) do serve to motivate and initiate people's involvement, the long-term goal is to build intrinsic motivation to willingly engage in *Enhancing* efforts with a heightened sense of safety mindfulness.

6.7 INITIATIVES AIMED TO PROMOTE SAFETY MINDFULNESS

Safety mindfulness is the moment-by-moment awareness or focus on quality and safety during routine work. To heighten people's safety mindset, we try to continually reinforce a system's perspective (e.g., our daily departmental huddles are a constant reminder of the interconnectivity of our actions). Further, we provide people with continual feedback on how they and the system are performing (e.g., through the daily metrics), and personally and publically thank and celebrate *Enhancing* behavior (e.g., through A3 and Good Catch awards, employee of the month, etc.). By continually discussing these issues, and by seeking people's input wherever possible (e.g., with safety rounds, Good Catch initiatives), we hope to send the message that management cares about safety mindfulness.

6.7.1 Departmental, Clinical Team, and Physics/Dosimetry Huddles

Huddles between team members have been observed to be useful in healthcare.[8,9] A centerpiece of our improvement culture is our daily departmental clinical huddles. These (1) are interdisciplinary (attended by physicians, dosimetrists, physicists, students, and representatives from the therapists, nurses, and clerical support staff); (2) occur at a standard time each day; (3) are conducted in a consistent location; (4) are brief; and (5) attendance is strongly encouraged. Although attendance is not taken, Larry speaks to physicians who are not attending regularly and to the leaders of groups that are not consistently represented. The expectation is clear that people attend. The goal of this huddle is to communicate and share information about the upcoming day's work and, as Larry likes to say, "preempt chaos." We review the pertinent issues of the day, go over the schedule, and plan for anticipated challenges. Even a cursory review of the pending day's schedule will identify likely bottlenecks, conflicts, and so on, and it is better to preemptively address these issues. As needed and as able, work is reassigned, schedules are modified, and "loose ends" are identified or addressed. We believe that these huddles result in a smoother flow to the day with fewer interruptions and delays. As issues are raised, anyone (in particular stakeholders) can be part of the discussion and assist in decision making (e.g., physicians and the chief therapist may adjust the treatment schedule to accommodate an emergency inpatient).

Medicine has a hierarchical culture, and this can stifle communication. Huddling transcends this hierarchy and promotes communication. Our huddles are a place where face-to-face communication replaces e-mails and text pages and where people tend to come if they need to grab someone in person for a quick question or discussion. The informal format promotes the sense of teamwork and cohesiveness among the staff.

The key elements of an effective huddle include team member attendance and participation. Ideally, someone other than senior leadership should lead it. While initially Larry, and subsequently Bhisham, led most huddles, over time others regularly have led as well (e.g., one of the other faculty or residents). In reality, the huddle often proceeds without a formal leader; the chief therapist addresses the simulation schedule, a nurse the clinic schedule, and so on. The exact order in which the items are addressed is not critical. The agenda for the huddle is posted on the wall, but we have not referred to this formal agenda in several years because the "core content" is now ingrained in our work flow.

At UNC, we have had a several-decade tradition for peer review, with physicians reviewing each other's simulation films and image segmentation. As part of our broad quality initiatives, we broadened attendance at this meeting to include more of the nonphysician staff and have essentially extended the content of this meeting to include the huddle. Technically, we have our daily peer review session (that we term *sim review*) from about 8:40 to 8:55 a.m., and the huddle follows immediately after that. The huddle agenda typically includes the following:

- CT-sim schedule: The chief therapist notes patients whose records lack clear directives. Patients presenting unique challenges or learning opportunities are noted. The availability, or lack, of openings for add-ons is noted.
- The daily patient treatment census is noted along with special considerations that might affect clinical flow (e.g., anesthesiology or total-body irradiation cases).
- Announcement is made of patients who will need pre-RT films so that the responsible physicians can plan to be available.
- Dosimetrists alert the group regarding treatment plans that are proceeding more slowly than expected and seek direction.
- Nurses note the clinic volumes and anticipated staffing, or other, issues.
- Clerical staff report any challenges they have with scheduling, staff absences, and responsibility reassignments.
- The names of the "doctor of the day" (DOD) and "physicist of the day" (POD) are announced (i.e., the physician and physicist responsible for inpatient coverage and unanticipated clinical needs; see Section 6.7.4).
- The group is invited to raise concerns, make announcements, introduce visitors or new staff, and so forth.

As noted, this morning meeting serves the practical functions of trying to anticipate the upcoming challenges and avoid chaos in the clinic. It also serves a social and cultural function to bring the department together daily, fostering an environment of easy communication among all team members. A survey of attendees demonstrated broad support for our departmental morning peer review session and huddle (Table 6.2).

Similarly, we have requested that clinical teams huddle daily. These huddles are a multidisciplinary team discussion involving the faculty physician, nurse practitioner or resident, and clinic nurse early during the clinic day. They review that day's clinic schedule, noting anticipated challenges and scheduling conflicts; review specific patient's special needs; make adjustments to the schedule as needed; and so on. For example, occasionally the providers know something about a patient that should

TABLE 6.2

Survey Results Demonstrating Broad Support for Our Departmental Morning Peer
Review Session and Huddles

Question	Strongly Disagree (%)	Disagree	Neutral (%)	Agree (%)	Strongly Agree (%)
Convenient time of day for me			7	59	34
Collegial debate/conversation			4	70	26
Provides me with quality/value			15	56	29
An excellent learning environment			4	52	44
Improves departmental "safety" culture	4		15	44	37
Helps clinical operations run smoothly			4	59	37
Fosters communication within the department			11	59	30
I am satisfied with morning huddle and peer review session				74	26

Source: With permission from Chera BS, Jackson M, Mazur LM, et al. *Semin Radiat Oncol*
2012;22:77–85.[10]

be shared with other team members, and this is a good time to share
this knowledge (e.g., "I got a call this morning from radiology about Mr.
XX, and they are having a hard time with his biopsy, so he might be
late," or, "Oh, I did not realize that Ms. YY is coming in today; I got
a fax from her home surgeon and it is on my desk; let me grab that so
you do not waste time looking for the outside records."). Typically, our
nurses lead the clinical team huddles; they often know what is going on
with the patients and best understand the global clinical activities and
needs. Furthermore, this empowers the nurse as a leader and coordinator
of that clinical team and fosters multidisciplinary collaboration within
the department. This was initially met with resistance from the physicians because they perceived it as a barrier to starting the day (e.g., "I
do not find it helpful."). However, the other team members, especially
the nurses, found the daily clinical team huddles helpful, and because
the nurses lead the huddle, they took the initiative to seek out the team
to ensure the huddle would occur. The physicians were forced to participate, and over time with persistence the nurses have made the daily
clinical team huddle a routine habit for the physicians. In the end, all
parties began to view this huddle as an important component to their

daily clinical activities. In fact, we monitor compliance with daily clinical team huddles for each physician as one of our daily quality metrics, and we are typically close to 100% compliant.

Recently, our physicists and dosimetrists have started their own daily huddle to review their specific clinical tasks for the upcoming days, challenges, and so on. This occurs immediately after, and in the same room as, the departmental huddle, so it is convenient and well attended.

These daily huddles serve as a continual reminder to all of our interdependence as a team, our mutual respect, and our desire to avoid the unexpected (and the often-associated chaos).

6.7.2 Safety Rounds

A practical and relatively easy way for an organization to demonstrate its commitment to building a culture of safety is to conduct regular safety rounds. Safety rounds, led by senior leaders (e.g., physician, administrator, physicist), are regular (e.g., monthly, quarterly) informal conversations between the leadership and front-line workers *at their work site* (treatment machine, simulator, dosimetry, clinic, etc.). Basically, leadership is regularly spending time with staff talking about the safety or operational issues that concern the staff. The front-line staff broadly define the agenda as they are free to bring up whatever issues concern them. The benefits of safety rounds are multifold: (1) They demonstrate leaders'/organizational commitment to safety, quality, and efficiency; (2) they fuel an organizational safety culture; (3) they foster communication; (4) they allow for rapid safety-based improvements; (5) they are educational for leaders. After each safety round, it is important for the leadership to follow up (and it is hoped address) the issues raised. Timely follow-up with tangible/visible quality improvements by the leadership will foster buy-in from the front-line staff and help drive the safety culture. We hope that this will increase reporting of errors, safety concerns, and so on (e.g., through the Good Catch program).

In 2010, we initiated a safety walk rounds program, with Robert as the coordinator. He defines the areas to be visited, gives the workers in those areas "advance notification" (so that they can think about what they might want to discuss), catalogues the issues raised, and tracks or coordinates follow-up. We did this initially every 6 months and then increased to quarterly. Typically, we will visit two or three locations, each with one to three workers present. Each location is visited for about 5–15 minutes, depending on how much the workers would like to discuss, so leadership spends roughly 60 minutes actually visiting with the staff. Leadership prompts the staff to discuss any safety or operational concerns, near misses, or unsafe conditions that may cause potential or real harm (or inconvenience, annoyance) to patients or staff.

At first, front-line workers were reluctant to disclose their concerns about safety or errors because of fear of blame, reprimands, and job security. Also, they had the predisposed notion that because they work in a state system, change is unlikely and slow to occur. But, we repeatedly assured them with each safety round that we were not on a "witch hunt," and that we wanted to improve their workplace and processes to improve quality of care of the patient. Robert was effective as a leader and facilitator of this initiative. He has been in the department for over 30 years, and as the director of our RT school, he trained many of our current therapists. Thus, he is trusted by much of the front-line staff. Over time, we believe that staff has become more comfortable with this initiative.

One of the first concerns raised was that there were occasional collisions of stretchers and wheelchairs transporting patients around "blind corners" in our department. The next day, we had maintenance install dome safety mirrors on the ceiling at corners of several hallways. Our rapid response to this easily fixable problem impressed our staff and increased leadership credibility (see Figure 5.13 in Chapter 5).

Since 2010, we have had 14 safety rounds sessions, visited all work spaces, collected over 200 suggestions or concerns, and provided follow-up on most of these. Robert continues to keep track of the initiative and ensures that we visit all areas of the department over time. Active participation of the leadership in the huddles and safety rounds is an example of standard work for managers. Safety and quality will not happen spontaneously. Rather, leadership needs to dedicate time and effort to make this happen (see Section 4.2.3 in Chapter 4).

6.7.3 Daily Metric

The daily metric is a work in progress. The concept is that we should have some metrics that describe how well or poorly our clinic is performing. When trying to define metrics, Larry often asks, "At the end of the day when you get home and your partner says, 'How was your day?' what goes through your mind? What quantifiable measure best reflects how good or bad your day was?" For those involved with the treatment machines, maybe it is, "Were we on time, or running late? How much later than planned did we treat? Was the machine functioning as needed?" For our clinic, maybe it is, "Are we on time? How many add-on consults were seen?" For the simulator staff, maybe it is, "What fraction of our patients could not be started on time because of lack of directives from the provider?" For dosimetry-related individuals, maybe it is, "How many replans did we do today? How many emergent calculations were done?" We have been trying to publicly announce, and have created the infrastructure to publicly display these operational metrics. These provide (it is hoped positive) feedback to the department regarding how we are doing and that we care about operations.

It is important to emphasize that this should not be considered as an individual's or team's "score card," as clearly these metrics are not totally in our control. Patients come late, machines break, emergencies happen, and so on. Rather, these are broad measures of operational performance and reflect the stresses (and successes) that our workers feel each day. To the degree that we can control these metrics, we should strive to optimize them. For things that we cannot control, we should define systems that can proactively, optimally, and flexibly address these issues. For example, if we are consistently having a large number of add-on consults on particular days, we can structure the schedule with excess capacity or review patterns of the referring physicians to see if a larger number of these patients can be scheduled ahead of time.

6.7.4 Physicist of the Day (POD) and Doctor of the Day (DOD)

The POD initiative is best illustrated by a short story. A therapist was having their typical workday on the treatment machine. Into their fourth patient of the day, the linear accelerator threw a fault and stopped working. In the past, they would have had a list of phone numbers to consider calling. They might have thought about which physicist they recently saw in the hallway, who tends to be the most responsive, or who recently has seemed the least hassled. On this day, however, they knew exactly who to call—the POD. The POD was responsive, immediately came to the machine, assessed the problem, and called the vendor. Because the linear accelerator was going to be down for a while, the physicist and therapists contacted dosimetry and the attending physicians, and a plan to treat some of the patients on a different machine was initiated. In the past, the ultimate result would have been the same, but the path might have been more haphazard. The POD plan was implemented to clearly define the "go-to" physicist to address these types of "technical" issues during the workday.

Similarly, the DOD allows our department to have a go-to physician to address arising issues. The DOD is assigned to be on site by 7 a.m. (the time we commence treatment) and stays until all treatments are completed. The DOD is responsible for things such as reviewing port films for providers who are out of town, checking clinical setups and simulations for providers who are unavailable, seeing the inpatient consultations, and dealing with any general clinical issues that need to be addressed during the day.

This has been particularly helpful to ensure physician oversight of simulations. We historically had some major challenges with patient flow through the simulator, in part related to timely attending oversight. This may not seem like a big issue, but when schedules are "tight," and one patient is delayed, it has a negative domino effect on all downstream processes, requiring adjustments to multiple schedules and so on. These operational challenges also had a negative effect on morale (particularly of the simulator therapists), and the staff and physicians had lost faith in the simulator schedule. The DOD has largely addressed these issues. The simulator therapists can better control their schedule, and our simulator is often busy and efficient. Further, by reducing uncertainty in the performance or oversight of simulations (also aided by reviewing the upcoming simulation schedule in our morning huddle; see 6.7.1), we believe that we have reduced replans and rework (Figure 6.12).

The POD and DOD are announced during our departmental morning huddle, and their names are posted on schedules throughout the department. Overall, the implementation of the POD and DOD has been successful, and we perceive it has reduced uncertainty in our clinical operations. It provides reassurance to the staff that they will have access to physics and physician support. Further, we believe that the POD/DOD provide some formal "coverage" for the people who are *not* the POD/DOD of the day. For example, if a physician has some clinical responsibility on a "nonclinical day" that they are not able to attend to, the DOD affords a default coverage option for that clinic responsibility.

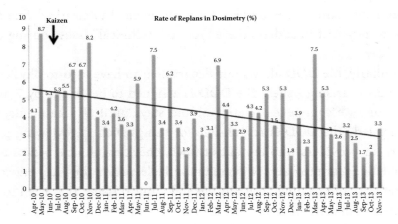

FIGURE 6.12
Rate of replans by dosimetrists over time. (Adapted from Chera et al., *PRO*, with permission.)

6.8 PATIENT ENGAGEMENT

We recognize the power of involving patients in improving our operations and in building a team culture.[10] Our self-registration system (Section 5.2.5), the monitors in the maze entryways to the treatment machines to facilitate verification of patient identification (Section 5.5.1), and the ringing of the gong (Section 5.5.5) are examples of initiatives whose success requires active patient participation. The sounding of the gong is a form of patient-to-patient encouragement. Similarly, we have a book in our lobby where patients and their families are invited to share their thoughts (Figure 6.13).

A similar wall-mounted area for patients to write public comments is being planned. When Larry is having what he perceives to be a "bad day," he will occasionally read a few entries in this book and his perspective is usually rapidly adjusted. We invite patients to provide us with formal feedback on our operations via comment cards and telephone surveys. We have not yet included a patient on our QA/quality improvement committees, but this is something that we should do as well.

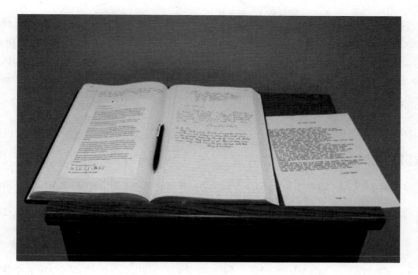

FIGURE 6.13
The book in our lobby where patients and their family can share their thoughts.

6.9 SUMMARY

The power of safety mindfulness is derived from its ability to leverage the knowledge within all of the people in an organization. Motivating people to be part of the continuous quest to improve our systems is the central challenge. It is hard work, and it is ongoing (i.e., it is never done), so people need to be continually encouraged and supported both to become involved and to stay involved.

This chapter reviewed many of the initiatives that we have taken at the people level to address this challenge. Although we focused on the A3 and Good Catch programs and our efforts to transform behaviors, we emphasize that these are just a few of the many components of our program that are focused on our people. Our daily huddles require broad participation to be effective, and their recurring (daily) nature is a constant reminder of the importance of each individual person in our improvement initiatives. The same is true of the smaller huddles for each of the clinical teams and the visual displays of our Lean improvement activities (i.e., the daily metrics, the Good Catch basketball in the trophy case, etc.). They are each consistent reminders of our roles and responsibilities, both as individuals and as part of a team, working together to build our safety culture.

The focus on people presented here is facilitated by the activities of the leadership (see Chapter 4) and the structure of the workplace (see Chapter 5). Safety mindfulness at all three levels (Figure 6.1) needs to be nurtured to build a successful and sustaining continuous quality improvement program.

REFERENCES

1. Mazur L, McCreery J, Chen S-J. Quality improvement in hospitals: what triggers behavioral change? *J Healthcare Eng* 2012;4:621–648.
2. Tabuchi H. Eiji Toyoda, promoter of the Toyota Way and engineer of its growth, dies at 100. *New York Times* September 17, 2013.
3. Sobek D, Smalley A. *Understanding A3 Thinking: A Critical Component of Toyota's PDCA*. New York, NY: Productivity Press; 2008.
4. Mazur LM, Chen S-J, Prescott B. Pragmatic evaluating of Toyota Production System (TPS) analysis procedure for problem solving with entry-level nurses. *J Indust Eng Manage* 2008;1:240–268.
5. Mazur LM, Chen S-J. Evaluation of industrial engineering students' competencies for process improvement in hospitals. *J Indust Eng Manage* 2010;3:603–628.
6. Church J, Adams R, Hendrix L, et al. National study to determine the comfort levels of radiation therapists and medical dosimetrists to report errors. *Pract Radiat Oncol* 2013;3:165–170.
7. Agency for Healthcare Research and Quality (AHRQ). *Hospital Survey on Patient Safety Culture*. Prepared by Westat, Rockville, MD; 2004.
8. Cooper RL, Meara M. The organizational huddle process: optimum results through collaboration. *Health Care Manager* 2002;21:12–16.
9. Dingley C, Daugherty R, Derieg MK, et al. Improving patient safety through provider communication strategy enhancements. In: Henriksen K, Battles JB, Keyes MA, Grady ML, eds. *Advances in Patient Safety: New Directions and Alternative Approaches, Vol. 3: Performance and Tools*. Rockville, MD: Agency for Healthcare Research and Quality (US); 2008;90–107.
10. Chera BS, Jackson M, Mazur LM, et al. Improving quality of patient care by improving daily practice in radiation oncology. *Semin Radiat Oncol* 2012;22:77–85.

7

Research*

LEARNING OBJECTIVES

After completing this chapter, the reader should be able to:

1. Understand the relationship between workload, performance, and safety;
2. Broadly appreciate the potential utility of additional research in these areas;
3. Develop ideas for future research within organizational transformation to high reliability and value creation (e.g., how to best build personal safety mindfulness, optimally lead change, optimally perform improvement cycles, and optimally organize radiation oncology centers); and
4. Understand some of the challenges associated with human-computer interactions and opportunities to improve and conduct research in the areas of interface design and usability.

7.1 BACKGROUND

Studying the causes of error in medicine can be challenging. Ideally, one might want to conduct research in the real clinical environment. However, the incidence of serious events is (thankfully) low, so the yield on such direct clinical observations might be small (tracking less-serious, or near-events might provide a larger yield). The clinical realm also presents many

---

* **Acknowledgment:** Portions of this chapter summarize our previously published research and permission was obtained for reproduction of text, tables, and figures.

confounding variables that make attribution of errors to specific factors uncertain (controlled experiments with well-controlled variables are not typically possible). Further, research in clinical areas is necessarily limited because one needs to be sure that the study itself does not affect worker performance and patient care.

Therefore, to better understand some of the causes of errors within the radiation oncology clinic, we have performed a series of research studies in both the real clinical realm (if practical) and in a simulated environment (where more detailed and controlled experiments were possible). In this chapter, we broadly review the results of these studies. All of these studies were done prospectively as part of trials approved by the internal review board (IRB).

7.1.1 Workload during Information Processing

A fundamental assumption in most of our research is that workload influences situation awareness and that both impact performance, which in turn impacts patient safety. Thus, we study workload and performance, both as surrogates for patient safety. This association is widely accepted in other industries, and the same is almost certainly true in healthcare (although this area of study is far less developed in healthcare versus other industries; Table 7.1).

Models have been created to describe how individuals make decisions and perform physical actions based on input variables and their

TABLE 7.1

Summary of Published Materials on Subjective (NASA-TLX) and Physiological Workload Measures

		Number of Citations Noting These Measures of Mental Workload in the Different Fields Shown	
Term: Mental Workload	**Total Number of Citations**	**Subjective (NASA-TLX)**	**Physiological (e.g., eye data, EEG)**
Aviation	5,490	2,450	527
Transportation (driving)	7,240	2,200	642
Power plants	844	1,650	42
Healthcare	1,480	331	87

Source: Data from Google Scholar (October 2013).
NASA-TLX, National Aeronautics and Space Administration Task Load Index.

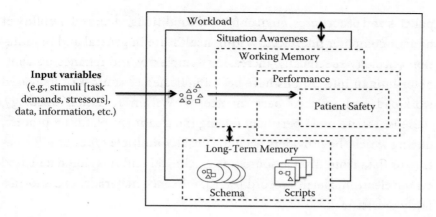

FIGURE 7.1
Fundamental assumption underpinning our research program.

long-term and working memories (Figure 7.1). A full explanation of this is beyond the scope of this book, and the interested reader is referred to other sources.[1,2] In brief, throughout this process, individuals exposed to suboptimal workload levels might have suboptimal situation awareness, both leading to suboptimal performance, with the potential for patient harm. Workload is a hypothetical construct representing the overall cost incurred by a human operator to achieve a particular level of performance.[3] A relationship between workload and performance was originally described in 1976 by Meister[4] and further explored and refined in 1988 by Reid and Colle.[5] Their work suggests that individuals exposed to relatively low levels of demand might experience suboptimal workload caused by low environmental stimulation and boredom, and thus reduced performance; individuals exposed to relatively moderate demands are expected to operate under optimal workload and thus achieve adequate performance; individuals exposed to relatively high demand are expected to be operating through stresses at a suboptimal workload and thus reduced performance. Reid and Colle proposed that an upper limit of workload be set (often termed a workload "redline, see Figure 3.9").[5]

7.1.2 Factors Influencing Workload

Mental workload and performance are affected by stressors (e.g., task complexity, time pressures, interruptions, etc.); workflow designs (e.g., policies and procedures, environmental conditions, etc.); and usability of human-computer interfaces. Within healthcare in general and in radiation oncology specifically, increasing complexity and reliance on computer-human interactions have been implicated as sources of increased workload and reduced performance.[6-13] Within radiation oncology, these issues are often pertinent during the treatment-planning process, during which the providers need to consider multiple types of information or data from diverse sources (e.g., clinical and imaging data based on the electronic health record [EHR], reference materials) to perform a fairly precise task.[8-11]

7.1.3 Research Endpoints and Broad Overview of Results

In our studies, we have measured workload for various radiation oncology professionals (focusing somewhat on tasks related to treatment planning), quantified stressors that might influence workload, and related several measures of workload to several measures of performance.

We initially present a broad overview of our IRB-approved studies, conducted in "real" clinical and simulated environments, followed by a more detailed formal presentation of the data. Overall, we have:

- demonstrated that there is a marked variation in workload among radiation oncology professionals performing a variety of routine clinical tasks.
- demonstrated that the National Aeronautics and Space Administration Task Load Index (NASA-TLX), a tool that is commonly used in other industries to measure subjective mental workload, appears valid in radiation oncology settings as well.
- demonstrated that there is an association between NASA-TLX and performance.
- quantified sources of stressors affecting radiation oncology professionals during routine clinical tasks.
- generated supporting evidence suggesting that physiological responses (i.e., pupil diameter) can be used to measure workload.

7.2 RESEARCH PERFORMED IN THE CLINICAL ENVIRONMENT

7.2.1 Subjective Evaluation of Mental Workload

The NASA-TLX is widely considered to be a valid and reliable subjective measure of mental workload and is used across many disciplines.[14–16] The NASA-TLX considers six dimensions: Mental, Physical Demands, Temporal Demands, Frustration, Effort, and Performance. NASA-TLX scores of 50 or above have been associated with reduced performance in numerous settings,[17–21] including (based our data) radiation oncology.[11,22–24]

In a real clinical environment, we collected 171 NASA-TLX assessments from 21 radiation oncology professionals (Figure 7.2).[11] Marked

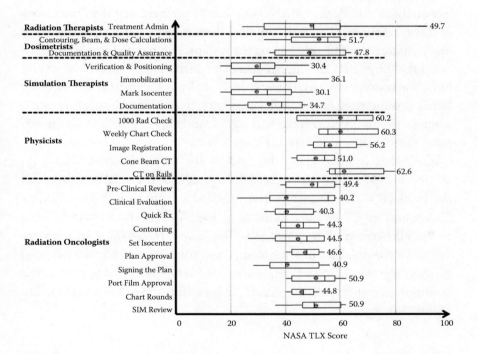

FIGURE 7.2
Mental workload levels (NASA-TLX score) for various radiation oncology professionals, for a variety of tasks, as shown. For each task, the average is marked by the circle with a cross inside and written to the side of the entry. The box plot itself demarcates the extent of the 25%–75% confidence interval with median (50%) marked by the vertical line and the full range of data by the thin horizontal line. (With permission from Mazur LM, Mosaly P, Jackson M, et al. *Int J Radiat Oncol Biol Phys* 2012;83:e571–e576.)

interprofessional variations were noted (analysis of variation [ANOVA], $P < .01$). Overall, simulation therapists had low workloads (NASA-TLX range 30 to 36) and physicists had high workloads (NASA-TLX range 51–63). We hypothesized that the suboptimal workloads for the simulation therapists may be caused by several factors, including (1) repetitive nature of some tasks, (2) an occasionally underbooked schedule, and (3) relatively lower criticality of some of their tasks (e.g., those not directly focused on the physical patient, such as scheduling). On the other hand, the relatively high workload (NASA-TLX > 55) for physicists may reflect the technical complexity and time demands of their tasks (e.g., pretreatment image registration) and the criticality of some of their work (e.g., QA activities mostly done in isolation).

Considering the individual dimensions of the NASA-TLX, the multivariate analysis of variance (MANOVA) results revealed that the dimensions of mental demand ($P < .001$), physical demand ($P = .001$), and effort ($P = .006$) differed significantly among the groups. Further, Duncan's test indicated that physicists had higher scores for mental demand and effort and radiation oncologists had higher scores for physical demand. On the other hand, dosimetrists had significantly lower scores for physical demand, whereas simulation therapists had significantly lower scores in all dimensions except physical demand (Figure 7.3).

Interestingly, considering the data by the tasks, the ANOVA analysis on the NASA-TLX scores revealed no significant difference between the tasks ($P = .12$). Duncan's test revealed significantly higher NASA-TLX scores for *CT on rails*, followed by *weekly chart check* and *1,000-rad check*, all performed by physicists. The lowest NASA-TLX scores were found for the *quick Rx* task performed by radiation oncologists, followed by *marking isocenter* and *simulation and setup verification* performed by simulation therapists (see Table 7.2 for definition of tasks included in Figure 7.4).

7.2.2 Relationship between Mental Workload and Performance

The World Health Organization (WHO) has created a large repository of information regarding 7,741 incidents affecting patients (consisting of 3,125 adverse events and 4,616 near misses) occurring over approximately 30 years in clinical radiation oncology.[25] For each, WHO attempted to identify the apparent stage of the treatment continuum at which the "root

NASA TLX Dimensions (average)

Study Group	Mental Demand	Physical Demand	Temporal Demand	Perfor-mance	Effort	Frustra-tion
Simulation Therapists	52	21	46	79	46	28
Radiation Therapists	65	36	65	64	67	37
Dosimetrists	70	5	54	95	59	47
Physicists	80	23	68	77	75	45
Radiation Oncologists	59	40	58	60	57	49

FIGURE 7.3

The graphical representation of average NASA TLX scores for the individual dimensions, shown for each radiation oncology professional subgroup. The width of the bar is approximately proportional to the score. (With permission from Mazur LM, Mosaly P, Jackson M, et al. *Int J Radiat Oncol Biol Phys* 2012;83:e571–e576.)

cause" of the incidents happened. The stages noted in the WHO report were mapped to the tasks studied in our clinic (see Table 7.3).

For each stage noted in the WHO report, we computed the average NASA-TLX score for the tasks that mapped to that stage. Eleven percent (828/7,741) of the incidents in the WHO report that could not be readily mapped to the tasks we assessed were excluded from the present analysis (e.g., cobalt machine commissioning, brachytherapy incidents). Considering the remaining 6,913 incidents, Figure 7.4 demonstrates the potential positive association between the average NASA-TLX scores of the different tasks in our analysis with the frequency of these tasks as the primary source of the incident in the WHO report (Pearson's correlation coefficient = 0.877, P value = .045).[11]

We recognize that there are inherent limitations to this approach. There are biases in attribution that make it difficult to identify the "precise cause" of a given incident. Indeed, most incidents result from the confluence of several events. Further, the mapping of the WHO stages to the

TABLE 7.2

Description of Tasks Analyzed in the Study

Responsibility	Task Name	Number of Assessments	Short Task Description
Simulation therapist	Verification and positioning	12	Identification and positioning of patient for CT
Simulation therapist	Immobilization	12	Fashioning devices such as molds and masks
Simulation therapist	Marking isocenter	12	Physical tattoo by simulation therapist (placement decision by radiation oncologist)
Simulation therapist	Simulation and documentation	12	Scheduling, completion of QA checklist
Radiation therapist	Treatment administration	23	Radiation therapist delivers the radiation to the patient
Dosimetrist	Contouring, beam and dose calculations	5	Contouring, beam placement, dose calculation in consultation with radiation oncologist
Dosimetrist	Documentation and quality assurance	5	Documentation and uploading plan from planning software to treatment software; completion of QA checklist
Physicist	1,000-rad check	3	Review treatment plan, delivery, and special instructions in R & V software after the first fraction of treatment and prior to the patient receiving 1,000 rads
Physicist	Weekly chart check	3	Confirm weekly that treatment was delivered as planned in the R & V software
Physicist	Image registration	4	Fusion of external images to treatment planning CT to assist MD in target localization
Physicist	CT on rails	4	"Real-time" image fusion (patient on treatment table) with immediate coordinate shifts to implement the treatment plan
Physicist	Cone beam CT	4	Image preparation for target localization on treatment machine

(Continued)

TABLE 7.2 *(CONTINUED)*

Description of Tasks Analyzed in the Study

Responsibility	Task Name	Number of Assessments	Short Task Description
Radiation oncologist	Preclinical review	8	Review of outside records, coordinating, and teaching discussion with students and residents
Radiation oncologist	Clinical evaluation	8	New consult—clinical evaluation, including decisions to treat or not and consent; interval follow-up care and status checks of active treatment patients
Radiation oncologist	Quick Rx	7	Entering orders and special instructions in electronic medical record for simulation
Radiation oncologist	Contouring	7	Target volume and sensitive organ definition (defining the borders of organs)
Radiation oncologist	Simulation—set isocenter	7	Selection of the isocenter at the time of simulation
Radiation oncologist	Plan approval	7	Review selection and approval of plan in treatment-planning system with dosimetrist
Radiation oncologist	Signing the plan	7	Electronic signature of prescription in the R & V system
Radiation oncologist	Port film approval	7	Port film or CBCT approval in the R & V system or at the treatment machine
Radiation oncologist	Chart rounds	7	Weekly peer review of new starts, boosts or other changes
Radiation oncologist	Sim review	7	Daily peer review of contours for patients recently simulated

* R & V = record and verify.

tasks considered in our clinic is somewhat uncertain. Clinical practice has certainly changed markedly over the last several decades and varies between clinics. Nevertheless, this is a reasonable first step to considering the possible utility of using the NASA-TLX to assess risks in clinical radiation oncology.

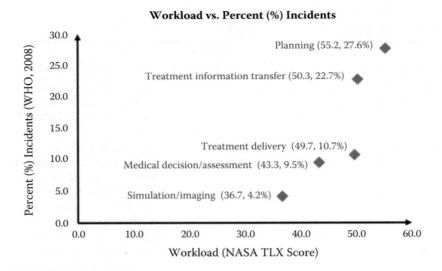

Workload vs. Percent (%) Incidents

FIGURE 7.4

The association between the average NASA TLX scores of the different tasks in our analysis with the frequency of similar tasks as being the primary source of the error in the WHO report. (With permission from Mazur LM, Mosaly P, Jackson M, et al. *Int J Radiat Oncol Biol Phys* 2012;83:e571–e576.). The mapping of processes in our analysis to those in the WHO data set is inexact (e.g., clinical practice has changed over time); thus, this analysis is imprecise. Nevertheless, the apparent association is thought provoking. See text for further discussion.

7.2.3 Stressors

We spent 32, 56, 24, 80, and 32 hours formally observing simulation therapists (therapists working on the computed tomographic [CT] and conventional simulator); radiation therapists (therapists working on the treatment machine); dosimetrists; physicists; and radiation oncologists, respectively, during their daily routines.[11] During each session, we recorded the number and sources of stressors, segregated based on a typical taxonomy of sources of stressors, defined as follows:

- Technical stressors caused by software or hardware malfunctions (e.g., computer program "freezes");
- Environmental stressors caused by conditions in the work environment (e.g., physician cannot focus because of the noise in the room);
- Teamwork stressors caused by a delay in information exchange or a delay in physical presence for task completion (e.g., therapist waiting for physician to approve a film);

TABLE 7.3

Summary of Adverse Events and Near Misses

Radiation Therapy Stage During Which the Event/Near Miss Occurred	WHO Errors (2008)			
	Adverse Events	Near Misses	Total Count	Percentage of Total
Assessment of patient, decision to treat, and prescription		736 (16%)	736	9.53
Positioning and immobilization		473 (10.2%)	473	6.12
Simulation and imaging				
Commissioning	790[a] (25.4%)		790	10.22
Treatment planning	1,717 (55.2%)	649 (14.1%)	2,366	30.62
Treatment information transfer	284 (9.1%)	1,909 (41.3%)	2,193	28.38
Patient setup and treatment delivery	320 (10.3%)	849 (18.4%)	1,169	15.13
Treatment review				
Total	3,111[b]	4,616	7,727	

Source: Data from the WHO (2008).
[a] Excludes cobalt 60 related errors.
[b] Excludes 23 cases of brachytherapy.

- Time stressors caused by the need to expedite work (e.g., a recalculation needed for a patient already under therapy);
- Patient stressors caused by the unexpected needs of patients (e.g., patient experiences a high level of pain, leading to a delay in scheduled procedure);
- Interruption stressors caused by physical interruptions during work activities (e.g., pages and incoming phone calls requiring attention).

Following each observational session, we reviewed the collected data with the participants to ensure accuracy of the recorded events. These observational data were analyzed to reveal frequencies of sources of stressors. On average, five stressors per case (defined as one cycle of analyzed tasks) occurred during the observed work of simulation therapists, radiation therapists, and dosimetrists and three per case for physicists and radiation oncologists. Figure 7.5 illustrates the percentages of different sources of stressors. For most team members, interruptions were the most common stressor. Some of our initiatives to reduce these stressors, in particular interruptions, are described in Chapter 5.

Stressors (%)

Study Group	Technical	Interruption	Teamwork	Time	Patient	Environmental
Simulation Therapists	20	40	10	10	20	
Radiation Therapists		71		16	13	
Dosimetrists	30	30	20	20		
Physicists	18	20	16	31	8	7
Radiation Oncologists		46	12	8	4	30
All Pooled	13.6	41.4	11.6	17	9	7.4

FIGURE 7.5

The graphical representation of different sources of stressors. The bar width is approximately proportional to the percentage of the different types of stressors experienced by each radiation oncology professional subgroup. The last row in the table represents the pooled average. (With permission from Mazur LM, Mosaly P, Jackson M, et al. *Int J Radiat Oncol Biol Phys* 2012;83:e571–e576.)

7.3 RESEARCH PERFORMED IN THE SIMULATED ENVIRONMENT

We have created a simulation laboratory within the Radiation Oncology Department that enables us to study providers performing routine clinical tasks. The design of the laboratory emulates the real clinical environment (Figure 7.6). Our group has assessed mental workload, subjectively based on the NASA-TLX; (Section 7.3.1) and objectively based on pupil diameter (Section 7.3.2). We have successfully related both subjective and objective mental workload measures to performance.

7.3.1 Subjective Evaluation of Mental Workload

In a laboratory setting, nine physician volunteers (four faculty and five residents; incentivized by $100 gift card) each performed a series of

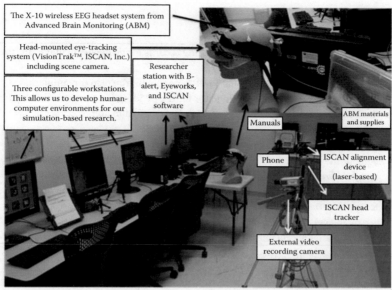

The X-10 wireless EEG headset system from Advanced Brain Monitoring (ABM)

Head-mounted eye-tracking system (VisionTrak™, ISCAN, Inc.) including scene camera.

Three configurable workstations. This allows us to develop human-computer environments for our simulation-based research.

Researcher station with B-alert, Eyeworks, and ISCAN software

Manuals

ABM materials and supplies

Phone

ISCAN alignment device (laser-based)

ISCAN head tracker

External video recording camera

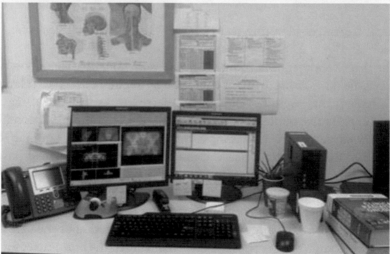

FIGURE 7.6

The simulation laboratory is a 250-square-foot dedicated room within the Department of Radiation Oncology (see top). The laboratory is immediately adjacent to the clinic, so it is in close proximity to the subjects needed for research studies. The laboratory is equipped with three workstations that closely emulate the real clinical environment. Each workstation includes a computer monitor (configurable; see bottom picture for a sample physician workstation), keyboard, and computer mouse (exactly what the subjects use in the real clinic), thus increasing the validity of our simulations. The laboratory also includes the researchers' workstation, which allows recording and analyzing the data from the experiments in "real time."

TABLE 7.4

Clinical Treatment-Planning Tasks[a]

1.	Review patient's written reports, including records in the departmental EHR, the clinic notes, and radiology reports.
2.	Type a note into the departmental EHR to document the plan for simulation, including instructions to the simulator for the pending CT and to dosimetry for the anticipated doses (done in the Quick Orders section and Notes sections of EHR, respectively).
3.	Review diagnostic images within the planning system.
4.	Segment the CT image to define the target volume (if desired; *not needed for two-field brain, but needed for a curative four-field postoperative pancreas*). Review contours/segmentations (of the normal anatomy) generated by the dosimetrist.
5.	Design your treatment field(s).
6.	Review the generated plan.
7.	Approve plan if acceptable in treatment. You might decide not to approve it.

[a] Performed for each of the three cases by each of the nine subjects.

clinical treatment-planning tasks (Table 7.4) for three clinical scenarios (thus resulting in 27 evaluations).[22–24]

The three treatment-planning scenarios were (1) palliative opposed lateral two-field whole brain under condition of "regular coverage" (planning for a patient they were familiar with; referred to as the "brain/regular" case); (2) palliative opposed lateral two-field whole brain under condition of "cross coverage" (planning for a patient they were not familiar with; referred to as the "brain/cross" case); and (3) curative four-field postoperative pancreas (referred to it as the "pancreas" case). Participants were asked to complete planning within 5, 10, and 15 minutes, respectively; however, they were permitted to complete the cases even if they extended their work beyond the allocated time. At the completion of the cases, the physicians completed the NASA-TLX. We included the brain cases for this study because they are common clinical scenarios for radiation oncologists and are generally considered "easy." However, because such patients often need to initiate their treatment urgently (and the physician may have less flexibility in scheduling the start of therapy), the pretherapy planning tasks might be likely to be "handed off" to a colleague.

Workload levels for brain/cross case were relatively moderate (NASA-TLX overall average 49) and were significantly higher for the pancreas case (NASA-TLX overall average 66; $P < .05$) and significantly lower for the brain/regular case (NASA-TLX overall average 27; $P < .05$). ANOVA revealed significant differences in NASA-TLX scores between cases ($P < .001$) and experience level ($P = .09$; with residents' scores trending higher than faculty).

Considering the different components of the NASA-TLX in all 27 assessments, the Mental Demand was higher than the Physical Demand in 27/27, higher than the Performance in 24/27, higher than Frustration in 22/27, higher than the Temporal Demand in 17/27, and higher than the Effort in 16/27. Thus, the Mental Demand dimension was a major source of the overall NASA-TLX score. We also learned that Temporal Demand and Frustration dimensions were the greatest sources of intersubject variation.

During the conduct of each task, subjects were observed by two research-ers and video recorded for subsequent formal objective review (using an external video camera and screen capture video software [via Camtasia Studio 7 software©]). Based on these direct observations ($\approx$18 hours) and video reviews ($\approx$30 hours), researchers noted errors. For each error that was recorded and not corrected before plan approval by the subject, a severity grade (based on its potential clinical impact) was assigned by con-tent experts (an experienced dosimetrist and physician) as follows:

- Grade 0: omitting or forgetting to perform certain steps but result-ing in no errors (e.g., rechecking that the directive to the dosime-trist accurately reflected the planned beam arrangement and desired doses, failing to comprehensively review image segmentation);
- Grade 1: entering an incomplete/suboptimal clinical note or planning directive/prescription (e.g., missing prescription requirements as required by a departmental standard: site, dose per fraction × number of fractions, total dose) but no direct clinical consequence expected;
- Grade 2: approving a treatment prescription without correcting a purposefully embedded error (e.g., evident as an inconsistency between the treatment-planning system and the treatment delivery/verify system but not likely to have a meaningful clinical impact).

Among the 27 cases studied, 18 had no noted errors, 7 had severity grade 1 errors, and 2 had severity grade 2. There were no higher-grade errors noted (e.g. errors likely to cause serious consequences).

The relationship between workload levels (as quantified by NASA-TLX) and the performance (as quantified by severity of errors) is shown in Figure 7.7 (relationship test statistic = 5.37; P value = .02; goodness-of-fit test statistics: chi-square [Pearson] = 49.4; P value = .45).[23]

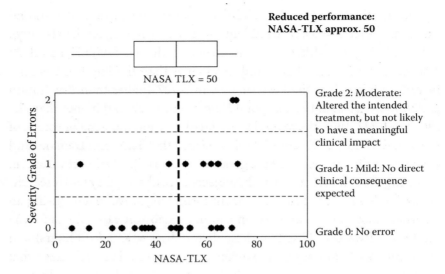

FIGURE 7.7

Marginal plot of NASA-TLX scores versus severity grade of errors. *x* axis, NASA-TLX scores; *y* axis, severity grade errors. Top, box plot of NASA-TLX scores (vertical line in the box defines the median, the box borders define the 25%–75% confidence interval, and the horizontal line indicates the range of the data). Dashed line at NASA-TLX score of 50 indicates workload score where errors appear to be more common (as per receiver operating characteristic analysis) and is the threshold value used in some other industries (e.g., aviation).

Our results suggest a relationship between workload and performance, with errors more common when NASA-TLX scores approach about 50. This same approximate threshold has been seen in other industries[14,15,20,21] and suggests that workload may be an important factor contributing to errors in treatment-planning tasks.

7.3.2 Objective Evaluation of Mental Workload

There are several methods that have been proposed to measure mental workload objectively (eye-based data, electroencephalography [EEG], heart rate, changes in temperature, galvanic skin response, etc.). Initially, we were particularly interested in the eye data, as it perhaps is most relevant to studies of human-computer interactions.

Changes in task-evoked pupil response (TEPR) have been suggested to provide an objective measure of mental workload in various experiments, including arithmetic; short-term memory tasks; pitch discriminations;

standard tests of concentration; sentence comprehension; paired-associate learning; imagery tasks with abstract and with concrete words; cognitive strategy shifts; and design of interfaces.[26-37]

In our simulated environment, we successfully measured TEPR in nine radiation oncologists (four faculty, five residents) using the head-mounted eye-tracking system (VisionTrak™, ISCAN, Inc., Burlington, MA; with pupil diameter sampled at 60 Hz).[22,24]

Clinicians performed treatment planning for a patient in need of simple palliative two-field opposed lateral brain fields during regular versus cross-coverage scenarios (see Section 7.3.1 for rationale). Three tasks performed and assessed for each scenario were: (1) review of patient's medical record within the documents section of our EHRs, review of the patient's diagnostic images; (2) review of the planning CT images and creation of the target volume and associated treatment beams within our treatment-planning system; and (3) retrieval and review of the completed three-dimensional (3D) treatment plan (created by dosimetry) and approval/disapproval of the treatment plan.[24,38]

The initial experiment was considered a cross-coverage scenario because the clinicians had no prior knowledge about the case. After 48 hours, the clinicians returned and planned the same case, now represented as a regular coverage scenario in which they had some prior knowledge about the case to be planned.

After collecting the data, we utilized standard procedures to process the pupil dilation data.[26] Baseline pupil dilation data were captured prior to the start of each experiment for all the participants. The TEPR was computed by subtracting the baseline from the task pupil dilation data. TEPR during cross coverage was significantly higher compared to regular coverage for all subjects and for the overall group (see Figure 7.8A; $P < .01$). However, how does one assess if the TEPR is too high? A common way to assess an "upper bound" for TEPR is to ask subjects to perform increasingly difficult cognitive tasks and to note the TEPR values just prior to when performance starts to decline. A well-known and valid method approach is based on an "operation span" (essentially the subject is asked to remember an increasing number of digits; in our experiments, we used letters). In our lab, we conducted an operation span experiment on 15 subjects and found that TEPR increased with the number of letters memorized, up to a maximum of six letters. Beyond six, performance uniformly declined, and TEPR also rapidly declined. Thus, the TEPR at the level of six letters might represent a reasonable upper bound (work-load "redline"). The data are shown in Figure 7.8B.

We can now use the data from Figures 7.8A and 7.8B to assess if the TEPR values during the clinical tasks were "too high." As shown in Figure 7.8C, the TEPR values during the cross-coverage scenario more closely approach the upper bound compared with the regular coverage scenario. These results suggest that a cross-coverage scenario was cognitively *more* demanding compared to regular coverage ($P < .01$). The cross coverage can be thought of as a task equivalent to memorizing approximately five digits, which seems doable but is at the point that potential performance degradation may be expected if there is continued working in this state. More research is needed in this area to advance our under-standing of mental workload and make findings generalizable to other areas in medicine.

7.4 PLANNED FUTURE RESEARCH ON WORKLOAD AND PERFORMANCE

We believe that it is most reasonable and timely to quantify workload, and study the relationship between workload and performance, within radia-tion oncology. We suggest that workload be considered as a metric for quality and safety because suboptimal workload levels appear to be asso-ciated with reduced performance. The results from these types of stud-ies can inform things such as work assignments, work duty hours, and the development of alternative procedures to either reduce workload (e.g., task redesign, usability improvements, etc.) or bolster QA efforts (e.g., checklists, huddles, double checks, hardware-/software-supported "hard" stops, etc.) for tasks with particularly high workloads. This research may have implications for other medical settings with similar tasks. Additional studies with a larger number of subjects, an increased diversity of tasks, and alternative measures of both workload and performance are planned.

Our future research will include measures of more *sophisticated* met-rics of pupil dilation. To date, we have been largely considering "average" pupil dilations. However, because radiation oncology providers perform numerous sequential tasks, the common indices such as time-weighted mean pupil diameter may *not* accurately capture high mental work-load for relatively short individual tasks (i.e., large dilations in the pupil

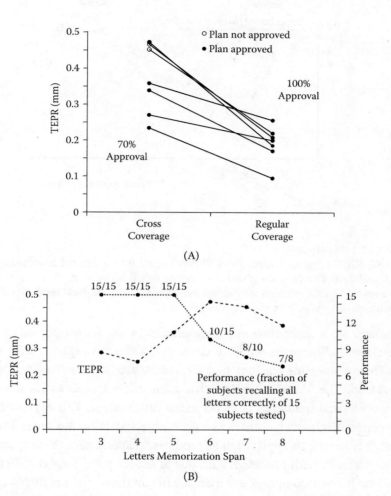

FIGURE 7.8
(A)–(C) The y axis in each figure quantifies mental workload using task-evoked pupillary response (TEPR), the degree of pupil dilation beyond the baseline. (A) Higher levels for cross coverage versus regular coverage ($P < .01$). The patterns are similar for faculty and residents. (B) Increases in TEPR and decline in performance with the length of the letter span in the memorization-recall experiment. Performance is perfect up to six letters. Beyond this, performance declines, and TEPR declines, apparently reflecting reduced workload as subjects "give up." *(Continued)*

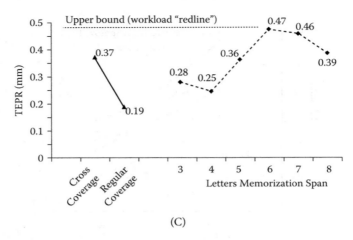

(C)

FIGURE 7.8 (CONTINUED)

(A)–(C) (C) The "upper bound" for a TEPR of about 0.47, estimated from panel B, is shown as the dotted line, along with the average data from panel A. This suggests that the workload level during cross coverage may approach the maximal level of workload consistent with a high level of performance.

diameter for a short time might be diluted by the longer period of data acquisition). Therefore, we have developed alternative quantitative indices from these time tracings that we believe are better related to mental workload. The "class" of indices that most interest us quantify the dilation peaks and frequency of peaks in the time tracing. This approach was suggested originally by others as a good objective index for mental workload.[26] However, its application beyond basic experiments (usually lasting a few seconds; with predesign stimulus to induce pupil response) to more realistic human-computer experiments in simulated environments (especially in healthcare settings) has been rather limited. Assessing the size and frequency of the peaks in pupil diameter might best reflect a person's overall mental workload. Consider a typical workday during which much of the time is spent performing routine tasks but is accentuated by several periods when the mental workload is much harder. Those "higher mental workload periods," the magnitude of the mental workload, and their frequency are likely going to be the major determinants of your perceived overall mental workload for that day.

We also started work on EEG-based metrics, which have been studied in many areas and appear to provide a somewhat-reliable measure of mental workload for individuals, including air traffic controllers, airline pilots, drivers, and participants performing basic cognitive tasks.[39–54]

We also plan to design and assess standardized and generalizable simulation-based training to enhance radiation oncology planners' performance (i.e., ability to detect and manage uncommon but potentially lethal events and to avoid potential omission/commission that can also lead to catastrophic events) and to improve mental workload. This may allow planners to acquire new skills and knowledge to proactively maintain their preoccupation with patient safety within optimal mental workload limits. Results from this research may also help improve user interfaces and cognitive work flows that might facilitate recognition of unanticipated unsafe situations (i.e. enhance safety mindfulness).

7.5 "LAUNDRY LIST" OF POTENTIAL RESEARCH PROJECTS

Sections 7.5.1 to 7.5.6 discuss research opportunities (a "laundry list" if you will) within the context of radiation oncology.

7.5.1 Personal Transformation to Safety Mindfulness

The successful implementation of safety mindfulness requires employees to be *initiators* and *enhancers*. Sections 3.4 and 6.6 highlight strategies for transitioning individuals from *Quick Fixing* to *Initiating* and how to develop *Enhancing* behaviors.[55] However, it is presently not known how best to do this. The potential impact of organizational-, workplace-, and people-level factors in promoting these desired behaviors is not well understood.

The American Society of Radiation Oncology (ASTRO) accreditation program will specifically assess the "culture of safety" and related factors. Therefore, this may provide a unique opportunity to gather data on the interplay between these various factors and the behaviors of radiation oncology professionals.

Potential research questions might include the following:

- What are the patterns of individual or organizational implementation efforts associated with successful transition to high reliability and value creation?

- What are the characteristics of an implementation efforts associated with individual or organizational readiness for transitioning people toward *Initiating* and *Enhancing* behaviors?
- How do workers perceive and respond to initiatives to alter behaviors?
- What theories for change implementation can we draw on, and what new theories must be developed, for successful implementation of high reliability and value creation in complex and technologically driven systems such as radiation oncology centers?

Challenges to these sorts of analyses will relate to the impact of many confounding factors. Thus, ascribing any apparent difference in behavioral outcome with specific input variables will be difficult at best. Nevertheless, with enough data, it might be possible to sort this out using advanced statistical approaches. But, why do this within radiation oncology at all? It is probable that research done in other areas of medicine or industry would yield similar results to any analyses done within radiation oncology. Unfortunately, there is little to draw on. Limited research has been done to gain understanding of the *dynamic interplay* between individuals and the organization within which they work and how that interplay influences individual or organizational behavior change. Thus, performing this work in our field is reasonable. If we are collecting the data necessary to perform this type of analysis during the accreditation process, the marginal costs might be small. Further, information learned in our field might be applicable to other areas as well.

7.5.2 Leadership Style and Behaviors

As discussed throughout this book, successful change management requires strong leadership. This is particularly true for the multiprofessional change effort needed in radiation oncology centers, where physicians, physicists, dosimetrists, therapists, nurses, administrators, and others each have specific needs and challenges to be addressed. However, what leadership style is most associated with an effective transition toward high reliability and value creation? Please recall a possible leadership paradox described to us by Larry in Chapter 4 (Sections 4.2 and 4.3). The paradox arises when Larry must make decision regarding his leadership style (to be "transformative" [build consensus, inspire others to follow, etc.] versus to be "transitional" [set a mandate and tell people what to do]). Which approach (or blend of approaches) is better and when?

We conducted some preliminary studies in healthcare organizations seeking high reliability and value creation.[56,57] The evaluation of leadership style and behaviors in rather successful organizations, as seen from raters' perspective, showed a slight tendency favoring transactional leadership. In general, employees viewed the leaders as somewhat task oriented with an emphasis on what needs to be done and how to do it. On the other hand, leaders viewed themselves as somewhat more transformational and concerned with motivating and inspiring employees to do more than expected. The leaders also perceived themselves as relatively charismatic and inspirational, communicating a clear vision of the future.

Our message to radiation oncology centers—to embrace these high-reliability and value creation concepts—will alter how staff members perform their jobs. This might be a difficult change for both leaders (to lead) and for employees (to accept). Such a fundamental change in behaviors of workers at all levels might be perceived to require transformational leadership as success depends on the leader building trust, motivation, and internal commitment throughout their organization. Nevertheless, our findings suggest that transactional leadership might be a more appropriate style to employ, with leader effectiveness depending on clearly defining what the change is, and monitoring performance against these expectations.[56,57]

It seems likely that good change management requires both styles. Research to better define the utility of each approach in the journey toward high reliability and value creation may be helpful. Perhaps there are settings in which one approach is clearly preferable? Potential research questions include the following:

- What are the patterns and magnitudes of leadership styles, actions, and decisions during different stages of implementation efforts associated with successful implementation of high reliability and value creation?
- Are there any radiation oncology-specific considerations that influence this question? Or, can we simply extrapolate from other industries?

Research along these lines might be conducted via standard tools to assess transformational and transactional leadership, such as the Multifactor Leadership Questionnaire (MLQ) developed by Avolio and Bass that has been used in numerous industries and research studies and has been shown to exhibit a strong level of validity.[58] The MLQ measures the extent the leader motivates others to extra effort, how effective the leader is perceived to be, and how satisfied the raters are with how the leader works with others. This might allow us to understand how different leadership styles and behaviors affect high-reliability and value creation organizations over time.

7.5.3 Plan–Do–Study–Act (PDSA)

Radiation oncology departments are complex entities with diverse groups of employees working simultaneously to achieve the common goal of treating patients safely, effectively, and efficiently. Within each group, there are opportunities to improve work flows. Although any improvement may have a positive effect within its specific group, there might be unforeseen negative effects on other groups or on intergroup activities. The Plan–Do–Study–Act (PDSA) cycle (see Section 3.2.3 for an overview), when correctly implemented, takes into account the complexity of the interrelationships between these groups and considers the unintended consequences that suggested improvements might have on the system as a whole. However, despite the enormous potential of the PDSA cycle for process improvement, little is known about characteristics of the PDSA cycle that make it effective while used on radiation oncology teams (especially teams that include multidisciplinary teams and physicians).

In theory, the PDSA cycle promotes the use of a small-scale, iterative approach to test interventions because this enables rapid assessment of change. This provides users with an opportunity to learn and act quickly, minimizing risk to patients. In line with the scientific experimental method, the PDSA cycle focuses on learning, and it is primarily achieved through interventional experiments designed to test a change.

There is reason to be concerned that this approach is not being used effectively in healthcare. In a systematic review of the application of the PDSA cycle to improve quality in healthcare, Taylor and colleagues found that only 73/409 published articles met the theoretical criteria, and less than 20% (14/73) fully documented the application of a sequence of iterative cycles; only 15% (7/47) reported the use of quantitative data at monthly (or more frequent) intervals to inform cycle progression.[59] Many of these studies lacked detail accounting for the variable denominator in these statistics.

In radiation oncology settings, it would be helpful to better understand the utility of improvement methods in general (e.g., failure mode effect analysis [FMEA], root cause analysis [RCA], etc.), including PDSA. A

PubMed search using the term *PDSA cycle* returned 52 matches; the term *PDSA and radiation oncology* returned zero relevant matches; the term *PDCA cycle* [with C standing for "check" instead of "study") *and radiation oncology* returned one match. Using Google Scholar and the terms *PDSA cycle* and *radiation oncology*, we found 17 matches. Thus, such potential deficits in knowledge can lead into improper use of PDSA cycles, leading to suboptimal results, frustration, and eventually misinterpretation of its utility in radiation oncology.

Potential research questions include the following:

- What improvement approaches are most associated with successful implementation of high reliability and value creation in complex and technologically driven systems such as radiation oncology centers?
- What are the characteristics of a PDSA cycle (or others) associated with successful implementation of high reliability and value creation?

Research along these lines could be conducted retrospectively or prospectively. Retrospectively, we could assess the past efforts of a variety of quality improvement tools (e.g., FMEA vs. RCA vs. PDSA vs. others) and relate them to actual improvement results. Prospectively, we could arrange a research study in which different centers would utilize different quality improvement methods and tools for similar issues, allowing us to gauge their effectiveness and efficiency in solving particular issues. However, interpretation of the data might still be difficult given the differences between centers and multiple other contextual factors that may have an impact on assessing actual improvement results. This could be overcome by a large number of centers participating in the study and proper design of the experiment.

7.5.4 Facility and Work Space Design

There are limited budgets to produce facility and workplace designs that meet the needs of patients, employees, suppliers, regulators, management, and so on. To our knowledge, there has not been a systematic review/ assessment of the optimal design of a radiation oncology facility. It is most interesting to recognize that there are marked differences in the physical design of most radiation oncology centers. An objective assessment of commonly used current designs, as well as alternatives, might be helpful. Is there a "superior" design that could optimize workload, performance, and lead to higher levels of patient safety? If yes, what are the key characteristics of such a superior design? Are these characteristics fairly uniform, or do they vary between environments?

Research along these lines could be conducted by assessing current designs of radiation oncology departments and relating them to key performance indicators (e.g., patient safety, employee safety, patient satisfaction, employee satisfaction, throughput, utilization rates, etc.). This could be done with centers varying in size ("large" vs. "small"), location (urban vs. rural), available services mix (radiation therapy only vs. multidisciplinary care; with different capabilities for treatment), and so on.

Equally important questions are *when* and *how* to generate and incorporate design characteristics into the design process. Many healthcare organizations utilize Lean thinking to help them design safer and more efficient facilities. A successful example is Virginia Mason Hospital in Seattle, Washington, where Lean-based redesign improved environments, quality, and operating margin.[60] The Center for Health Design and the Institute for Healthcare Improvement (IHI) both noted that such Lean-based approaches can promote quality, employee and patient satisfaction, and safety. Indeed, we relied heavily on this Lean thinking during our improvement work at UNC (described in Chapter 5).

However, there is little academic research regarding how to best incorporate Lean into the evidence-based design (EBD) process. Mazur and colleagues proposed an integration of the EBD process with Lean exploration loops, thereby creating a "Lean-EBD" design process.[61] At a high level, the Mazur et al. approach calls for development of broad sets of design alternatives, which allow architects to concurrently begin the EBD design process while receiving valuable information from Lean exploration loops, gradually narrowing the design alternatives and increasing the level of design details until an optimum design is revealed and refined. The goal underpinning the use of Lean exploration loops during the EBD process is the opportunity to postpone critical decisions while moving through the three critical EBD process design gates, namely, the footprint-planning gate, the layout-planning gate, and final design selection gate.

The design and construction of new radiation oncology centers across the United States and the world provide an opportunity for a prospective research study along these lines, testing and assessing Lean thinking during the EBD design process. Similar research opportunities exist across all other healthcare settings, which could accelerate our understanding of how best to use Lean thinking during facility design projects.

7.6 INTERFACE DESIGN AND USABILITY

Much of our work in radiation oncology has been computer based for many years (e.g., treatment planning, record-and-verify systems). The broader embrace of EHR systems throughout healthcare (e.g., Mosaiq˚ and ARIA within radiation oncology and Epic, Cerner, Allscripts, etc. more generally) has altered the manner in which we work. The transition from the traditional paper chart to an EHR raises many exciting possibilities for enhanced efficiency and performance as well as many challenges. In this section, we review some of the challenges and suggest how the application of usability engineering principles within the EHR might mitigate some of these challenges. Some of the lessons we have learned during the many years that electronic tools have been used within radiation oncology, and work done outside healthcare, can be used to improve the EHR. Research can be done to quantify the impact of some of these ideas within healthcare (or radiation oncology specifically). However, as these concepts have been shown to be generally valid in other settings, there is every reason to suspect that these approaches will be beneficial.

7.6.1 Lessons from Computer Science and UNC's Experience with Our Treatment-Planning Software

PLUNC (Plan UNC) is a radiation treatment-planning software program written, nurtured, and used clinically at UNC for over 20 years. This was the result of a long-term collaboration between visionary leaders in radiation oncology (e.g., Drs. Julian Rosenman, Edward Chaney, Joel Tepper, Sha Chang) and computer science (e.g., Dr. Steve Pizer) and the very hard work of many computer scientists (e.g., Drs. George Sherouse, Tim Cullip, Gregg Tracton). We are particularly fortunate that UNC has had a strong department of computer science, and we were successfully able to leverage its expertise. For many years, PLUNC was arguably one of the best radiation-planning software tools on the planet; as evidenced by its broad distribution to more than 200 centers internationally (including Duke, where Larry spent most of his career) and its use in more than 342 publications.

It is instructive to consider how PLUNC came to be such a good tool, particularly with regard to usability. Sure, we had good and motivated programmers, computer scientists, providers, and so on. However, critical factors were, and are the proximity of the programmers to the users and the ability for frequent iterations in development. Broadly speaking, users tell the programmers what they *think* they need and want. Programmers then watch how the users *actually use* the software, considering the intended and (perhaps even more important) the unintended uses. Modifications are continually considered, as clinical practice, and hence the needed software, evolves. Our PLUNC programmers routinely watch the software in use (e.g., in clinic, in our peer review sessions, etc.). It has been estimated that the PLUNC software currently being used clinically has been through 100 revisions for new features and improvements.

Presently, it is becoming difficult for us to maintain PLUNC's full clinical functionality with the increasing complexity and coupling of our practice. Indeed, UNC has both CyberKnife and TomoTherapy units, and we use their planning tools for stereotactic and complex intensity-modulated radiation therapy (IMRT). We will be adopting additional commercial software as well. These steps are being taken to address functionality, not usability. PLUNC is user friendly, more so than most commercial products.

The distinction between usability and functionality is important. *Usability* refers to the ability of the user to do the fundamental intended tasks (e.g., whether it is intuitive). *Functionality* refers to the capabilities of the software (e.g., the bells and whistles). Some of the most widely used software (e.g., Microsoft Word, Excel, PowerPoint) are both usable and functional. The basic functions are intuitive, and few people actually need to read the instruction manual. However, many of the more complex features within these programs are not intuitive and are likely not used by many people, but this is accepted because the basic functions (which most people need or use) *are* usable. Generally, users are more sensitive to usability than to functionality (assuming some basic utility is still provided). Consider the wide popularity of cell phone apps that often have focused and limited functionality but are loved because they are so easy to use. Users will tolerate functional limitations if the usability is good. Systems with suboptimal usability generally will not be voluntarily used. However, if users are forced to use such systems (e.g., poorly designed EHRs), they will likely experience escalating frustrations with each repeated use and perhaps increase the risk of human error. The user may come to resent their supervisors or institution for forcing use of the software and may have the impression that their time and efforts are not being respected.[12,13,62,63]

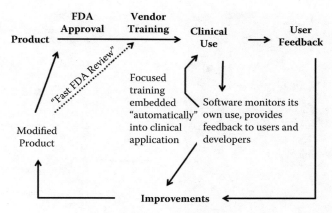

More Evolutionary Cycles → Better Product

FIGURE 7.9
The generic "product modification cycle" is crudely shown as the outer ring. The inner aspects reflect some modifications to facilitate more evolutionary cycles likely leading to better products.

The lessons for the EHRs are clear. We need to have frequent (and nearly continuous) interactions between users and developers, with corresponding relatively rapid evolution. We recognize that this can be challenging given regulations (e.g., of the Food and Drug Administration [FDA], etc.). Vendors, professional societies, and regulators need to work together to define systems that allow the power of evolution to improve these systems (Figure 7.9).

Further, we recognize that different users will perceive that they have different needs, and that the vendors feel a responsibility to meet those varied desires. We acknowledge that the software will need to provide some flexibility with regard to some features, but this needs to be carefully considered. Providing flexibility simply because the user asks for it might not be ideal. We offer the following considerations:

a. Heuristics have been used to define standards for software interfaces in other fields. There already is a body of literature to support some types of displays over others. This information should be used to define many (or even most) features in our EHRs. Certainly, additional assessments and research should be done to verify that these approaches are optimal in medicine/radiation oncology. But, until then, we would be wise to apply knowledge from other settings.

b. The software industry has broadly defined some best practices that are not universally applied in some EHRs. Consistency is a major

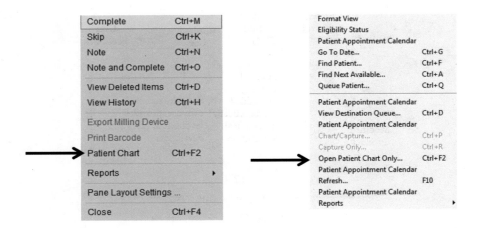

FIGURE 7.10

Example of an inconsistency in the nomenclature used in menus within a widely used software tool. Opening a chart is sometimes listed as "open patient chart" and in another place "patient chart." These sorts of inconsistencies, fairly common within medical software, tend to increase provider workload and frustration.

consideration. For example, buttons performing similar functions in different windows or views should be made to be as consistent as possible (wording, size, location, color, etc.). If not done, this may represent a source of persistent/growing frustration because the user never "gets used to it" as they are continually receiving "mixed messages" (Figure 7.10).

c. Variability in the manner in which information is input and displayed should be minimized. A good example of this is the variation in the manner in which the radiation prescription is displayed in some EHRs (discussed in more detail in the Appendix). Our field would be well served by adopting a standard manner for how we describe a radiation therapy prescription (e.g., Dose per fraction * Fraction number = Total planned dose). Our lack of consistency in this area is a major source of potential error and is analogous to the potential confusion resulting from inconsistent ways of describing dates (month/day/year vs. day/month/year) and distances/"weights" (meters/kilograms vs. feet/pounds).

d. Within an institution, some types of interuser variability should not be permitted. It would be foolish to allow one user to work in feet and another in meters within the same center.

e. Vendors should work together, and with the professional organizations, to define some standards and best practices (based on optimal usability) to address interinstitutional variations that might lead to error and inefficiency. Working with professional organizations and regulators should provide the vendors with a rationale to limit some of the choices provided to their customers. Again, the radiation prescription is perhaps an ideal example of this (discussed in the Appendix).

7.6.2 Lessons from Advertising and Education: Comprehension

Good communication is difficult, and we should do what we can to maximize the likelihood the readers will understand the message we are trying to convey. Scholars and practitioners have spent a fair amount of time studying this. A comprehensive assessment of this issue is presented in the book *Type and Layout* by Colin Wheildon, from the field of advertising.[64] Some of the information that follows is extracted from this book.

7.6.2.1 Capitalization

Studies have been done to better understand how humans comprehend text. Educational experts grapple with this issue as they try to ensure that our nation's young people learn to read effectively. The two major educational theories regarding reading comprehension are "phonics" and "whole language." Phonics contends that we read by sounding out, or decoding, the individual letters and syllables within words. Whole language contends that we learn to recognize words based on their entire look. For example, the word *giraffe* actually looks a little like a giraffe, with the *g* being the long tail to the left and the *f* being the animal's neck off to the right. The highly variable appearance of the lowercase letters (especially their upper halves) gives whole words unique shapes. Words written in all capitals have less-variable shapes of both their upper and lower halves (see Figure 7.11). Therefore, one is able to read lowercase letters better (even when the whole letter is not shown).

Here is what Larry has to say about this: "My understanding of these competing theories is that young people can learn to read by either method, but that as one becomes a more experienced reader, we rely largely on whole language to comprehend written text. This seems reasonable to me as I rarely sound out words based on their individual

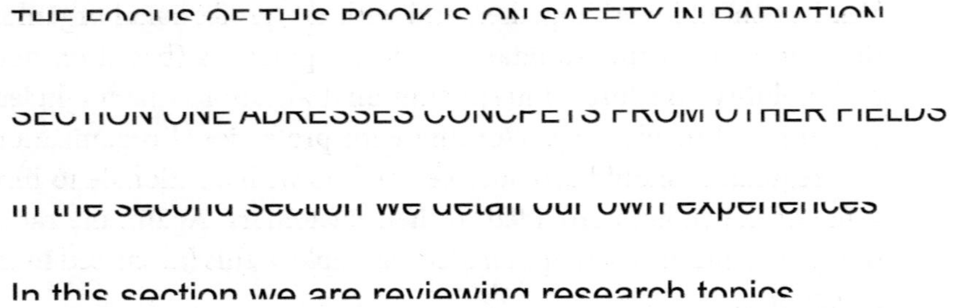

THE FOCUS OF THIS BOOK IS ON SAFETY IN RADIATION

SECTION ONE ADRESSES CONCPETS FROM OTHER FIELDS

IN THE SECOND SECTION WE DETAIL OUR OWN EXPERIENCES

In this section we are reviewing research topics

FIGURE 7.11
Sentences are shown four ways, with the upper and lower halves of uppercase and low-ercase letters. The upper half of the lowercase letters can be more readily comprehended than the others.

letters (although I do this whenever I struggle to read Hebrew at Torah study, but that is another story entirely). I've always been interested in this since I had trouble learning reading as a youngster, and both of my parents were teachers. I have not-so-fond memories of struggling to read and unsuccessfully decoding the letters in words. For many years, I dreaded the possibility of reading in public. Therefore, we should avoid the use of all capital letters wherever practical, as this makes it harder for the reader to understand our message."

IF YOU DON'T BELIEVE LARRY, ARE YOU HAVING DIFFICULTY READING THIS SENTENCE? HOW ABOUT THE PRIOR PARAGRAPH REPEATED HERE IN ALL CAPITALS. "MY UNDERSTANDING OF THESE COMPETING THEORIES IS THAT YOUNG PEOPLE CAN LEARN TO READ BY EITHER METHOD, BUT THAT AS ONE BECOMES A MORE EXPERIENCED READER, WE RELY LARGELY ON WHOLE LANGUAGE TO COMPREHEND WRITTEN TEXT. THIS SEEMS REASONABLE TO ME AS I RARELY SOUND OUT WORDS BASED ON THEIR INDIVIDUAL LETTERS (ALTHOUGH I DO THIS WHENEVER I STRUGGLE TO READ HEBREW AT TORAH STUDY, BUT THAT IS ANOTHER STORY ENTIRELY). I'VE ALWAYS BEEN INTERESTED IN THIS SINCE I HAD TROUBLE LEARNING READING AS A YOUNGSTER, AND BOTH OF MY PARENTS WERE TEACHERS. I HAVE NOT-SO-FOND MEMORIES OF STRUGGLING TO READ AND UNSUCCESSFULLY DECODING THE LETTERS IN WORDS. FOR MANY YEARS, I DREADED THE POSSIBILITY OF READING IN PUBLIC."

There are exceptions to this. For example, some words have been shown so often in capitals that we have become accustomed to understanding their meaning using a whole-language approach (e.g., EXIT, NO, YES, EHR, CME [continuing medical education], STOP, ASTRO, NIH [National Institutes of Health]). Short phrases in all capitals, such as a figure or table title or newspaper headline, are usually easily comprehended, but even in these cases, the use of lowercase letters would probably enhance comprehension. We find it harder to appreciate punctuation when all capitals are used. Thus, we suspect that a reason why one can "get away" with capitals in headlines and titles is that there is typically no punctuation.

There is an erroneous belief that the important information should be placed in capital letters. We see this often in pathology or radiology reports, where the diagnosis or interpretation is listed in all capitals, with the body of the main report in upper- and lowercase letters. Clearly, the creators of some of these reports believe that the diagnosis and interpretation are the more important aspects of the report and thus warrant being placed in all capital letters. We would suggest that this is the exact wrong approach as this reduces the reader's comprehension within the most important parts of the report. Within radiation oncology, we occasionally see error messages in computer software or alerts from industry vendors that are suboptimally presented in all capital letters. Alternative ways to make text stand out include things such as italics, increased font size, bold face, and color bordering, with italics apparently the optimal for comprehension.[64]

There are many places within our EHR where all capital letters are used without strong rationale and indeed is challenging to read. Medication lists raise particular challenges because one needs to comprehend words *and* numbers (Figure 7.12). Because numbers do not have upper and lower case and all are "tall," numbers naturally *do* stand out in a sea of traditional text. So, it is harder to appreciate the differences in the numbers within different entries if the surrounding text is in all capitals. In other words, the use of all capital letters negates this distinctive character of numbers. Note how the different medication dosages (i.e., the numbers) are more difficult to appreciate in the context of all capitals (Figure 7.12). This is a *major* latent error in the design of our health system. Medication errors are seen as one of the key hazards in our health system, and the use of all capital letters in this setting is only making matters worse. These are concrete examples

ACETAMINOPHEN PAIN RELIEF 500 MG TABLET
ACETAMINOPHEN PM 25 MG-500 MG TABLET
ACETAMINOPHEN PM EXTRA STRENGTH 25MG-500 MG TABLET
ACETAMINOPHEN-CAFFEINE 500 MG-65 MG DISINTEGRATING TABLET
ACETAMINOPHEN-CAFFEINE 500 MG-65 MG TABLET
ACETAMINOPHEN-CAFFEINE-PYRILAMINE 500 MG-60 MG-15 MG TABLET
ACETAMINOPHEN-DIPHENHYDRAMINE 500-25MG COMBO PRODUCT
ACETAMINOPHEN-DM 1,000 MG-30 MG/30 ML ORAL LIQUID
ACETAMINOPHEN-DM 160 MG-5 MG CHEWABLE TABLET
ACETAMINOPHEN-DM 160 MG-5 MG/5 ML ORAL LIQUID
ACETAMINOPHEN-DM 160 MG-5 MG/5 ML ORAL SUSPENSION
ACETAMINOPHEN-DM 160 MG-7.5 MG/5 ML ORAL LIQUID
ACETAMINOPHEN-GUAIFENESIN 1,000 MG-400 MG ORAL POWDER PACKET
ACETAMINOPHEN-GUAIFENESIN 325 MG-200 MG TABLET
ACETAMINOPHEN-GUAIFENESIN 650 MG-400 MG TABLET
ACETAMINOPHEN-PAMABROM 325 MG-25 MG TABLET
ACETAMINOPHEN-PAMABROM 500 MG-25 MG TABLET
ACETAMINOPHEN-PAMABROM-PYRILAM 500 MG-25 MG-15 MG TABLET

FIGURE 7.12
Example of a list of medications in all capitals. The dosages (i.e., the numbers) are somewhat difficult to comprehend in the context of all capital letters.

of challenges that are being brought on countless providers likely thousands of times per day. This is all so unnecessary and preventable.

7.6.2.2 Color

With regard to comprehension of written text on paper, a black font on a white background appears optimal. Subtle shading of the white background does not appear to alter comprehension much; however, darker shading of the background or the use of color leads to reduced comprehension (see Figure 7.13).

The data shown were derived from a randomized study done in over 200 subjects in Australia, where they were given a series of essays to read (about current events), with variable fonts, colors, and so on.[64] Comprehension was tested by a series of questions. Therefore, although the use of color might appear more pleasing to the eye, it tends to degrade comprehension. Certainly, we are not advocating for everything to be in black and white. Color certainly has its place in helping to highlight and distinguish components of text. However, it needs to be done judiciously and with recognition of the possible associated detriment in comprehension.

Font Style	Comprehension (%)		
	Good	Fair	Poor
Reading is a critically important means of communication that is ubiquitous in society.	70	19	11
Research demonstrates that things such as font type, style, and color influence the reader's ability to comprehend text.	30	20	50
Unfortunately, this information is not always considered when designing displays within electronic health records.	0	12	88

FIGURE 7.13

Comprehension as function of font, style, and background colors. Data (taken from Wheildon C. *Type and Layout: How Typography and Design Can Get Your Message Across—or Get in the Way*. Berkeley, CA: Strathmore Press; 1995.) are based on randomized studies involving human subjects assigned to read news articles about current events with different font characteristics as shown. Note that comprehension is generally better for nonbold black font on white background.

These concepts are well known in the commercial world. When the vendors want us to purchase something, they use clear formats and attractive graphics. Conversely, when they are giving us a coupon to be reimbursed (e.g., for a cancelled flight), it is provided to us in far-less-readable format (Figure 7.14). Other topics addressed by Wheildon that might also be relevant to the design of EHR displays include the optimal placement of figures and tables within text, optimal spacing between lines and words, and the readability of different fonts.[64]

7.6.2.3 Figure Labeling

Figures are often an ideal way to convey quantitative information. However, graphs are often not labeled well, making comprehension a challenge.[65] In an informal review of articles in the radiation oncology literature, 9% (13/145) of the graphs published lacked a title or a clearly defined endpoint on the *y* axis.[65] Further, 14% (20/145) lacked labels defining each line within the graph itself. For these, one needed to read the caption (text beneath the figure) to understand the meaning of the lines. Differentiation of the different lines shown was difficult in 8% (11/145) of graphs, typically because the multiple lines were too similar in size, texture, or color.

(A)

(B)

FIGURE 7.14

When companies want us to purchase something, they present the information in an easily readable manner to facilitate our purchase. Conversely, when a transaction with the company may cost them money (as opposed to earning money), they make the presentation of information more complex. (A) Screenshot from an airline's website facilitating purchase of a plane ticket. Note the usability of the site, with easily understandable text, mostly dark text on a white background. Color is used in the nice picture, to make the website appear attractive. (B) A coupon from an airline for reimbursement for a cancelled flight. Note the instructions to the customer in this setting are given in all capital letters that are not easily understood.

A similar issue makes it challenging to understand dose-volume histograms in several radiation treatment-planning systems. We need better ways to display this type of quantitative data to make them more understandable. Ideally, the meaning of each line should be readily apparent to the user. Because the user is typically looking at the line, placing labels directly on the line itself might be optimal as in Figure 4.2. If the graph has multiple lines, the ideal location of the labels depends on the number of lines and their proximity. This can become cumbersome if there are many lines, in which case using arrows or having a legend may be necessary. Placing the legend within the figure itself is almost always preferable (vs. placing the information in the caption). The closer the labels can be to the lines to which they refer, the better it is because that minimizes the distance that the user needs to gaze.

7.6.3 Context

A particular challenge with EHRs is in understanding the context of the information. Although individual portions of the record (e.g., clinic notes, test results) can be readily viewed, viewing *multiple items simultaneously* is more challenging. Further, even when viewing multiple items is possible, the user often needs to actively seek the context; the EHR does not necessarily facilitate such contextual review. Thus, it is sometimes difficult to obtain a clear picture of the patient's overall situation. Reading a medical history in the EHR sometimes seems like reading a novel but being permitted to only look at one paragraph at a time, and with the need to actively seek or request each subsequent paragraph from the card catalogue.

Many visual or tactile cues inherent within the paper chart provided useful information (albeit often imprecise or incorrect). For example, the size or thickness of the chart (e.g., the number of notes, test results, or number of radiation therapy prescriptions on the prescription page) provided a crude estimate of the severity or duration of a patient's illness or the duration of the hospital admission for an inpatient. The color of the binder holding the paper could be used to denote on which machine a patient was being treated. Different medical services sometimes used different color paper for their notes, so one could readily identify notes from these different services and readily know that some specialty service had seen the patient (a useful piece of data irrespective of what that note actually said). Handwriting was also useful in readily identifying groups of notes from the same person and in differentiating notes from different people. Notes were readily appended, corrected, annotated, or emphasized (e.g., underlined, circled), often enabling the reader to infer (albeit perhaps incorrectly) where the author was uncertain, items deemed particularly important, and so on. We are not suggesting that we go back to the days of the paper chart. The EHR offers great benefits to patients, providers, and society at large. Further, sick patients often had thin paper charts, many reports were often missing, and handwriting often could not be read. Nevertheless, it is worth acknowledging that some contextual information is often more challenging to appreciate in the EHR compared to the paper record.

This section outlines several ideas aimed to enhance contextual understanding with EHRs. The idea is to assist with the interpretation of data, reduce the workload of data interpretation, facilitate in prioritization of data review, and overall make it easier to navigate the electronic record. The approaches described largely provide additional information in places where the user is already working (i.e., the passively and automatically) and do not require additional "clicks." These tools rely largely on the use of things such as variable font sizes, spacing, color, and justification to convey information.

The underlying concept is to systematically and automatically embed within the existing displays of data files (e.g., lists of clinic notes, laboratory reports) visual cues providing increased context regarding the data size, temporal nature (time), context, and value. Examples of some of these concepts are shown in Figures 7.15–7.17.

- Size: Using font size or a symbol to reflect the size of the file it represents.
- Time: Using spacing or formatting (such as lines of different thicknesses) to reflect time between different entries.
- Authorship: The creators of notes or reports in the medical record can be portrayed by unique "handwriting" (e.g., some combinations of font style, font size, color, shading, etc.). This can be done at a per user level, by discipline, or by other segregation. It might seem silly to consider, but I suspect that over time users would become accustomed to recognizing their colleagues' unique "handwriting styles."
- Value: For numerical values, one can use justification/location and font size to represent the value (e.g., lower values in a table are smaller or are justified lower in their "cell."
- Content (discretization of data from notes or reports and the "Sneak Preview"): Most clinic notes and reports presently lack discrete data that summarize that note or report. But, this can change. Consider mammogram reports as a model example for which each report is ascribed a BI-RADS score (an objective quantification of the

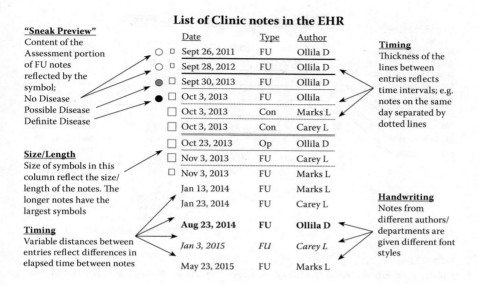

FIGURE 7.15

Several examples shown for ways to embed additional information into a list of clinic notes; e.g. content of the notes (symbols in upper left), timing between the notes (lines of variable thickness in the top portion, or spacing between entries in bottom portion), length of the notes (size of symbols in upper left for the top portion), and authorship (variable font styles depicted in the lower portion). Any or all of these concepts, in various combinations, might be useful. FU = Follow-up notes.

radiologist's overall impression). A list of mammogram reports then can include a hint, or "sneak preview," of that report's content that is based on the BI-RADS score. The same can be done for any list of documents (e.g., clinical notes or pathology reports). By incorporating discrete data within a report (e.g. a diagnosis of cancer in a pathology report, or a statement that there is evidence of a disease recurrence in a clinic note), that discrete data element can be used to "determine the color or symbol" that reflects the content of the report.

There is likely benefit in using discrete data elements in the EHR notes or reports that is independent of whether the sneak preview is used. It would certainly make it easier for someone reading a note to readily understand what the author of that note was thinking if the author had been forced to select one of several discrete items from a series of menus. This would make retrospective chart reviews much easier and might facilitate

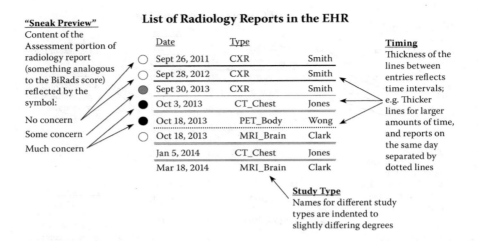

FIGURE 7.16

Information embedded in the list of radiology reports as shown; including the content, timing and type of imaging study. Indenting different study types to a variable degree might make it easier to identify prior studies of similar type.

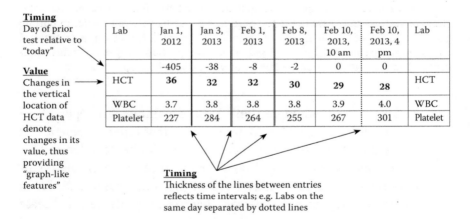

FIGURE 7.17

Information embedded in a table of laboratory results as shown including the value and timing.

large-scale review of medical records using natural language-processing assessments of the record (e.g., searching for common phrases within records). For example, imagine if every radiation therapy completion note summary were to have a menu with items such as these, where the author can choose one or more noncontradictory items:

- Completed therapy as planned without interruption
- Completed therapy as planned with interruption for acute toxicity
- Completed planned therapy with interruption for other reason
- Did not complete therapy
- Unplanned hospital admission during therapy
- Died during therapy

Then, software could be used to identify groups of patients who (for example) died during therapy or to calculate the rates of treatment completion and so on. This and other examples are provided in Figure 7.18. The exact formulation of these menus is debatable, and they certainly can be modified to be consistent with other grading systems for tumor response or normal tissue effects. The utility of the concept seems clear.

Certainly, we do not know for sure which, if any, of these strategies might prove to be useful. These concepts should be further developed by various experts, refined using usability principles and experiences from other settings, and implemented for testing in the experimental and possibly clinical environments. It is critical that we do what we can to improve the usability of the EHRs, and some of these initiatives are reasonable to consider.

7.6.4 The Need for Rapid Action

We understand and respect that the vendors have multiple demands and that EHRs are relatively new products. Evolution will happen over time. Usability will improve. However, there is reason for concern and a need to push for more rapid improvement. There are tens of thousands of providers struggling with these systems every day. There almost certainly have been and will be errors related to the use of EHRs. We recognize the great benefits that the EHRs provide (e.g., accessibility, data analysis, population management, decision support), and we are awed by the potential. Nevertheless, the benefits of the EHRs do not reduce our responsibility to make improvements quickly. It is the separation presently between the reality and the possibility that makes us anxious. It is because we know it can be better that we want to push for improvements rapidly. We worry that once suboptimal systems are in place, they may be difficult to change (because of inertia or regulatory issues) and will become entrenched. Competing products will be difficult to consider given the high cost of replacing existing systems.

In all radiation treatment management notes
- Continue treatment as planned
- Planned break for acute toxicity
- Discontinue therapy for toxicity
- Discontinue therapy for tumor progression
- Alter therapy for disease progression
- Other

In all radiation completion note summaries
- Completed planned therapy without interruption
- Completed planned therapy with interruption for acute toxicity
- Completed planned therapy with interruption for other reason
- Did not complete therapy
- Unplanned hospital admission during therapy
- Died during therapy
- Other

In all follow-up notes (present disease status)
- No evidence of cancer
- No evidence of progression
- Suspected recurrence or progression; continue current regimen
- Continue surveillance
- Consider change in therapy
- Other

In all follow-up notes (present normal tissue status)
- No meaningful clinical toxicity
- Toxicity, no intervention taken
- Toxicity, intervention taken
- Toxicity, requiring hospitalization or surgery
- Other

(These can be altered to follow recognized toxicity scales.)

FIGURE 7.18

Example "standardized text" menus that can be used routinely in certain types of clinic notes to provide discrete information related to that visit. This would make it easier for the readers to comprehend the author's impression, facilitating retrospective chart reviews and larger record reviews using natural language processing (e.g., enabled by standardized language usage). The user would choose one or several of the options shown. The standardized text that is chosen for each note can be used to determine the sneak preview concept in Figures 7.15–7.16.

REFERENCES

1. Endsley MR. Toward a theory of situational awareness in dynamic systems. *Human Factors* 1995;37:32–64.
2. Wickens CD, Hollands JG. *Engineering Psychology and Human Performance.* 3rd ed. Upper Saddle River, NJ: Prentice-Hall; 2000.
3. Hart SG, Staveland LE. Development of NASA-TLX (Task Load Index): results of empirical and theoretical research. In: Hancock PA, Meshkati N, eds. *Human Mental Workload.* Amsterdam, the Netherlands: North Holland Press; 1988;139–183.
4. Meister D. *Behavioral Foundations of System Development.* New York, NY: Wiley; 1976.
5. Colle HA, Reid GB. Mental workload redline in a simulated air-to-ground combat mission. *Int J Aviat Psychol* 2005;15:303–319.
6. Karsh BT, Holden RJ, Alper SJ, et al. Human factors engineering paradigm for patient safety: designing to support the performance of the healthcare professional. *Qual Saf Health Care* 2006;15:59–65.
7. Rasmussen J, Pejtersen MA, Goodstein LP. *Cognitive Systems Engineering.* New York, NY: Wiley; 1994.
8. Hysong SJ, Sawhney MK, Wilson L, et al. Provider management strategies of abnormal test result alerts: a cognitive task analysis. *JAMIA* 2010;17:71–77.
9. Marks LB, Light KL, Hubbs JL, et al. The impact of advanced technologies on treatment deviations in radiation treatment delivery. *Int J Radiat Oncol Biol Phys* 2007;69:1579–1586.
10. Marks LB, Jackson M, Xie L, Chang SX, et al. The challenge of maximizing safety in radiation oncology. *Pract Radiat Oncol* 2011;1(1):2–14.
11. Mazur LM, Mosaly P, Jackson M, et al. Quantitative assessment of workload and stressors in clinical radiation oncology. *Int J Radiat Oncol Biol Phys* 2012;83:e571–e576.
12. Ash JS, Sittig DF, Dykstra RH, Guappone K, Carpenter JD, Seshadri V. Categorizing the unintended sociotechnical consequences of computerized provider order entry. *Int J Med Inform* 2007;76:S21–S27.
13. Ash JS, Kilo CM, Shapiro M, Wasserman J, McMullen C, Hersh W. *Roadmap for Provision of Safer Healthcare Information Systems: Preventing e-Iatrogensis.* Washington, DC: Institute of Medicine; 2011.
14. Byun SN, Choi SN. An evaluation of the operator mental workload of advanced control facilities in Korea next generation reactor. *J Korean Inst Indust Eng* 2002;28:178–186.
15. Yurko YY, Scerbo MW, Prabhu AS, et al. Higher mental workload is associated with poorer laparoscopic performance as measured by the NASA-TLX Tool. *J Soc Sim Healthcare* 2010;5:267–271.
16. Rubio S, Diaz E, Martin J, Puente JM. Evaluation of subjective mental workload: a comparison of SWAT, NASA-TLX, and workload profile. *Appl Psychol Int Rev* 2004;53:61–86.
17. Lee KK, Kerns K, Bones R, Nickelson M. Development and validation of the controller acceptance rating scale (CARS): results of empirical research. Paper presented at the Fourth USA/Europe Air Traffic Management Research and Development Seminar (ATM-2001); Santa Fe, NM; December 2001.
18. Leiden K, Keller J, French J. *Context of Human Error in Commercial Aviation.* Report prepared for National Aeronautics and Space Administration System-wide Accident Prevention Program. Moffett Field, CA: Ames Research Center; 2001.

19. Calkin BA. *Parameters Affecting Mental Workload and the Number of Simulated UCAVs that Can Be Effectively Supervised* [master's thesis]. Troy, AL: Troy University; 2002.

20. Hoffman E, Pene N, Rognin L, Zeghal K. Introducing a new spacing instruction, impact of spacing tolerance on flight crew activity. *Proceedings of the 47th Annual Meeting of the Human Factors and Ergonomics Society*; Santa Monica, CA; October 2003:174–178.

21. Young G, Zavelina L, Hooper V. Assessment of workload using NASA Task Load Index in perianesthesia nursing. *J Perianesth Nurs* 2008;3:102–110.

22. Mazur LM, Mosaly P, Hoyle L, et al. Subjective and objective quantification of physician's workload and performance during radiotherapy planning tasks. *Pract Radiat Oncol* 2013;3:e171–e177.

23. Mazur LM, Mosaly P, Hoyle L, et al. Relating physician's workload with errors during radiotherapy planning. *Pract Radiat Oncol* 2013:71–75.

24. Mosaly P, Mazur LM, Jones E, et al. Quantification of physician's workload and performance during cross-coverage in radiation therapy treatment planning. *Pract Radiat Oncol* 2013;3:e179–e186.

25. World Health Organization. *Radiotherapy Risk Profile*. Geneva, Switzerland: WHO; 2008. http://www.who.int/patientsafety/activities/technical/radiotherapy_risk_pro-file.pdf. Accessed October 2013.

26. Beatty J, Lucero-Wagoner B. The pupillary system. In: Cacioppo JT, Tassinary LG, Berntson G, eds. *Handbook of Psychophysiology*. Cambridge, UK: Cambridge University Press; 2000:142–162.

27. Beatty J, Kahneman D. Pupillary changes in two memory tasks. *Psychon Sci* 1966;5:371–372.

28. Kahneman D, Beatty D. Pupillary responses in a pitch-discrimination task. *Percept Psychophys* 1967;2:101–105.

29. Bradshaw LJ. Pupil size and problem solving. *Q J Exp Psychol* 1968;20:116–122.

30. Colman E, Paivio A. Pupillary dilation and mediation processes during paired-association learning. *Can J Psychol* 1970;24:261–270.

31. Goldberg JH, Kotval XP. Eye movement-based evaluation of the computer interface. In Kumar SK, ed. *Advances in Occupational Ergonomics and Safety*. Amsterdam, the Netherlands: IOS Press; 1998;529–532.

32. Hess EH. Attitude and pupil size. *Sci Am* 1965;212:46–54.

33. Hess EH, Polt JH. Pupil size in relation to mental activity during simple problem solving. *Science* 1964;143:1190–1192.

34. Marshall SP. The index of cognitive activity: measuring cognitive workload. *Proceedings of the 2002 IEEE 7th Conference on Human Factors and Power Plants* 2002:7-7-7-9.

35. Paivio A, Simpson HM. Magnitude and latency of the pupillary response during an imagery task as a function of stimulus abstractness and imagery ability. *Psychon Sci* 1968;12:45–46.

36. Steinhauer SR, Siegle GJ, Condray J, et al. Sympathetic and parasympathetic innervation of pupillary dilation during sustained processing. *Int J Psychophysiol* 2004;53:77–86.

37. Wright P, Kahneman D. Evidence of alternative strategies of sentence retention. *Q J Exp Psychol* 1971;23:197–213.

38. Mosaly P, Mazur LM, Chera B, Marks LB. Assessing cognitive effort using task evoked pupillary response during physicians' interaction with electronic medical records. Presented at the Human Factors and Ergonomics Society, 2014 International Annual Meeting; Chicago, IL; October 2014.

39. Gevins A, Smith ME, Leong H, et al. Monitoring working memory load during computer-based tasks with EEG pattern recognition methods. *Hum Factors* 1998;40:79–91.

40. Gevins A, Smith ME. Neurophysiological measures of cognitive workload during human-computer interaction. *Theor Issues Ergon* 2003;4:113–131.

41. Gevins A, Smith ME, McEvoy L, et al. High-resolution EEG mapping of cortical activation related to working memory: effects of task difficulty, type of processing, and practice. *Cereb Cortex* 1997;7:374–385.

42. Brookings JB, Wilson GF, Swain CR. Psychophysiological responses to changes in workload during simulated air traffic control. *Biol Psychol* 1996;42:361–377.

43. Brookhuis KA, de Waard D. The use of psychophysiology to assess driver status. *Ergonomics* 1993;36:1099–1110.

44. Berka C, Levendowski DJ, Cvetinovic MM, et al. Real-time analysis of EEG indexes of alertness, cognition, and memory acquired with a wireless EEG headset. *Int J Human-Computer Interact* 2004;17:151–170.

45. Berka C, Levendowski D, Lumicao MN, et al. EEG correlates of task engagement and mental workload in vigilance, learning, and memory tasks. *Aviat Space Environ Med* 2007;78:B231–B244.

46. DuRousseau DR, Mannucci MA. *eXecutive Load Index (XLI): Spatial-Frequency EEG Tracks Moment-to-Moment Changes in High-Order Attentional Resources. Foundations of Augmented Cognition.* Mahwah, NJ: Erlbaum; 2005;245–251.

47. Parasuraman R, Rizzo M. Introduction to neuroergonomics. In Parasuraman R, Rizzo M, eds. *Neuroergonomics: The Brain at Work.* New York, NY: Oxford University Press; 2007:3–12.

48. Smith ME, Gevins A, Brown H, et al. Monitoring task loading with multivariate EEG measures during complex forms of human–computer interaction. *Hum Factors* 2001;43:366–380.

49. Sterman MB, Mann CA. Concepts and applications of EEG analysis in aviation performance evaluation. *Biol Psychol* 1995;40:115–130.

50. Sterman MB, Mann CA, Kaiser DA. Quantitative EEG patterns of differential in-flight workload. In: *Space Operations, Applications, and Research Proceedings*; Sepulveda VA Medical Center: NASA conference publication; 1992;466–473.

51. Slagle J, Weinger MB. The effects of intraoperative reading on vigilance and workload during anesthesia care in an academic medical center. *Anesthesiology* 2009;110:275–83.

52. Wilson GF. An analysis of mental workload in pilots during flight using multiple psychophysiological measures. *Int J Aviat Psychol* 2001;12:3–18.

53. Wilson GF, Eggemeier FT. Psychophysiological assessment of workload in multi-task environments. In: Damos DL, ed. *Multiple Task Performance.* London, UK: Taylor & Francis; 1991:329–360.

54. Wilson GF, Russell CA. Operator functional state classification using multiple psychophysiological features in an air traffic control task. *Hum Factors* 2003;45:381–389.

55. Mazur L, McCreery J, Chen S-J. Quality improvement in hospitals: what triggers behavioral change? *J Healthcare Eng* 2012;4:621–648.

56. Mazur LM, McCreery J, Rothenberg L. Exploring the power of social networks and leadership styles during Lean program implementation in hospitals. Paper presented at the IIE Annual Conference and Expo; Reno, NV; May 2011.

57. Mazur LM, Rothenberg L, McCreery J. Measuring and understanding change recipients' buy-in during Lean transformation program. Paper presented at the IIE Annual Conference and Expo; Reno, NV; May 2011.
58. Avolio BJ, Bass BM. *Multifactor Leadership Questionnaire*. Redwood City, CA: Mindgarden; 1995.
59. Taylor M, McNicholas C, Nicolay C, Darzi A, Bell D, Reed J. Systematic review of the application of the plan–do–study–act method to improve quality in healthcare. *BMJ Qual Saf* 2013;0:1–9.
60. Kenny C. *Transforming Health Care: Virginia Mason Medical Center's Pursuit of the Perfect Patient Experience*. New York, NY: CRC Press, Taylor & Francis Group; 2011.
61. Mazur LM, McCreery J, Vaughan M, Lefteris C. Adapting Lean principles and practices to evidence-based design during hospital design projects. *Indust Eng* 2013;45:40–45.
62. Nielsen J. *Usability Engineering*. London, UK: Academic Press; 1993.
63. Vicente K. *Cognitive Work Analysis: Toward Safe, Productive, and Healthy Computer-Based Work*. Mahwah, NJ: Erlbaum; 1999.
64. Wheildon C. *Type and Layout: How Typography and Design Can Get Your Message Across—or Get in the Way*. Berkeley, CA: Strathmoor Press; 1995.
65. Marks LB. A plea for clarity. *Int J Radiat Oncol Biol Phys* 2012;82:1307–1309.

8

Conclusion

8.1 SUMMARY OF THE BOOK

Our book was structured around the Swiss Cheese Model (Figure 8.1) to emphasize the need for improvement efforts at all levels: organizational, workplace, and people.

In Part 1 of this book (Chapters 1–3), we introduced the basic concepts, methods, and tools that underlie our approach to high reliability and value creation and provided an overview of key safety challenges within radiation oncology.

In Chapter 1, we learned that high reliability and value creation require formal strategies and actions at all three levels (organizational, workplace, and people) to prevent patient harm. In Chapter 2, we reviewed the "past" and "current" challenges of patient safety issues within radiation oncology. Although we recognize and applaud the multiple technology-based initiatives aimed at improving patient safety, we also convey our belief that technical solutions, automation, and forcing functions alone (at least for now) are not going to bring our field to the desired level of reliability and value creation. Rather, we need a comprehensive approach applied to improvement throughout the Swiss Cheese Model. As software evolves, the role of automation and forcing functions will increase.

Chapter 3 introduced the theories/concepts of normal accident theory (NAT), high-reliability organizations (HROs), and the Toyota Production System (TPS; or Lean). We learned how Perrow's NAT model describes systems based on the dimensions of linear versus interactive complexity and loose versus tight coupling (see Figure 3.2C and Section 3.1). Applying this model to radiation oncology practices, we reviewed the rationale for various quality assurance (QA) strategies in our field. In summary, we support the following:

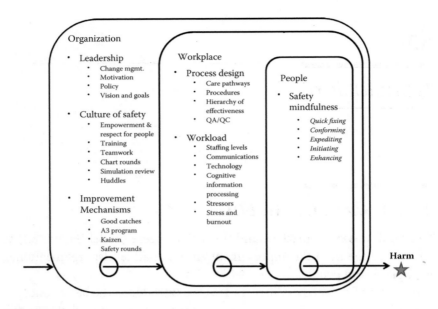

FIGURE 8.1
Summary of our book using the Swiss Cheese Model with key concepts highlighted for each level (organizational, workplace, people levels).

a. Automation with human oversight and forcing functions wherever possible, especially for tightly coupled processes (e.g., data transfer, dose calculation/optimization);

b. Strict process standardization and monitoring of processes, supported by vigilant testing and verification before any change implementation, for tightly coupled processes where automation and forcing functions are not possible (e.g., system commissioning, intensity-modulated radiation therapy [IMRT]);

c. People-driven QA (e.g., huddles, time-outs, checklists, etc.), flexible process standardization, and "selective/strategic" monitoring of processes, supported by relatively "rapid" continuous quality improvement (CQI) methodologies such as Lean for the loosely coupled (and to some degree more creative) aspects of our practice (e.g., treatment planning, image segmentation, clinical decisions, and routine clinical care).

In Part 2 (Chapters 4–6), we detailed some of our specific experiences in applying these approaches at the University of North Carolina (UNC). In Chapter 4, Larry reviews his journey in coming to lead this initiative at UNC and the struggles that leaders can face in promoting this type of change. We described and emphasized the critical role leadership plays in actively and overtly supporting quality improvement initiatives, both directly through their actions and indirectly by inspiring others.

Chapter 5 highlighted our efforts to optimize our workplaces. We wanted to make it "easy to do the right thing" so human error can be minimized. We relied heavily on Human Factors Engineering and the hierarchy of effectiveness for error prevention as our guiding principles. These principles have been effective in many other industries and need to be more widely applied in medicine. Nobody goes to work thinking, "Hey, I am going to make a mistake today." Rather, we put workers into suboptimal environments and then wonder why things go wrong. Improving the workplace affords an opportunity for innovation and creativity that can be both fun and rewarding.

Chapter 6 reviewed our initiatives focusing on people and their decision-making processes and behaviors. We offered ways to engage, transform, and respect people during transition to high reliability and value creation. Because many aspects of our clinical care are interactively complex and tightly coupled, we simply do not know how our systems can fail us. Thus, we need a sense of safety mindfulness in all people so that the entire team can be effective advocates for improvement.

Chapter 7 summarized our research program on workload and performance that is synergetic with our clinical activities and provided ideas for future research. This is an exciting area that blends aspects of diverse fields (e.g., psychology, computer science, engineering, medicine) to address complex issues that are ubiquitous in our workplace and in our everyday lives.

8.2 CONTEXT OF THE BOOK

a. The focus of this book was our experiences in radiation oncology at UNC and not a review of the world's literature or the experiences of others. There are other venues for the interested reader to learn more about quality improvement initiatives within radiation oncology broadly.[1–18] Some particularly exciting initiatives have moved some of our core tasks "up" the hierarchy of effectiveness. For example, initiatives are under way (and some fairly well developed) to add automation and standardization to components of the treatment-planning process.[17] On a simple level, the consistent use of goal sheets (see Section 5.2.2) and adherence to department treatment policies are moves toward standardization. On a more advanced and exciting level, others are using libraries of previously planned cases to facilitate planning in new cases.[8,10,12,13] These can all be considered attempts to move the planning process up the hierarchy of effectiveness and represent an exciting area of research and development. Similarly, automatic image segmentation is an attempt to move that specific task up the hierarchy of effectiveness as well.

b. We also limited our discussion to our organizational, workplace, and people levels *in the department of radiation oncology at UNC*, that is, where we had the most influence. There are additional layers of the Swiss Cheese Model that we have *not* specifically addressed (see Figure 8.2). For example, broader/related organizations (e.g., our hospital, health system, other medical school departments, state and federal governments, the Food and Drug Administration, and professional organizations) have an impact on our departmental organizational, workplace, and people levels.

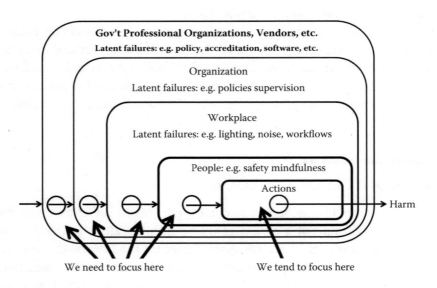

FIGURE 8.2
Venn-like diagram of the Swiss Cheese Model with an additional outermost layer consisting of societal, governmental, professional, and so on factors that have an impact on organizational, workplace, and people levels.

Locally, we have been fortunate that our hospital and health system have been supportive of the improvement activities in our department as well as in many other areas in our health system. The UNC healthcare system has a growing group of quality improvement experts embedded in various areas, as well as central resources to train and assist others. There is also cross-fertilization between areas; for example, personnel from our department are working with others in promoting improvement initiatives elsewhere in our cancer hospital and health system. Indeed, we were fortunate to receive funding from the Centers for Disease Control and Prevention (CDC) to use Lean-based principles to improve specific aspects of our multidisciplinary breast cancer program.[11] Similarly, we are actively learning from, and engaging with, others throughout the health system with similar interests.

National organizations (e.g., professional societies, industries) have a potentially large impact on our practices (and hence quality, safety, efficiency, etc.) through activities such as accreditation, educational programs, the generation of guidelines, advocacy, regulation, and so on. One area that has been of particular interest to us, and where we support more national input, is the ambiguity of some of our communication, particularly regarding radiation treatment prescriptions. This issue is discussed in more detail in the appendix.

8.3 CONCLUDING REMARKS

We have been working at improving quality and safety for several years; this has been a lot of work, filled with successes and failures. We had two main motivations to write this book:

a. We believe that we had an important message to send—that the patient safety and quality concerns within our field are not merely technical issues. We will not be able to make dramatic improvements with only technical fixes. Rather, a more global change in culture and attitude are needed. We thought that our experiences might be helpful to others considering similar initiatives. We are excited and proud of what we and our group have achieved, and we wanted to share this experience and enthusiasm with others. We hope that the reader senses our true enthusiasm for our improvement work because it is real.

b. We wanted to systematically assess and review the impact of our improvement initiatives. Ideally, we would like to assess for an impact on patient outcomes. Unfortunately, we do not have data along these lines. However, we do have a modest amount of patient satisfaction information. Since 2010, UNC hospitals recognized its "Top Five Clinics" quarterly, based on patient satisfaction scores. Our radiation oncology clinic was awarded this distinction in one quarter in fiscal year 2011, one quarter in 2012, three quarters in 2013, once in 2014, and at least once in 2015. We obviously do not know if these recognitions are a result of our improvement work. Nevertheless, our relatively high patient satisfaction scores are encouraging (Figure 8.3). Employee satisfaction and departmental financial performance have generally improved over time as well.

Writing the book had several unexpected benefits. First, it provided a good opportunity for us to look back at what we had done, not only to be proud of many things but also to identify many areas where we could have done things better. In this regard, the writing was cathartic and reflective.

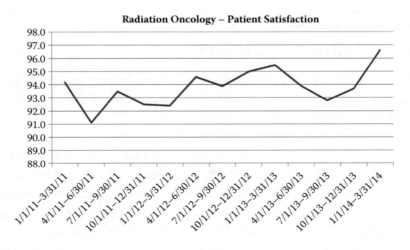

FIGURE 8.3
Patient satisfaction scores over time.

Second, it forced us to reassess how we did things. Although we have been broadly considering the basic theories of high reliability, formally mapping our initiatives to the NAT (Chapter 3) and the hierarchy of effectiveness (Chapter 5) was enlightening. This has helped us to better understand the potential utility and limitations of our strategies to date and has led us to reassess some of our initiatives.

Our experience strongly supports the position that radiation oncology professionals take pride in their work and care deeply about patient safety and positive patient outcomes. In general, the people who resist our initiatives are motivated by their sincere belief that specific initiatives are either unnecessary or suboptimal. **In this regard, it is not really the people who are the "problem," but rather the lack of a robust infrastructure to support people's own journeys toward safety mindfulness.** Thus, leaders need to create and nurture a culture that promotes this journey to help all people move from *Quick Fixing*, *Conforming*, and *Expediting* behaviors to *Enhancing* and *Initiating* behaviors. Leaders (in the broadest sense) need to acknowledge that they are responsible for modeling and developing these desired improvement behaviors. They should help build organizations that promote these values and, as needed, use their authority to enforce these values as well.

After experiencing many of the frustrations in promoting these initiatives, we can understand why some people give up and accept the status quo. Bringing change to healthcare is challenging as many existing systems have evolved over decades, and inertia can be strong. Nevertheless, we are energized by our occasional successes and motivated by the knowledge of what can be. We need to continually remind ourselves that things can be better, and that there are proven approaches that can be more systematically applied to help reach our goals (Figure 8.4).

We believe that the broad application of the principles described in this book to healthcare can make us more efficient and effective as caregivers. This will benefit all of us—our staff and patients. Society has entrusted us with an enormous responsibility, and we want to make it easier for us to perform at the high level that is expected and that our patients deserve.

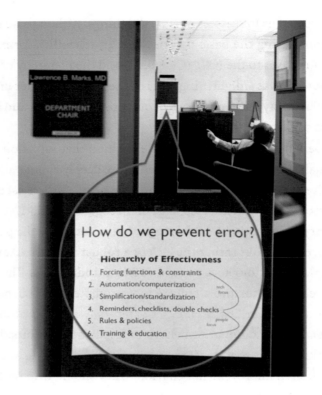

FIGURE 8.4

Looking into Larry's office, the hierarchy of effectiveness is prominently posted on the side of a bookcase. It serves as a constant reminder (and motivator) to Larry of the safety principles that he and his team are promoting at UNC. Further, Larry often refers to it while speaking with visitors about operational concerns and the like.

REFERENCES

1. Albert JM, Das P. Quality indicators in radiation oncology. *Int J Radiat Oncol Biol Phys* 2013;85(4):904–911.
2. Chao ST, Meier T, Hugebeck B, et al. Workflow enhancement (WE) improves safety in radiation oncology: putting the WE and team together. *Int J Radiat Oncol Biol Phys* 2014;89(4):765–772.
3. Chan AJ, Islam MK, Rosewall T, et al. Applying usability heuristics to radiotherapy systems. *Radiother Oncol* 2012;102(1):142–147.
4. Efstathiou JA, Nassif DS, McNutt TR, et al. Practice-based evidence to evidence-based practice: building the National Radiation Oncology Registry. *J Oncol Pract* 2013;9(3):e90–e95.
5. Ford EC, Gaudette R, Myers L, et al. Evaluation of safety in a radiation oncology setting using failure mode and effects analysis. *Int J Radiat Oncol Biol Phys* 2009;74(3):852–858.
6. Ford EC, Fong de Los Santos L, Pawlicki T, et al. The structure of incident learning systems for radiation oncology. *Int J Radiat Oncol Biol Phys* 2013;86(1):11–12.

7. Fraass B, Marks L, Pawlicki T for the ASTRO Multidisciplinary Quality Assurance Subcommittee. Safety considerations in contemporary radiation oncology: introduction to a series of ASTRO safety white papers. *Pract Radiat Oncol* 2011;1(3):188–189.

8. Good D, Lo J, Lee WR, et al. A knowledge-based approach to improving and homogenizing intensity modulated radiation therapy planning quality among treatment centers: an example application to prostate cancer planning. *Int J Radiat Oncol Biol Phys* 2013;87(1):176–181.

9. Létourneau D, McNiven A, Jaffray D. Multicenter collaborative quality assurance program for the province of Ontario, Canada: first-year results. *Int J Radiat Oncol Biol Phys* 2013;86(1):164–169.

10. Lian J, Yuan L, Ge Y, et al. Modeling the dosimetry of organ-at-risk in head and neck IMRT planning: an intertechnique and interinstitutional study. *Med Phys* 2013;40(12):121704.

11. Mayer DK, Taylor K, Gerstel A, et al. Using Lean methods to increase access to support services in younger breast cancer survivors. Poster presentation at the San Antonio Breast Cancer Symposium; San Antonio, TX, December, 2013.

12. McNutt TR, Wu B, Moore J, et al. Automated treatment planning using a database of prior patient treatment plans. http://amos3.aapm.org/abstracts/pdf/68-19822-230349-85703.pdf.

13. McNutt TR. Oncospace. http://iccr2013.org/cms/wp-content/uploads/2013/05/Todd-McNutt.pdf.

14. Pawlicki T, Harry T, Taylor M, et al. Investigation of RFID-based workflow analysis. *Int J Radiat Oncol Biol Phys* 2012;84(3):S543.

15. Potters L, Kapur A. Implementation of a "No Fly" safety culture in a multicenter radiation medicine department. *Pract Radiat Oncol* 2012;2(1):18–26.

16. Potters L, Kapur A. Six Sigma tools for a patient safety-oriented, quality-checklist driven radiation medicine department. *Pract Radiat Oncol* 2012;2(2):86–96.

17. Purdie T, Dinniwell R, Fyles A, et al. Automation and IMRT for individualized high-quality tangent breast treatment plans. *Int J Radiat Oncol Biol Phys* 2014;90(3):688–695.

18. Rivera AJ, Karsh BT. Human factors and systems engineering approach to patient safety for radiotherapy. *Int J Radiat Oncol Biol Phys* 2008;71(1):S174–S177.

Glossary

The Language of High Reliability and Value Creation: Please do not get frustrated by the terminology used. The field of quality improvement and patient safety can sometimes seem (particularly to the non-expert) to be mired in ambiguous nomenclature. As with all areas of study, scholars need to define terms specifically in order to facilitate communication and bring clarity to research. Thus, terms that seem broad to the non-expert, often have very specific meanings to experts, and this can hinder communication between the expert and non-expert. This issue is not unique to the study of quality and safety. Physicists use terms such as 'speed', 'velocity', 'work', 'heat' and 'weight' in a manner different than non-physicists. Medical professionals use the term 'stomach' in a manner much more specific than the general public. In this book, we have tried to use various terms in a specific manner consistent with experts in the field. The non-expert readers generally do not need to get bogged down in the nomenclature details to grasp the concepts being described. In the sections where such knowledge is needed, we have tried to clearly define the pertinent terms. For the initiated reader, an appreciation of the differences between the seemingly similar terms (e.g., quality control vs. quality assurance) can lead to a more in-depth understanding of the field. We include a detailed glossary of key concepts and terms to help guide the reader.

Active failure: Individual's acts that can be directly linked to an error.
Active failure pathway: The actual process of committing the unsafe act that can be directly linked to an error.
Behavior (or quality/safety behavior) is one of the following:
> **Quick fixing:** This behavior consists of detection and correction of defects often accompanied by a discussion or description – most often in the form of a complaint – of the problem to coworkers and the immediate manager, but without formal reporting of defects.
> **Initiating:** This behavior involves formal reporting of defects and the initiation of an improvement effort to improve the system.

Conforming: This behavior is characterized by compliance with standard procedures and processes under the conditions of a system free of defects.

Expediting: This type of behavior describes non-compliant procedures performed to complete the work (e.g., "shortcuts") under the conditions of a system free of defects.

Enhancing: Enhancing behavior is seen in efforts to make long-lasting system improvements with regard to work efficiency, effectiveness, or patient safety under the conditions of a system free of defects.

Charismatic and transformational leadership style: Leaders who stimulate and inspire employees to both achieve extraordinary outcomes and, in the process, develop their own leadership capacity.

Continuous Quality Improvement (CQI): A set of philosophies, methods, and tools for continuous quality improvement efforts. *Lean* and *Six-Sigma* are examples of CQI programs.

Crew Resource Management (CRM): A training program focused on culture, teamwork, communication and inevitability of errors and ways to avoid, trap, and mitigate hazards before they lead to serious or catastrophic harm.

Culture of safety: A set of values, beliefs and artifacts allowing workers feel comfortable in raising concerns about safety, efficiency, quality, reliability, value, etc., without concern of retaliation or reprimand.

Defect: The lack of something in the system (i.e., information, material, etc.) necessary or desirable for task completion.

Event (or Safety Event) is any of the following:

Incident that reached the patient: An incident that reaches the patient, with or without harm;

Near-miss: An incident that comes close to reaching the patient but is caught and corrected beforehand; or

An unsafe condition: Any condition that increases the probability of an incident reaching the patient.

Failure: Any of the following: Active failure, active failure pathway, latent failure, latent failure pathway.

Flexible standardization: Design of a highly standardized process that allows for flexibility and creativity when needed.

Forcing functions: An automated error reduction strategy that tries to correct human errors as they occur.

Hazard: Potential source of error.

Harm: Physical injury or damage to the health of people, or damage to property or the environment.

Hierarchy of effectiveness: A Human Factors Engineering concept for error reduction strategies.

High Reliability Organization (HRO): Organizations that successfully manage their risks over prolonged time periods.

High Reliability Theory: Theory that emphasizes safety mindfulness as the primary approach to reduce the probability of errors.

Human error[*] (or error): Slips, lapses, and mistakes are all considered forms of error.

> **Slip:** actively doing something unintended (this is observable); e.g., inadvertently writing the prescription incorrectly.
>
> **Lapse:** failing to do something that was intended to be done (this is often *not*-observable); e.g., failing to write the prescription.
>
> **Mistakes:** purposeful action (perhaps done flawlessly) that was based on incorrect knowledge, or judgment; e.g., prescribing radiation for a patient in a situation where it is not supported by the data.

Human Factors Engineering: An engineering knowledge domain that covers three major areas: (1) physical ergonomics concerned with physical activity, (2) cognitive (or information processing) ergonomics concerned with mental processes, and (3) organizational ergonomics (also called macroergonomics) concerned with socio-technical system design.

Improvement cycles: An improvement cycle consists of four stages (Plan–Do–Study–Act [PDSA]) that the investigator(s) must go through to get from 'problem faced' to 'problem solved'.

Latent failure: Contributory factor in the system that may have lain dormant for a long time (days, weeks, months, or years) until they contributed to the accident.

Latent failure pathway: The actual process through which contribution factors that may have lain dormant for a long time (days, weeks, months, or years) that contributed to the accident.

Leadership: Means of developing and executing overall vision, mission and goals. It is also one of key drivers for organizational change.

---

[*] Error definition is adapted from J. Reason, *Human Error*. Cambridge, England: Cambridge University Press, 1990.

Lean: A continuous quality improvement philosophy with a core idea to maximize system reliability and maximize value while minimizing waste.

Management: Means of producing consistency with policies and procedures. It is also one of the key drivers for problem solving.

Normal Accidents Theory: Theory that hypothesizes that systems in which elements are tightly coupled and interactively complex would be subjected to accidents in the normal course of operations.

PDSA: Plan–Do–Study–Act improvement cycle.

Quality Assurance (QA): All planned and *proactive* processes, techniques, and actions necessary to ensure adequate confidence that product or service meets the requirements for quality.

Quality Control (QC): All planned operational techniques necessary to *retrospectively* verify if provided product or service met the requirements for quality.

Quality Management (QM): Systems and processes used for decision making related to reliable functioning of continuous quality improvement (CQI), quality assurance (QA) and quality control (QC).

Risk: Product of the "probability of occurrence of error" and "the severity of that error."

Safety Mindfulness: A worker's broad awareness of, and appreciation for, the potential presence of latent failures pathways, the risk of active failures pathways, and the critical role that they play in improving their (and the broader system's) overall safety and performance.

Situational awareness: A hypothetical construct that represents the perception, comprehension, and projection of the system elements, their meaning, and their status in the environment within its volume of time and space.

Standard work procedures: Highly specified step-by-step instruction on how to perform tasks.

Sterile cockpit rule: An error reduction strategy that minimizes unnecessary workload during task execution.

Swiss Cheese Model: A conceptual error causation model based on four failure domains: organizational influences, supervision, preconditions, and specific acts.

Value creation organizations: Organizations that successfully remove waste in any form and shape and create value to their customers over prolonged time periods.

Workload: A hypothetical construct that represents the overall cost incurred by a human operator to achieve a particular level of performance.

Key abbreviations:

EHR: Electronic health record.
HRO: High Reliability Theory.
IGRT: Image guided radiation therapy.
IMRT: Intensity modulated radiation therapy.
NAT: Normal Accident Theory.
NASA-TLX: NASA Task-Load Index.
RT: Radiation therapy.
SRS: Stereotactic radiosurgery.
PSO: Patient Safety Organization.
WHO: World Healthcare Organization

Appendix A

This appendix presents an analogy of the normal accident theory (NAT) concept as applied to sports. We suspect that the reader might find this a more intuitive way to consider these issues. Individual actions in some track and field events (e.g., the sprint) have a clear impact on the race's outcome, and typically no unexpected things occur during the race. Conversely, in sports such as soccer and ice hockey, there are often unforeseen events, and (given the low scoring in most competitions) these often do have an impact on the outcome. Basketball and football are similarly unpredictable, but as there are many plays/possessions, any one of these unforeseen events is less likely to influence the outcome (compared to hockey and soccer). Golf and tennis are somewhat more predictable. Boxing can be quite unpredictable, with one "good" punch deciding the outcome of the competition. We place baseball near the center as shown in Figure A1.1.

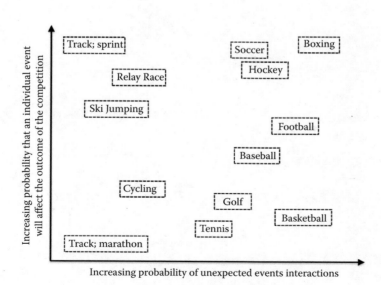

FIGURE A1.1

An analogy of NAT concept, as applied to sports.

Appendix B

Our national organizations have spent much time ensuring that computers communicate well with each other. This is totally understandable and critically important given the need for computer interconnectivity and for automatic data transfer (i.e., this facilitates moving things up the hierarchy of effectiveness). However, we believe that additional efforts are needed to better standardize computer-to-human and human-to-human communication (Figure B1.1).

The appropriateness of some of our long-standing jargon should be reexamined in light of changes in practice. For example, the increased use of hypofractionation increases the "breadth of reasonably acceptable prescriptions" and increases the risk of misinterpreting each other. For example, what does "3 in 10" mean? Is that 3 Gy times 10 fractions or 3 fractions of 10 Gy?

Accurate unambiguous communication among members of the radiation oncology team is critical to ensure patient safety. This is especially true as our current practice often requires numerous handoffs. The means of communication used within programs providing care at multiple locations can be variable (and usually not face to face), thus increasing the risks for miscommunication.

There are many opportunities to improve our interpersonal communication. Given the central nature of the Radiation Treatment Directive, we suggest that a good first step would be to adapt a standard format, or order, for basic directives. Presently, there is no standard within our field for how to do this; there is much variation between and within different organizations (e.g., Figure B1.2).

A sample format addressing the most basic components of the prescription is shown in Table B1.1. The core principle is that all prescriptions will have the general format of

$$(\text{Dose per fraction}) * (\text{Number of fractions}) = \text{Total dose}$$

We recommend that units be applied to avoid ambiguity. We are not wed to this exact formalism but rather to the concept of a uniform formalism. A similar formalism can be used for brachytherapy and radiosurgery

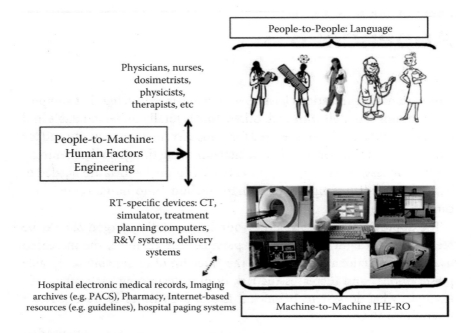

People-to-People: Language

Physicians, nurses, dosimetrists, physicists, therapists, etc

People-to-Machine: Human Factors Engineering

RT-specific devices: CT, simulator, treatment planning computers, R&V systems, delivery systems

Hospital electronic medical records, Imaging archives (e.g. PACS), Pharmacy, Internet-based resources (e.g. guidelines), hospital paging systems

Machine-to-Machine IHE-RO

FIGURE B1.1

The three types of communication between or within people and machines are shown. The IHE-RO (Integrating the Healthcare Enterprise-Radiation Oncology) initiative addresses communication between devices. In the lower corner are listed additional electronic systems (e.g., hospital electronic medical records) where communication or connectivity issues can also be challenging. Also important are communication between people and between people and machines. The proposed standard format/language for radiation therapy prescriptions is intended to facilitate clear human-to-human and computer-to-human communication. CT, computed tomography; PACS, picture archiving and communication system; RT, radiotherapy; R&V systems, radiotherapy record-and-verify system. (Adopted with permission from Marks and Chang, *Pract Radiat Oncol* 2011;1:232–234.)

procedures as shown in Table B1.1. A proposed format for a more comprehensive prescription, addressing some additional parameters, is shown in Table B1.2.

These types of initiatives need to be done at the national level, with support from our professional organizations and the vendors. Formalizing and standardizing the basic elements of a radiation prescription will help to reduce the risk of errors nationally. This, and similar initiatives to harmonize other aspects of our communication (e.g., nomenclature for anatomic structures), will complement existing standards in the manner that

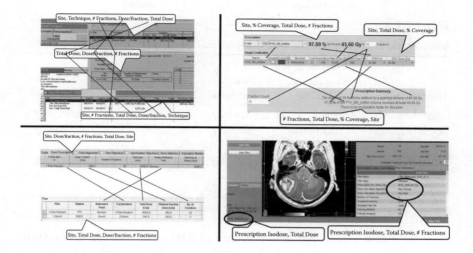

FIGURE B1.2

The need for such standardization in how we communicate a radiation therapy prescription is illustrated. Screen shots are shown from four vendors' planning and record-and-verify systems: Clockwise from upper left: Elekta's Mosaiq®, Accuray's Tomotherapy, Accuray's CyberKnife planning, and Varian's Aria. Note the variation in the manner (content and order) of how the key components of the prescription are depicted. The lack of standardization likely requires an increased level of mental effort by those who input or review information from these different displays. Some clinics (including ours at UNC) have software from multiple vendors. The highlights, lines, and callout balloons are added to emphasize the point. (Portions adopted with permission from Marks and Chang, *Pract Radiat Oncol* 2011;1:232–234.)

we describe things such as tumor extent (e.g., staging system) and normal tissue responses (e.g., Common Terminology Criteria for Adverse Events).

A similar issue that can be best addressed nationally relates to the use of the abbreviations Gy versus cGy. There is inconsistency in the field in the use of Gy versus cGy, and users often have strong preferences for one or the other. The use of cGy has many advantages, including the following:

a. Numbers that are larger in size (i.e., more digits) are consistently larger in value than numbers with fewer digits.

b. It should largely avoid the need for decimal points. Decimal points are a potential problem because they

   1. Are small and might be relatively easy to overlook, leading to misreading of numbers;

TABLE B1.1

A Recommended Format for the Basic Components of a Radiation Therapy Prescription

Treatment Site	Treatment Technique/ Modality	Dose per Fraction	Total Number of Fractions	Total Dose
Right chest wall	Tangents	200 cGy	25	5,000 cGy
Vaginal mucosa	Brachytherapy cylinder	600 cGy	5	3,000 cGy
Left frontal brain metastasis	Radiosurgery	1,800 cGy	1	1,800 cGy

Source: Adopted with permission from Marks and Chang, *Pract Radiat Oncol* 2011;1:232–234.

2. Raise issues related to presence and number of leading and trailing zeros that can make numbers harder to read and prone to misreading (e.g., 0.8 vs. 0.80 vs. 0.8 vs. 8 vs. .80), as well as the number of digits placed to the right of the decimal point (e.g., 8 vs. 8.0 vs. 8.00).

With decimal points, the same numerical value can be shown in numerous ways, with a varying number of digits, and hence variable lengths. Thus, the "fail-safe" use of decimal points requires strict adherence to rules regarding the number and placement of zeros and is thus more prone to error than a system that is not reliant on decimals.

Inconsistencies in the radiation prescription format and radiation dose units are provided as examples of issues that can have an impact on safety and that can best be addressed on a broad scale (e.g., nationally or internationally).

TABLE B1.2

Proposed Format for a More Comprehensive Prescription, Addressing Some Additional Parameters

	Core					Frequency		Immobil-ization	IGRT/Localization		Localization				
Treatment Site	Treatment Technique/ Modality	Beam Energy	Dose per Fraction	Total Number of Fractions	Total Dose	Fractions per Day	Fractions per Week	Immobil-ization	Localization Type	Frequency	Localize via	Action Directive	When to Start	Date Stamp to Signature
Right chest wall	Tangents	6X	200 cGy	25	5,000 cGy	1	5	Custom cradle on angle board	Field portal films	Weekly	NA	Per MD	Oct 17	
Area of gross disease	Smaller tangents	6X	200 cGy	8	1,600 cGy	1	5	Custom cradle	CBCT	Daily	Chest wall mass	Shift for ≥ 2 mm, call MD for ≥ 10 mm	Follow-ing prior field	

Index